Life, as Viewed from the Goldfish Bowl

BEVERLY HYLES

SWORD of the LORD
PUBLISHERS
P. O. BOX 1099, MURFREESBORO, TN 37133

DEDICATION

To all the wives of men in service for God — whether those men be deacons, bus directors, Sunday school workers or in some other area of Christian service. Especially do I dedicate this book to all those special ladies who are called, "pastors' wives." You are so important even if you are tucked away in a small, fundamental church in a rural area. If you are staying by the stuff, **you** may receive greater rewards than some who are more well-known. God bless you.

■　■　■

A great big thank you goes to two ladies who have literally suffered birth pangs as they spent hours and hours typing, proofing, prodding me and seeing that this book became a reality. They are Mrs. Linda Stubblefield and Mrs. Angie Zachary.

Also, thank you to these ladies and men without whom the work would not have been as well done: Mrs. Joanne Bass, Mr. Doug Cook, Mrs. Joyce Pins, Miss Laura Plummer, Mrs. Naomi Roberson, and Mr. David Stubblefield.

In conclusion, I could never fail to mention my pastor, Jack Hyles, who has taught me more than any other human being has ever taught me.

— Beverly Hyles

TABLE OF CONTENTS

Foreword
Introduction

SOME THINGS I HAVE LEARNED *11*
  An Education in a Country Church
  Doesn't Everyone Love the Preacher, Lord?
  So You Don't Want Testing?
  Cutting the Umbilical Cord
  Don't Be Surprised at Fiery Trials

YOU CAN'T STORE IT, FREEZE IT,
OR DEHYDRATE IT! *25*
  Goals Should Make You, Not Break You
  Even the Mundane Needs Planning
  What Are Your Priorities?
  Have You Called Your Father Today?
  Who Is Your Neighbor?
  Hold Things Loosely
  Your Child Has a Right — You!
  Don't Be Superwoman
  Don't Put Me On a Pedestal, Please!
  How To Get it All Done
  What Will Your Diary Say?

DON'T BURN YOUR OWN BRIDGE *52*
  "Be Ye Kind,. . .Tenderhearted"
  The Greatest Example in Forgiving
  Deadly, Destructive, Depressing

KEEP AWAY! PRIVATE PROPERTY! *66*
  Who Is the Strange Woman?
  Words Like Apples of Gold

A FEW DULL MOMENTS, PLEASE 77

SO YOU'RE NUMBER 10,031 ON HIS LIST, HUH? 83
    God's Wonderful People
    Content in Any State

ARE YOU ALL WOUND UP? 94
    The Weary Round of Life
    Quit Crying Over Spilled Milk
    Practical Ways to Deal with Stress
    Relax? What's That?
    Expect God to Keep His Word
    Get a Brand New Start

STOP, LOOK, AND LISTEN! 115
    The "Eyes" Have It
    "Study to Shew Thyself Approved"

WHAT MAKES CHAMPIONS? 133
    Unclench That Fist
    Boot Camp
    Total Commitment

TOUGHNESS WRAPPED IN FEMININITY 144
    Don't Spend Your Life at the Complaint Counter
    Get Your Second Wind
    What Is the Battleground?
    Watch Out for Wounded Animal!
    Our Weapons

DAUGHTER OF THE KING, I BOW TO YOU! 153
    Life Began at Forty
    Opposites, But Insecure
    Agape Love

TRUST AND OBEY 162
    The Way Up is Down
    Look For God in Your Dailies

REACH OUT AND TOUCH 170
     A Personal Question
     What Good is a Whatnot?
     ". . .Ye Did It Unto Me"

OH, TO BE LIKE JESUS 183
     Learn To Turn a Deaf Ear
     What's Your Test Grade?
     Job Made An A+
     Chosen in the Furnace of Affliction
     Wrong Ways to Take Tests
     Ways to Pass With Flying Colors

MAN LOOKETH ON THE OUTWARD APPEARANCE 199
     Does God Want Us to Look Beautiful?
     Preserving the Distinctives

THE X FACTOR 210
     How About Your Heart?
     Changing Your Point of View
     The Praise Principle

HOW TO KEEP ON KEEPING ON 221
     You're a Diamond in the Rough
     Observations About Quitting

BEHAVIOR THAT BECOMETH HOLINESS 231

LIFE, AS VIEWED FROM THE GOLDFISH BOWL 241

FOREWORD

No one is more qualified to author a book of this nature than is Beverly Hyles. She has been the "First Lady" in parsonages — "fish bowls"— of country churches, small-town churches, and a large city church. She has shared with me from a "fish bowl" that was about to fall down to the lovely "bowl" in which we now live. Through all this scrutinization, not one time in forty-three years has there been in any of our churches even the slightest problem that was caused by Mrs. Hyles.

One could return to the Marris Chapel Baptist Church of Bogata, Texas; the Grange Hall Baptist Church of Marshall, Texas; the Southside Baptist Church of Henderson, Texas; the Miller Road Baptist Church of Garland, Texas; and the First Baptist Church of Hammond, Indiana, to enquire about Beverly Hyles. The words that would be used to describe her would be "proper," "gracious," "queenly," "sweet," and "lovely."

You have seen the "fish bowl" from the outside. Now, Beverly takes you inside to show you what we have seen from within for these many years.

What Michelangelo is to the brush, what R. G. Lee is to the pulpit, what the Mayo brothers are to health, what Lee Roberson is to church building, what John Rice is to the pen, Beverly Hyles is to the parsonage or the "fish bowl."

Now, come on in to our "bowl" for a few chapters, and let us show you the joy and sorrows of *Life, as Viewed from the Goldfish Bowl.*

— *Jack Hyles*

INTRODUCTION

"The aged women likewise, that they be in behaviour as becometh holiness, not false accusers, not given to much wine, teachers of good things; That they may teach the young women to be sober, to love their husbands, to love their children, To be discreet, chaste, keepers at home, good, obedient to their own husbands, that the word of God be not blasphemed." (Titus 2:3-5) These verses tell you why I am writing this book. I am one of those "aged women." I hate to admit it, but I have been in the ministry for more than forty years.

Hebrews 13:5 and 6 says, "Let your conversation be without covetousness; and be content with such things as ye have: for he hath said, I will never leave thee, nor forsake thee. So that we may boldly say, The Lord is my helper, and I will not fear what man shall do unto me." If you haven't already learned to rely on those verses, you need to learn it now. You are going to need them many times as a Christian leader's wife. Because of these verses, I believe I can have the boldness to give you the things in this book. He has said to me, "I will never leave you, so you may boldly say to the women who read this book the things I have put on your heart as something they need." I will use many Scripture verses to back up what I teach in this book. If I can't back it up with the Word of God, it's just "Beverly Hylesology" and that won't stand. However, if backed with the Word of God, it will stand.

Who is the pastor's wife? I want to share a poem with you from the book *Help! I'm a Pastor's Wife.*

Daily works from morn 'til night,
Perfect children, act just right,
House is always neat and clean,
Company may soon be seen,
Cheerfully at every meeting,
Smiling nicely with her greeting,
Slim, trim and always fit,
Confident and quick with wit,
Thrifty, smart and pretty, too.
Knows the Bible through and through,
Cooks and entertains with zest,
Never worried, never stressed,
Talent, charm and patience, too,
Nothing that she cannot do,
Never existing in real life,
She's the mythical preacher's wife.

Now that's true! That kind of woman **is** mythical. She doesn't exist. There is no such animal. There is no perfect pastor's wife because we are human. We come in all shapes and sizes and colors and personalities. And isn't that good?

Throughout my life I have had several pastors' wives and they were all different — very different. Some were very outgoing and visible; some stayed behind the scenes. They all performed different duties as pastors' wives. I want you now, for about two minutes, to decide what you think your duties will be as a pastor's wife or as a Christian leader's wife. Get a piece of paper and write them down as they come to your mind.

Now, if you had only one duty, you had the right answer. You are to be the pastor's wife or the wife of that full-time Christian leader. That is your only duty. Isn't that interesting? Of course, there are other things you can take on, but your only required duty is to be your husband's wife. I realize the great commandment tells us we should first love the Lord our God with everything that is within us. And I am taking it for granted you are a Christian and you love God. But as far as your duty as a pastor's wife, it is **only** to be the pastor's wife. Any other things you take on are simply things that go with your talents and your gifts and the things you enjoy.

When it comes to taking on other things, I don't believe God wants to make us miserable in what we do. For example, I have never liked to work with small children. I just don't enjoy working with primaries and beginners. I **do** enjoy working with teenagers and I have worked with them for years and years because it is the age I love. I don't think God stands up there in Heaven looking down saying, "Just what can I put on her to make her so miserable she is a grouch at home and will never smile." I believe He gives us talents in the area in which He wants us to serve. Of course, that doesn't mean we shouldn't **love** all ages. I am nice and sweet to little children — and then I want them to go away!! No, I really do love little children. I have fun with them. I enjoy my grandchildren. I am simply saying though we do have other things God will ask us to do, our main requirement is to be exactly what our name implies — the pastor's wife. Having proper priorities will help you decide how you can be the pastor's wife and then how much else you can take on without becoming overburdened or becoming less than you ought to be to your husband.

—*Beverly Hyles*

SOME THINGS I HAVE LEARNED

In this chapter I am going to give you some important lessons I have learned during my forty years as a pastor's wife in the five pastorates we have had. First of all, **I learned very, very early that when I went to church, my husband was not my husband — he was my pastor.** It is very important for you to learn this too. If you look at that neatly dressed man expounding the Word of God and think of him as your husband, you are going to think of all those whiskers he left in the sink that morning, the clothes he left lying on the floor, and the sharp words between the two of you on the way to church. Then you are going to think, "How does he dare stand up there and expound the Word of God like he thinks he's perfect?!!" No, you forget all that. In your mind, he must cease to be your husband; he must become your pastor. This has been a great help to me. I can listen to my husband preach and be fed in all kinds of circumstances — even when I've hit him over the head with the frying pan just before we left home!! (Of course I have never done that — but I have wanted to!) It's very important for you to realize your husband is God's man for you. You've got to be fed just like everyone else, so you must let your husband be your pastor.

An Education in a Country Church

We must learn that we can learn from anyone. The first church we pastored consisted of 19 members. We were there almost a year, and it grew to 19 during that time! One little girl was saved, but she wasn't allowed to join the church or be baptized; therefore, she couldn't be put on the church roll so we didn't grow. The church was way out in the country. Perhaps you have heard my husband tell a little bit about it, but you've never heard about it from **my** viewpoint! We were paid $7.50 every two weeks, and I just don't know what we did with it all. I guess we blew it because we surely didn't save any of it! A lot of that $15 a month went for gas because we drove a hundred miles from our college town to the church. We would get up on Sunday morning and drive to Bogata, which was a little community close to Marris Chapel Baptist Church. Then, if it wasn't raining, we would take the dirt roads to our church. But if we got to Bogata and it was raining, we couldn't get to our church. There was nothing but dirt roads and we would get stuck in the mud if we tried to make it.

I remember one time in particular when it was raining at our home a hundred miles away from the church. We assumed it was raining at our church too, so we didn't go. Then during the week our people called and said, "Where were you last Sunday?"

We said, "Well, wasn't it raining there?"

To our chagrin, they replied, "No! It was beautiful here!"

This church was in the country, and I was a city girl. I had never drunk out of a dipper in my life and especially not after somebody else! I was used to indoor plumbing.

I remember our first visit to our new church. It was a hot summer afternoon — and if you have ever lived in Texas, you know how hot it can get! There was no hotel or motel, so we stayed with our only deacon and his wife. Before retiring that night, I asked, "Where's the bathroom?" This was after looking through the house and finding none.

My husband said, "Look outside for something that looks like a telephone booth!" Of course he was grinning inwardly all the while. So I went outside and I looked and looked and looked some more. No little telephone booth was found! There wasn't one! The whole outdoors was the bathroom, and there aren't many trees in Texas!

Things seemed so primitive to me, but I learned so much from those precious people. **I learned to be teachable.** I came to realize you can learn from people even though they might seem to be backwards.   No, they didn't have the accommodations I was accustomed to as a city girl, but they had love. They were just the salt-of-the-earth kind of people who took me in as a nineteen-year-old girl trying to be a pastor's wife and loved me. They just acted like I was the smartest thing in the world and treated us with such respect.

I learned there is no one from whom you cannot learn. The person may not smell as good as you do, he may not look like you look, but he can teach you something. I know had those people not just accepted me, I would not have accepted them. It really started me off on a good footing as a pastor's wife when I realized I could love all kinds of people and they would return that love.

Now I have already said we didn't make a great big salary. But our church people loaded our car at the end of the day with chickens, vegetables, fresh milk and butter. Every Sunday we went home with enough food for at least three or four days. **Through that, I learned to be grateful.**

Don't ever get to the place where you expect things because you are in a position of leadership. Always be grateful. Be grateful even when you are given something that makes you think, "I wonder what that is?"

I remember one time when we had dinner with a very, very poor dirt farmer. There were open windows, no screens and flies everywhere. If I remember correctly, there were even chickens in the kitchen. We had hamburgers and cold chili for lunch and I remember the man saying, "Boy, I wish we had the preacher every Sunday because we really eat when the preacher comes." As we ate, I noticed a pie — and it looked like it might have been raisin pie. So at the end of lunch I said, "And I'll have a piece of the raisin pie." And as the wife drove the flies off the top of it she said, "This isn't raisin pie; it's custard." Now, I had already asked for that pie; what else could I do? I ate it. I hate flies! I remember saying as that pie went down, "Lord, bless it as it goes down and help it stay there!" Sometimes it's hard to be grateful, but it's a lesson we must learn. It will be especially necessary if you end up on the mission field. You might be in a place where dog is a great delicacy like it is in the Philippines! Just learn to be grateful.

We must learn to be grateful for whatever is offered to us and never expect anything. We have, since we came to Hammond, been given the privilege at one of the local department stores of purchasing things with a ten percent discount. To this day, I have not ever asked for it. Now if a clerk remembers and says something about it, I take it. However, I never ask for it. The people in the store even tell me to ask when I come in, but I don't and I never will.

Far too many preachers and preachers' wives expect their people to bow at their feet and give them too much. And people will; they are generous. People love their pastor's wife. But don't expect it. Don't ever get to the place you think you are above everybody and that everything should be given to you. It's just not true. Be grateful for what you do receive.

Then at that little church I learned to accept different customs. I learned to accept things like going to the bathroom in the great big outdoors and drinking out of a dipper after others and to accept people who came to church driving tractors and wearing overalls. We were probably the only ones who arrived at church in a car. And, of course, I didn't wear overalls! I didn't even dress sloppily. I was probably a little less dressed up than was usual for me, but I always went looking as I thought they would want their pastor's wife to look — neat and well-groomed. I tried not to be too "fussy" in that particular area because I wanted them to feel comfortable; yet, I wanted to keep up what I thought were my standards. I feel a pastor and his wife ought to look the part. Nevertheless, there are times when we would not want to wear our really "fussy duds" around people who don't have them.

I also learned to adjust to their different ways without compromising convictions. You must never compromise your real convictions. Now you can compromise your preferences if they aren't based on the Bible, but never compromise your convictions.

Before we leave this little church, I want us to consider verses 2 through 4 of the second chapter of James. "For if there come unto your assembly a man with a gold ring, in goodly apparel, and there come in also a poor man in vile raiment; And ye have respect to him that weareth the gay clothing, and say unto him, Sit thou here in a good place; and say to the poor, Stand thou there, or sit here under my footstool: Are ye not then partial in yourselves, and are become judges of evil thoughts?" (James 2:2-4)

To me, these verses fit this little church. They were very, very different people. But I learned to love them as much as if they had worn satin and lace and driven Cadillacs.

I learned not to be partial. As a pastor's wife, there will always be in your church a mixture of country people and city people, or well-dressed people and poorly-dressed people. However, they all have the same needs, the same love to give and the same need of your love. We must learn not to be partial to people because of the way they look or dress and to accept their different customs.

Doesn't Everyone Love the Preacher, Lord?

The second church to which we were called was the Grange Hall Baptist Church located in our college town. We went there with forty-some-odd members — and some of them didn't like us! (I **said** they were odd.) We were called by a majority but, as my husband has mentioned before, the three main members of the church didn't want us. They didn't vote for us and, therefore, we were not paid for several weeks! We didn't even get the $15 a month we had gotten at the other church! But do you know what? **I learned that God does take care of His own.** He takes care of you and He will never let you go without your needs. Now you may not get your wants, but your needs will be met.

I remember one Sunday as we left church we didn't know how in the world we were going to get back to church that night. We were living in town in an apartment at that time — we hadn't moved out by the church to the parsonage yet — and we needed gas to get back to the evening service. And God provided that gasoline **and** some money. As we left the church that morning, a man who had visited the morning service pulled up beside our car at a stoplight and said, "Bro. Hyles, God has impressed me to give you this $10. It's not for the church; it is for you personally." Now, that man didn't know us; and he certainly didn't know about our need. So we said, "Thank you, Lord, for gasoline." I learned that God provides. It may be raisin pie, but He will provide.

I learned at Grange Hall that not everyone loves God's man. Now it's usually not personal; it's because of what God's man stands for and because of what he preaches. In our first little country church everybody had just always loved us. They were good to us. However, this second church taught me not everyone loves God's man.

John 15:20 says, "Remember the word that I said unto you, The servant is not greater than his lord. If they have persecuted me, they will also persecute you; if they have kept my saying, they will keep your's also." The servant is not greater than his master. If Jesus at times suffered hatred and criticism, you will too. You may as well expect it. In remembering that not everyone loves God's man, we should remember that not everyone loved Jesus.

I learned here that it is possible to learn in the midst of persecution. In II Samuel 16 a man named Shimei cast stones and dust on David. Instead of ordering the man's death, David said Shimei should be left alone. He realized there might be something he should learn from the man's attitude toward him.

It's important to learn criticism is sometimes justified. We can learn from it. Perhaps the things people are saying about us are things that need to teach us something.

I think we also need to realize the criticism is really not directed at us personally. It's because of Whom we represent. They hated Jesus and they will hate the ones who represent Him.

I also learned there, the hard way, to be careful about criticizing my husband's sermons. You can be his greatest critic, but you need to learn when to do it and how to do it. I learned that right after his message was no time to tell him anything I disagreed with or thought could have been said differently. Right after a sermon he is still under the load of the day and the message. The next day is better if you honestly feel there is something you must say. By the way, before the next day comes you may have changed your mind anyway. My husband said to me one day when I started to critique him, "Now, look, I can't take that right now. If you want to tell me tomorrow, that's fine."

So I said, "Alright, I'm sorry. I'm glad you told me that." And I think by the next day I had forgotten and didn't feel like he needed the criticism.

When your husband is being criticized by others, that is not the time to criticize anything he says — not on Monday, Wednesday or any other day. He has enough criticism coming from other areas at a time like that.

There are times when we should just let the Lord take care of criticizing his sermons! I do remember one particular night in this church when my husband so vividly portrayed the person about whom he was preaching, you could have just turned around and looked right at her. If you think he preaches hard now, you should have heard him back then! On that particular night, everybody knew who he was preaching against. He didn't make any bones about where he was aiming his sermon. There was a lady in the church who had done something — I don't even remember what — that had really riled him. So he just spent the whole sermon preaching at her. (Of course, he doesn't do that anymore.) But not too many people got fed that night. She just got chafed really good. He came home after church, but I had already learned I was not supposed to criticize him right away. So I didn't say anything. But he said, "Well, I let her have it, didn't I?"

I said, "Mm hmm."

He said, "She deserved it too, didn't she?"

"Mm hmm."

And he said, "Bet she won't ever do that again, will she?"

"Huh mm."

By this time, he was already in his pajamas, but he said, "Okay, I'll put my clothes on and go apologize!"

Now I had not said one thing but "Mm hmm" and "Huh mm." And I had said it nicely. But the Lord took care of convicting him; I didn't need to. You make him happy and let God make him good. If I had said, "Boy, you surely did," it might never have been resolved; we probably would have lost a good lady. I knew he had handled it wrongly; but it would have been wrong for me to have lied and sided with him. Yet, it would have also been wrong of me to criticize him. So all I did was sweetly say, "Mm hmm" and "Huh mm" and the Lord convicted his heart. He can do that, you know!

So learn to be careful about being critical of your husband's sermons.

I learned many things about hospitality at Grange Hall. Now maybe you are one who loves people running in and out of your home. You can put down pallets here, there and everywhere and just have a crowd. But I am not that way. I like my home to be in order and, if I am going to have company, I want to have just enough beds and sheets. I don't want to have to put anyone in the bathtub to sleep!

I read once about a woman who said her home was open house all the time. She said out of the 365 nights in one year one of her children slept 297 nights in a place other than his own bed. She said he once took his bedclothes to the bathtub! Now, I think that's wrong for a child. I don't think it's wrong for a child to give up his bed occasionally; I think it teaches a pastor's child something good to give up his privacy once in a while. But asking a child to give up his bed for almost a whole year is wrong.

However, we must learn to be hospitable with whatever we have. When we had visiting evangelists at Grange Hall, they had to stay in our little country parsonage. And it was **not** the Waldorf Astoria! We even had a pet. It was about four or five inches long, it was gray and furry and, as you can guess, it was a rat! We'd put out poison and he just loved it! One time Mel and Dorothy Rutter, missionaries from Mexico, were staying with us when the toilet got stopped up. So we all just laughed and went over to the church to use the facilities. We were hospitable with what we had. We couldn't send guests to a hotel or motel — there weren't any. If there had been one, we couldn't have afforded it. Visiting pastors and evangelists would probably prefer motels if the church can afford it. But when the church is small and you can't, you have to learn to be hospitable with what you have.

Realize your guests have been where you are now. You look at me and you think, "Mrs. Hyles cannot possibly understand what it is like to go out in the country to a little church." Yes, I can! I've been there! So when people come and you don't have the best of accommodations, they've been there. They understand. You just make things as clean as you can and your guests will enjoy your hospitality.

I learned at Grange Hall I had to do jobs behind the scenes that just wouldn't get done otherwise. We had a janitor there who was in his seventies. His walk could best be described as a slow shuffle and he didn't get much done. But he had been the janitor for years, so we didn't want to fire him. Anyway, the restrooms were never clean enough to suit me. They didn't smell good. So during the week I would take some cleanser and clean the toilets. No one knew it — no one saw it — and I didn't want them to see it. I also didn't think our small nursery smelled like it should. So I would wipe the beds off well and take the sheets off and wash them. I felt like those two areas must be clean and smell clean, so I would often work on them. No one ever knew it. I didn't do it to be seen. I did it because I thought it was a necessity. I knew our janitor couldn't move fast enough to get it all done, so I did it.

Do jobs that you see need to be done without recognition. Now that doesn't mean you are to do everything you see that needs to be done. You have to remember your primary job is to be the pastor's wife. But you can do some things behind the scenes that won't get done if you don't do them.

So, You Don't Want Testing?

Then we moved to Southside Baptist Church in Henderson, Texas. When people think of churches we have pastored, they very seldom think of Southside Baptist Church. Well, I don't either! That's because there were no problems there. It was a wonderful little church. There was a little brick building, the people were good, it was an established church in the community, everyone loved us and there were no problems. The church grew a little; someone joined every Sunday. People were saved here and there. And that's exactly why we don't remember it!! Because there were no problems. There were no testings. Now we loved the people and, as I think back to it, I think of it with happy memories. But when I look back over the years, I most often remember the Marris Chapels where the great outdoors was the bathroom and the Grange Halls where three men sat and made faces at my husband as he preached. I remember these places more than I remember the peaceful, wonderful little community church where everything went smoothly. And you will too.

Now I'm so glad that in our more than forty years of pastoring we had almost a whole year where we had a peaceful existence and everything was just "hunky-dory." (That's Texan for "great.") And as I said, I loved it! However, I don't think of that church as often as I do the others. My husband doesn't mention it often; it's almost as if we had a period of rest to get us ready for the years ahead.

Even though things went so smoothly, I can look back on that time and think of several things I learned. **First of all, I learned that the greatest lessons come out of testing.** We just don't usually learn when everything is going well. That's probably because we don't run to the Bible with the same sense of urgency when all is well as we do when there are problems. **Secondly, I learned not to be a martyr by always keeping the nursery.** Now if the women there had let me, I could have become the only one who kept the nursery. By that time I had a child, and they would have gladly let me do it. But I gladly didn't do it! We made up a roster and we all took turns each Sunday and Wednesday. Of course I did my share, but I learned people will let you do anything you want to take on. However, I knew I needed some preaching. I knew I did not dare stay out of the church services all the time because I needed it as much as anybody.

Cutting the Umbilical Cord

We had been at Southside almost a year when my husband left to go to Garland, Texas, so he could attend Southwestern Seminary and finish his education. So he started pastoring at Miller Road Baptist Church. To begin with, it was a small church. I don't remember exactly how many there were when we first went, but it began to grow and grow and grow.

Here I learned that you can't and shouldn't have special friends

among the members of your church with whom you fellowship more than others. By that I mean you shouldn't go out with them and have them over to your house to the exclusion of other people.

In every church God will give you at least one couple who will just be there for you. They seem to have an almost uncanny sense of what you need when you need it. There was a couple like this at Miller Road and they began to ask us over for meals occasionally. We felt like we surely ought to have them over in return. Well, we soon learned that was not the thing to do. People criticized us. The work was small enough to make it appear we were showing favoritism, and that just does not work. Of course we did repay that couple over and over for their hospitality. We did it in ways other than having them over to our home. You can repay the hospitality of your people by teaching their children and serving them in the church, but it isn't a good idea to fellowship with any certain couple to the exclusion of others. It is even a different matter if you have a church with a staff and you socialize with your staff. The church members seem to view that in a different light and they don't object to it.

I also learned at Miller Road that you must keep your feet on the ground when popularity comes — because popularity did begin to come our way there. I think we saw success in the world's eyes as well as in God's eyes. Many, many people were saved. We became known as the fastest-growing church in Texas. My husband has told you that he spoke at the conventions of the Southern Baptist Convention. He was the "fair-haired young man," and I liked that. I was his wife! But popularity comes and popularity goes. And it goes more quickly than it comes.

Hebrews 11:26 is a wonderful verse for you to keep in mind. I love it. This is the place in Hebrews where the Bible is talking about the heroes of the faith. This verse is speaking of Moses who grew up in a palace among riches with all the conveniences and the surroundings of wealth. The verse says, "Esteeming the reproach of Christ greater riches than the treasures in Egypt: for he had respect unto the recompence of the reward." (Hebrews 11:26)

Ladies, success times will come. And the good times have far outnumbered the bad in our ministry — and they will in yours if you will look for them and recognize them. The assets of the ministry far outweigh the liabilities. When popularity comes, that's good. When success comes, it's a result of soul winning. Some people come to the First Baptist Church of Hammond and say it's too big. But if you are going soul winning, a church is going to get big. That is part of the price you pay. Nevertheless, when you get too popular, that is not always a good sign. Christ wasn't popular! If you are popular for doing right, winning souls, preaching the truth and standing for that which is right, fine. If it is because of compromising, then watch out! That is not the right kind of popularity.

Moses turned his back on the great riches he could have had to run with his people and to suffer the reproach of Christ; yet he esteemed it greater riches than the popularity of ruling in Egypt. We need to realize that to serve Christ, whether we are on top or on bottom, is riches. It really is.

There will be times in your ministry when the world might say you are "on the bottom." But during those times of suffering reproach, it is feasible to feel the closeness and wonder of God's hand as never before and to enjoy your walk with the Lord more than ever. During the low times you can rejoice in what God is doing in your own heart. It is possible — and we must learn — to esteem the reproach of Christ greater riches than to walk with the world.

I learned the truth of John 12:24: "Verily, verily, I say unto you, Except a corn of wheat fall into the ground and die, it abideth alone: but if it die, it bringeth forth much fruit." There came a time at Miller Road in Garland where we had to die to our denomination — the one in which we were both reared. We had to die to friends of a lifetime. Losing the life-giving support of a denomination was much like having the umbilical cord cut. We had to die to family. When we were kicked out of the Southern Baptist Convention, we were kicked "outside the camp." But you know, we found Someone else Who was outside the camp. Jesus was outside the camp, so we were in good company. Yes, it made the headlines and we lost a lot of good people over it. In one day, all my husband's speaking engagements were canceled. Friends of a lifetime turned their backs on us. Even relatives questioned what had happened. However, it was a springboard for the people of that church to do greater things than they had ever done before. After this we were free to serve God as we felt the Bible told us to, and the church flourished and grew and prospered.

We must also remember it isn't always bad when a church attains a bit of notoriety and people leave. Sometimes a church needs purging.

God **did** turn to prosperity what seemed to us to be evil. Miller Road grew and grew. We were situated for life — we **thought!** Both of our families lived nearby; my brother was superintendent of the Junior department and my husband's mother, sister, and other relatives were among our members.

But into our comfortable situation came a series of calls from a nominating committee and, after feeling the definite leading of God, we came north to Hammond, Indiana.

When we came to First Baptist Church, it was about 70 years old. It was a good church, but it was a formal church. Now they had won souls through the years. They had had good pastors — they had good people. But there were two factions in the church. There were those people who said, "We want to keep it just as it is — the First Baptist Church with the mayor and the councilmen and the department store owners." And then there were those who had always wanted to be a soul winning, aggressive, forward-going church. These two factions had always tried to coexist, yet there was not really harmony. And guess who God chose to break those two factions apart? Yes — us! So just a year after we got here, we had the crucial vote as to whether or not we would go back to Texas. Now frankly, we both voted yes! We even signed the petition that was circulating. We wanted to go back! But we lost the vote, so we stayed.

All this didn't happen without a lot of heartache, and the heartache was not only ours. Families were split, and we hurt for them. But it had to come, so we left another convention — the American Baptist Convention.

An exodus like this doesn't come without persecution. Remember this: persecution often comes, and most often comes, **for doing right.**

Don't Be Surprised at Fiery Trials

What caused Daniel's persecution — right or wrong? What about Shadrach, Meshach and Abednego — right or wrong? Or Joseph in the Old Testament? What about Job whose testing came because God said to Satan, "Have you considered my servant Job?" And Satan said, "I surely have. So let's just test him." What about Stephen, Paul and Peter? What about all the apostles who died unnaturally in some way or another?

Let's not be guilty of pointing fingers at people when they are going through testing, saying, "Wonder what they've done?" Always remember when it comes to you, you are going to want people to realize even though God does sometimes chasten and spank, persecution often comes for doing right. We always need to remember that.

Then I learned early on — and should have learned it way back yonder — that Christianity is a warfare, not a picnic. II Timothy 2:3 and 4 says, "Thou therefore endure hardness, as a good soldier of Jesus Christ. No man that warreth entangleth himself with the affairs of this life; that he may please him who hath chosen him to be a soldier."

Now granted, we are not the ones who fight on the front lines; our men do. But in Psalms 68:11 through 13 we see that we are still soldiers. "The Lord gave the word: great was the company of those that published it. Kings of armies did flee apace: and she that tarried at home divided the spoil. Though ye have lien among the pots, yet shall ye be as the wings of a dove covered with silver, and her feathers with yellow gold." (Psalm 68:11-13) These verses are precious to me. Of course, we don't go out to the front lines and get in the trenches. We are the ones who stay home with the pots and cook good meals and keep the home fires burning — but we are still soldiers. The guy who stays home in the mess tent and cooks for those who go out — he is a soldier. The man who packs the

parachutes for the men who jump is just as important a soldier —
though he may never have jumped.

We are in a warfare. I'm not talking about just the pastor and his
wife, but all Christians. Ephesians 6:10-17 are valuable verses for
teaching us how to equip ourselves for this warfare we are in.

**I also learned not only is Christianity a warfare, but there is no
discharge.** You can't go AWOL. Oh, you may, but you won't be
very happy. Do you know what AWOL means? It means absent
without leave. There is no discharge and there is never a time to
quit.

Of course there are fun times in the army too. R and R is fun.
Service isn't all bad. In fact, it's great — depending upon who your
captain is. And we have the best Captain of all!

YOU CAN'T STORE IT, FREEZE IT, OR DEHYDRATE IT!

In this chapter we are going to deal with scheduling your time. Before we do, let me give you an important quote: "The Christian ministry is not composed so much of **doing** as **being**." Now James 2:17 tells us faith without works is dead. We know that if we are Christians who love the Lord, we will be doing. But doing can never replace being. That's why it's so important for you to be what you appear to be; be real.

I suppose the prayer I have prayed most in the last ten or fifteen years is, "Lord, make me real. Make me what people think I am." People often say to me, "You are so sweet and gracious." That is kind, but I am just like you are. I am made of the same stuff you are. It is so important for us to learn to be real.

Another important thing to remember is this: "You will do what you ought to do if you are what you ought to be." Yet so often "doing" is a problem because of a seeming lack of time. We all have the same amount, yet it still seems sometimes that we don't have enough. That's why we need to deal with priorities and using our time wisely.

I am going to read a few quotes from Ann Ortlund's *Disciplines of the Beautiful Woman*. First of all, she says, "The great majority of women in this world, not understanding that God has specific plans for their lives, would tell you they just take it as it comes." Does that sound like you? Does life just happen to you? She goes on to say, "Because their lives have only a horizontal, humanistic dimension — not vertical between them and God — they readily agree that they just live one day at a time." Now we are told to do that, but it is possible to do that and still be planning our lives. She goes on to say, "Actually, that's what's known as drifting down the lazy old river, man, and it feels so good — only it ends up at Niagara Falls. You are going over and you don't even have a barrel."

Now going over the falls is rough — with or without a barrel! So I say, "Don't let life just happen!"

You need to be somewhat scheduled every day. You ought to learn to have priorities in your scheduling.

Now when that first baby comes, be prepared! It is very hard to follow a schedule. All you can expect is the unexpected. But Romans 13:11 and 12 says, "And that, knowing the time, that now it is high time to awake out of sleep: for now is our salvation nearer than when we believed. The night is far spent, the day is at hand: let us therefore cast off the works of darkness, and let us put on the armour of light." Colossians 4:5 teaches us that we must redeem the time. We need to be conscious of our days, our moments, and our time and learn to use them wisely.

Jack Lalanne, the fitness guru, made this statement: "You are the sum total of the books you read and the people you meet." I also agree with Mr. Lalanne that how you use your time is a great part of what you are. That's because, more than you realize, the way you use your time reveals what's important to you.

Goals Should Make You, Not Break You

Someone said, "Women must balance their time because they don't have wives." That, too, is true. If you are the mother and wife of the home, it is even more important for you to know how to balance your time, readjust schedules and be flexible; you have many duties calling from many directions. Therefore, you need to learn to make realistic goals every day. Proverbs 29:18a says, "Where there is no vision, the people perish." You **need** a vision for every day. But don't try to do your spring cleaning in one day if you know you must also tend to a husband and child and go to a college class. You can't do it. And do you know what? If you have made that your goal, you will feel completely defeated by the end of the day because you didn't reach it. Make realistic goals you feel you can probably reach in a day, and you won't be defeated so often.

Five times I have had the happy privilege of cruising on a large cruise ship from New York to the Caribbean. Now the interesting thing is the captain had always planned the exact course that great ship would take through the waters of the Atlantic, but he had to rechart that course continually because of the contrary winds or storms that would come. He had to keep his eyes and mind open constantly to rechanneling that ship so we would reach our destination.

It is the same in your life. Though you make realistic goals daily, you have to learn to be flexible, to rechannel. You must be flexible because people are more important than prescheduled things. If your husband needs you, if your children need you, if someone has an emergency need for you, people are always more important than your rigid schedule.

Now I had to learn that people are always more important than a schedule. I like schedule and I am a perfectionist. I just wasn't very flexible. When it was housecleaning day, it was housecleaning day if the whole world was lost; I didn't care. But we must learn to rechannel and take a different course when contrary winds come up. I guess that's why I love Proverbs 3:5 and 6 that says, "Trust in the Lord with all thine heart; and lean not unto thine own understanding. In all thy ways acknowledge him, and he shall direct thy paths." The Lord will help us when it's necessary to make changes. He will tell us when we need to go just a little bit to the left or right in our days.

Values and priorities — how do we determine them? It is very hard. Time is life and it is our most valuable commodity. We all have 1,440 minutes a day. Why is it some people can accomplish so much and some say, "I just don't have time!" We all have the same amount of time; the key lies in learning to use it well. That's the problem. No one seems to have enough, and yet all of us have all there is. It's a paradox, isn't it? You know, people often say, "I need more than 24 hours in a day!" Well, I don't! Believe me, that's all I can handle. By the time I get to bed at night, I think, "Boy, I am glad there are no more hours in this day!"

But our time must be spent. You can't store it, freeze it or dehydrate it for another day. How are you spending yours? Psalm 90:12 says, "So teach us to number our days, that we may apply our hearts unto wisdom." Now, how many more days do you have left? Nobody knows, but the normal life span is seventy years. Where are you? You know, the farther along you get, the more important it is that you use every day to the fullest and in the wisest way. Even when you are young, there is no time to waste. Every day ought to be filled. Now that doesn't mean you don't take time to play and time to laugh. One of the most important things you will learn in life is to laugh. It's a lot better than crying! Many times it releases the same pent-up emotions. A wise person will learn to use his or her time well.

Matthew 25:1-12 gives us the parable of the virgins. There were five foolish and five wise. What was the difference? The five wise virgins took time to prepare. The five foolish virgins were caught empty-handed because they didn't use their time wisely.

We can tell if we are using our time to the fullest by determining whether we are making and reaching daily, weekly and monthly goals. If you periodically get a spurt of energy and good sense, and make some goals but you never reach them; then you may as well not make them. If you aren't reaching goals, you are not using your time wisely.

Another way to use your time wisely is to know your priorities and to use your time accordingly. I ask you again, "Does life just happen to you?" Do you just get up and say, "Que sera, sera." I believe that means, "Whatever will be, will be."

Let's think about it a moment. What is your greatest goal as a Christian lady? Write it down. Perhaps because you are reading this book, yours is to be the best full-time Christian worker's wife you can be. Probably above that would be to serve God to the best of your ability; that would make you the best pastor's wife you can be. But what is your greatest goal as a Christian leader's wife or a potential Christian leader's wife? Under that goal, write down a goal you are going to make for this year that will help you reach your ultimate goal. Then decide what you can do this week that will help you reach that ultimate goal by the time your life is over. After that you can set a goal for this day. That's how to make goals and schedules. Don't just set future goals. If you aren't reaching goals today, you won't reach future goals. Each step you take leads you toward your big goal, and each step you miss or take the wrong way deters you from reaching your goal. So you see, there are no unimportant days. There are no unimportant moments. Even the times of fun and laughter are important; laughter is an important part of your life. Don't think I'm talking about all work and no play, because that makes Jack a dull boy, believe me!!

Even the Mundane Needs Planning

When you cook, do you just think, "Well, I'll just get in there and stir a bunch of stuff together." Is that the way you cook? Of course not! You have planned to be sure you have the ingredients you need for whatever you are fixing.

I enjoy gardening. I just love to go out and get dirt under my fingernails and get nasty. However, I don't go out there and plant any old packet of seeds and hope I get tomatoes! If I plant zinnias, I'm not going to get tomatoes. So I plan.

I plan when I am going to take a nap. Young mothers, sometimes the most spiritual thing you can do is to plan a nap. I don't care if your children go to sleep in the middle of the morning. If you feel you have not gotten enough rest and you can nap for thirty minutes, take a nap. You will be fresher for your husband when he comes home and you will be better able to cope with your children.

Sometimes the most spiritual thing you can do is just to go out and throw the ball for your dog to fetch. While visiting my daughter, Linda, in Dallas, Texas, I had so much fun playing with their little terrier, Sugar Boy. I realized how much it relaxed me just to play with that little dog. One night you should have seen us! I'd bark at him, and he'd bark back. We just had the best time barking at each other! Those times are fun and you need to plan them. You need to plan some relaxation in your life. Every activity needs direction. According to the Bible, God is a God of orderliness. "For God is not the author of confusion, but of peace, as in all churches of the saints." (I Corinthians 14:33) "Let all things be done decently and in order." (I Corinthians 14:40) Now, how can you keep your life running decently and in order without having chaos and without running around in all directions? You do it by planning, by scheduling. Yes, there will be unexpected things. But your attitude will help you take even the unexpected events and keep your life in order. If you are a chaotic, unscheduled, hectic person, it says something is wrong inside; God is not the author of that kind of chaos. The world was in chaos when He created it, and He brought everything into order. He will do the same for your life, but you have to do your part too. You must ask Him to direct you and help you know how to make your schedule and your plans for the day.

Now, our priorities will be based on what we value. What you value will command time from you. If you think about how you spend most of your time, you can determine what you really value. Perhaps you spend most of your time primping in front of the mirror. Now you ought to spend a little bit of time doing that, but perhaps you spend far too much time. You will find that whatever you really value will demand time from you. It demands your time because you value it, and it will get done whether anything else gets done or not.

Let's see what God has to say in Matthew 22:35 through 38 about our values and priorities: "Then one of them, which was a lawyer, asked him a question, tempting him, and saying, Master, which is the great commandment in the law? Jesus said unto him, Thou shalt love the Lord thy God with all thy heart, and with all thy soul, and with all thy mind. This is the first and great commandment." That will sum up all the other commandments in the Bible. If we really get it in our hearts, it will help us to want to do all the other things we have been commanded to do. But then He said in verses 39 and 40, "And the second is like unto it, Thou shalt love thy neighbour as thyself. On these two commandments hang all the law and the prophets." And from these two commandments you can secure all your priorities and know in which order they should come.

First and foremost as Christian leader's wives, we should love the Lord our God with all our hearts, souls and minds. And we need to give God priority time every day. You won't make it if you don't.

People have often asked me what gives me strength when times are difficult in my Christian life. First, I know when the battles come I am undergirded with a lot of prayer. But I think my strength also comes because I learned a long time ago to go to the Word of God with a sense of urgency. I am not talking about going with a sense of urgency **when** the battles come. I mean we must go with a sense of urgency **all** the time. You see, it's easy to go with urgency when the battles are here. But we need to go to the Bible that way all the time because we never know what is just around the bend!

You can't wait until your child's fever is 107° plus to get into the Word. That is no time to be looking for food in the Word in order to strengthen your spiritual muscles. You can't wait until the battles come. I believe that going to the Bible with a sense of urgency on a daily basis has played a major part in my having the strength and peace to face the battles that have come my way.

What Are Your Priorities?

Let's make some guidelines then for our priorities according to these two great commandments. First of all, the greatest priority in our lives should be a personal relationship with our God — daily. Salvation comes first. I would not want to take it for granted that you know you are saved. Perhaps there is someone reading this book who isn't sure of your salvation. If that's true of you, get the matter settled today. You must have a personal relationship with God.

Mrs. Dawson Trotman, who was the wife of the founder of the Navigators, said that a wife's personal walk with her God is the greatest contribution she can give to her marriage or to any other thing she does. It is so very important. I had to learn that the hard way.

You know, as leaders' wives, especially when you get out into the work, you are in church all the time. You are there for Sunday morning, Sunday night, Sunday school, Wednesday night, soul winning, Phoster Club, choir practice, and perhaps even more than that. You are involved in it all. And you are hearing the Scripture read in every meeting. So you can get to the place where you think, "I have heard the Bible. I don't need to read it for myself." But that's just not true!

I have always had the privilege of having the best preacher in the world. (Of course, if your husband is a preacher, you don't agree — and you shouldn't!) But there came a time after all four of my children had been born when I came to the end of my day and realized, "Oh! I haven't read my Bible today!" So I would say, "Alright, I know what I'll do. I'll just let my Bible fall open and read wherever it opens." And of course it usually didn't mean a thing to me when I did that and I would say, "I just don't understand the Bible!" No wonder! If you read a book that way, you wouldn't understand it either! Even though you should be in the church services faithfully, it isn't enough to depend only on the Bible you hear at church for your spiritual food.

Of course, I am in no way trying to minimize the importance of church attendance. Dr. Lee Roberson's wife has said her main duty as given to her by her husband was just to be his wife and be in the services sitting in the same spot. That is what he mainly wanted her to do. So, through the years she was in charge of the church nursery and she attended the services. Those were her main duties and that is what she did. It is very important for you to be in the church services. In my book, *I Feel Precious To God*, I mention how important the public services are. We need them. I need preaching. ". . .faith cometh by hearing, and hearing by the Word of God." (Romans 10:17)

I am not saying you need to take your kids to church when their noses are pouring and they have temperatures of 104°. I think your children deserve the right to stay home in bed when they are sick and have mother love them and tend to them until they get well. If you keep them home, they will get well more quickly which will enable you to be back in church sooner. There have been times in the past when my husband hired a sitter to come in so that I could go to church when the kids had been sick one after the other for weeks in a row. We didn't have a lot of money then, but he knew

I needed to be in church and he knew the children needed to be home because they were sick. He knew I needed to hear the Word of God preached in church.

Do you know that in the days before Gerber and Heinz, mothers used to chew up food and put it in their babies' mouths? I don't think my mother had to do that, but that is similar to what is being done to you when you go to church. When you hear someone preach the Word, it has already been chewed up for you. That's wonderful, but you need to learn to do it for yourself! Yes, the pastor has indeed sought wisdom from God, and he knows the diet you need — sometimes better than you do. However, you also need to learn how to chew for yourself.

The Bible is your meat, your honey, your milk and your bread. It's a balanced meal that you need to be eating. You cannot live off your husband's spirituality. He may be the greatest Christian you have ever known, but you cannot live on his spirituality — you have to develop your own. You can only do that as you have a time with the Lord personally and learn to talk to Him and communicate with Him. After all, that's why He made us. I know He made the woman to be a helpmeet for the man, but He made all mankind to fellowship with Himself.

We must also realize that the Bible is a love letter. If you do not have a good sense of self-worth and you don't know how precious you are to God, it could be because you are not daily reading the letter of love that God uses to tell you how precious you are to Him.

I have already said the Bible is our meat. Meat is the protein in our diet. Of course, other things are too, but meat is one of the best sources of protein. Every cell in your physical body needs protein. Your spiritual body also needs protein for building strength, and you can only get it from the Bible — the meat of the Word of God.

The Bible also talks about Christians who are still babies. The milk of the Word is important to those people. What was the first food most of you had? You had milk from your mother's body or from a bottle. To me, that denotes not only the food and the nourishment that was the only kind we could take as babies, but it also denotes the time mother held us and cuddled us and sang lullabies to us as we were fed. I think of the milk of the Word of God in the same way. You may be a spiritual baby, but you need the Word. You need the nourishment and that "cuddling time" with the Lord.

Bread is called the staff of life. And the Bible is the staff of our spiritual lives. It is strengthening and we must have it.

Maybe you have a hard time staying sweet. I do! Well, the Bible is our honey — the sweetener! My husband has often said that each day he reads Proverbs for wisdom, Psalms to make him sweet and Acts to keep him on fire.

You need to get into the Word of God. I don't know what kind of plan will work for you. Some years I read through the Bible. Some years I just study portions of it. I do try to read a Psalm each day and the Proverb that corresponds to the day of the month every day each year. Proverbs is a book of wisdom and you can never get too much wisdom. Make a plan for reading the Word of God. If you don't plan, you won't do it. If you have not planned to do it, that means it is not a valuable thing to you. It ought to have top priority.

Joshua 1:8 says, "This book of the law shall not depart out of thy mouth; but thou shalt meditate therein day and night, that thou mayest observe to do according to all that is written therein: for then thou shalt make thy way prosperous, and then thou shalt have good success." Now that's a promise. Psalm 1 tells us if we will not walk in the counsel of the ungodly nor sit in the seat of the scornful nor stand in the way of sinners, but meditate on the Word of God, we shall have success. We must find a way to meditate on the Word of God.

Even when I am in a really big hurry, I must get at least one verse to chew on first thing in the morning until I can spend time in the Word of God. Perhaps I will meditate on a verse that I have underlined in the past. (If a verse is underlined in my Bible, it is very precious to me.) But I simply must start my day with the Word.

Are you a lark or an owl? A lark is a morning person; he just gets up singing. I'm not so much anymore, but I used to be a lark. An owl is a person who just wakes up at noon (even though he has been out of bed for hours), and he can go until the wee hours of the next morning. If you know you are an owl and you do not comprehend anything before noon, the early morning is not the best time for you to do your Bible reading. If you are an owl, the evening is probably better for you. If you are a morning person and you wake up fresh and alive, then morning would be the best time for you to read your Bible. You must decide when is best for you and **put it in your schedule**. Schedule it or you won't do it.

Have You Called Your Father Today?

We need to learn to talk to God. He talks to us by His Word; we talk to Him in prayer. It's so important. You can say anything to God. You can gripe to Him, you can fuss at Him (reverently, of course!), and you can tell Him just what you think about anything.

I remember one time when I felt someone had wronged me at church. I was so angry I wanted to see blood! So on the way home from church I said, "Lord, You know what that person did. I'm so upset, Lord. You know I'm angry. I tell You, what can I do?" And do you know that by the time I got through telling the Lord about it, I was laughing? It really helps to tell Him. I just simply wasn't mad anymore. I can't even remember who it was or what they did that made me so irritated now. But God knows all about it anyway. You might as well admit you just want to kill your husband! Dr. Bob Jones was known to have said he never wanted to divorce his wife but he often wanted to kill her!

You know, we can go to God, pour out all our mixed feelings — things we don't even understand we are feeling — and, often, just talking about it out loud to God gets it all sorted out. You don't have to go to another person. He is our Counselor. You would pay a psychiatrist a hundred dollars an hour to talk and he would just say, "Yes? Tell me more." And a psychiatrist couldn't even give you any specific answers as he charged you a hundred dollars an hour. However, you can get better results talking out loud to God, and He doesn't charge!

I can't pray silently for more than just a few seconds. If I try, I start wondering if I took the meat out to thaw for supper or some such thing. I just like to pray out loud. Maybe you need to get down on your face. Maybe you need to get on your knees. Do whatever works for you, but I can't emphasize this enough: **YOUR PERSONAL TIME WITH GOD MUST HAVE TOP PRIORITY IN YOUR LIFE.** You can't do without it. You'll never be able to cope without it. You won't make it without it.

So you **must** purpose in your heart to do it. Daniel 1:8 says, "But Daniel purposed in his heart that he would not defile himself with the portion of the king's meat, nor with the wine which he drank: therefore he requested of the prince of the eunuchs that he might not defile himself." He purposed in a seemingly small matter to do what he felt was right. It was his conviction not to eat of the strong meat and drink. It was a seemingly small decision, but when the great crisis decision came about whether he would keep on praying, he was strong enough to do it. He kept on praying because he had been strong enough to make the right decision in small matters as a result of having spent time with God. Then when the great crisis time came, he was ready for it. Don't wait for the crisis before you go to the Word with a sense of urgency; feel going to the Word is urgent every day — because it is.

Who Is Your Neighbor?

Now, our second priority following time with God is to love our neighbor as ourself. Assuming that you are a pastor's wife, who would be your closest neighbor? Your husband would be. He is the one God has placed over your home as the leader. He is the God-figure in your home. So he needs to be top priority. He is your nearest neighbor. Are you pleasing Him? In every way? Do you know what pleases him? Are you dressing the way he likes? If you don't know, why don't you ask him? I think he will tell you.

A very important part of making your husband your top priority is letting him decide what jobs you will take. Some husbands want their wives to be involved in everything. They want them to be church secretaries as well as being involved in every other way. But **my** husband said from the very beginning, "I want you to stay home. I want you to keep the home running smoothly. I want you to keep the kids in order, keep the clothes clean and keep the meals cooked. I want you to teach a class, and I want you to sing in the choir because I know you love to sing. Also, I always want you to be involved in a soul winning ministry." And that was all. So I teach a class, go soul winning, sing in the choir and be my husband's wife. That doesn't sound hard, does it? And it isn't. When someone would come and say, "Mrs. Hyles, we want you to take the WMS presidency this year because it has always been a custom that the pastor's wife take it for a term," then I could say, "No, my husband won't let me." And people will take that. Now if I had said, "No, I am doing too much to add more," they would have said, "She doesn't want to cooperate. She isn't going to be the kind of pastor's wife we want." But they didn't say that because I could say, "No, I'm sorry. My husband has given me some guidelines, and right now he doesn't want me to take on any more responsibilities." That was a great help. I am **not** saying you should use that as an opportunity to be lazy. There was a time when my children were older when my husband did ask me to be the WMS president. It was great training; I loved it. It was hard work, but it was good for me. Be sure you always try to follow your husband's guidelines concerning your priorities in the Lord's work. That is a very important part of making him **your** top priority.

I will never forget the first time Dr. John R. Rice asked me to speak at a Women's Jubilee. When he began the Jubilees a few years before his death, he called and asked me to speak at the very first one. My first response was, "No!" I mean, I didn't say it; but that is what was going through my mind as he talked. I was thinking, "No, I'm not a speaker — especially not one who travels. I mean, nobody would pay me to come speak to them with this accent!" But then I thought, "Beverly Hyles, how can you question a man of God like Dr. Rice? I am sure he has prayed and asked for God's guidance." And all the time I was thinking all this, I don't know **what** he was saying! But he was asking me to come and my answer was simply this: "Dr. Rice, I will ask my husband. If he says it is alright and you feel that I can be a help, then rest assured that I would love to do so." So I asked my husband and he said "Yes." Can you imagine having Dr. John R. Rice sitting in a service listening to you speak? The good thing was that he usually went to sleep! I was very boring!

But again I ask, "Are you pleasing your husband? Do you know what He wants? Do you periodically stop and ask him if there is something he would like to have changed or if you have become perhaps something other than he wants?" You should know what pleases him, and you should do everything you can to **do** what pleases him.

Next in making your husband top priority is to accept him as he is. Accept him unconditionally. Now I know he's not perfect; there is no such animal as a perfect person. If you see there are things he needs to change — perhaps there are character flaws — remember it is up to you to make him happy and up to God to make him good. If you'll pray for him and be to him all that he needs, God will work on those things. Your husband will usually help you if you will be to him what you ought to be. When the children were small, my husband changed as many diapers as I did. He washed dishes. They weren't always very clean, but he washed them. On Sunday mornings he dressed two of the children and I dressed two. I don't know how I would have made it without his help. I hear women say, "My husband's never changed a diaper — he won't!" And I don't know how they do it. But I think my husband wanted to help me because he knew I tried to do things that pleased him. They say marriage is a 50%-50% deal, but it's not. It's a 100%-100% deal. Part of the time you will give 100% and part of the time he will. That's a very important thing to remember.

You should satisfy your husband's physical needs. I mean all the time. Don't ever use physical intimacy as a reward or punishment. You just be there when he needs you. You be to that man what he needs you to be using the Bible as a guideline.

Be his friend and his confidante. Listen to him! At one point in our ministry, my husband thought it necessary to explain our personal finances to our church family. He came home that night and said, "Did I do right by explaining our finances?" I said, "If you feel that's what needed to be done, that's fine; you know more about the situation than I do." And of course I would rather not have sat through our people learning all about the money we didn't have!! I turned around to the choir that night after it was over and said, "Alms for the poor!" My sister-in-law, Earlyne Stephens, sent a note to me just before the closing prayer that said, "Don't kill him. He's not worth it!" I laughed through the whole prayer. But if he felt that was what was needed, that was alright with me. My job is just to support him.

Hold Things Loosely

Now this next statement is very important. Relinquish your husband to God. He is God's first. If you know you are going to marry a preacher, decide before you marry him you are going to be second. God is first. You must realize men love their work. Work is important to a man. In most cases, their work is the highest thing in their lives. But we should never feel put upon because we are second to God. When a man loves and serves God like he should, he will have more love to give to his wife. So relinquish him to God. There is an old proverb that says, "If you love something, set it free. If it's yours, it will come back to you. If it doesn't come back, it wasn't yours in the first place." Hold things loosely in your hands. You do not own that man! You set him free to become all he can be. The following poem says what I would like to convey to you.

> "Love without clinging;
> Cry —
> If you must —
> But privately cry;
> The heart will adjust
> To the newness of loving
> In practical ways:

Cleaning and cooking
And sorting out clothes,
All say, 'I love you,'
When lovingly done.

So —
Love without clinging;
Cry —
If you must —
But privately cry;
The heart will adjust
To the length of his stride,
The song he is singing,
The trail he must ride,
The tensions that make him
The man that he is,
The world he must face,
The life that is his.

So love
Without clinging;
Cry —
If you must —
But privately cry;
The heart will adjust
To being the heart,
Not the forefront of life;
A part of himself,
Not the object —
His wife.

So —
Love."

— Ruth Graham

This poem reminded me of Mrs. John R. Rice, because she said of all the years she and Dr. Rice were married most of them were spent apart from her husband. However, he never saw her cry when he left. She cried alone — privately. She relinquished him to God; and I believe she had a wonderful, wonderful marriage and a man who loved her dearly. But she didn't try to hold him back. She did not cry when he left her and we must learn to be that way. Set him free. Build your life around him. Now you might ask, "Is that fair?" Yes! Because remember, marriage is a 100%-100% deal. When he sees you giving, he's going to give back. "Give and it shall be given unto you." (Luke 6:38a) Now you aren't supposed to give just for that reason, but it will happen. Just make sure your husband has top priority in your life.

Your Child Has a Right — You!

Third, if you have children, they are your next closest neighbors. Love them. You can't love them too much. Of course, I'm not talking about spoiling them; spoiling is not loving. A lack of discipline is not love. Never spanking is not love. Loving them will seem harsh at times. It will seem like you are an old fogy and all that, but love them anyway. Discipline, teach and be an example.

Realize children pick up on what we do more than what we say. You will see what they have learned. As I look at my girls, particularly, and watch the way they keep house and rear their own children, I say, "Oh, horrors, they learned the bad as well as the good." They do learn by example; and you must realize you are always teaching your children. You have to be so very, very careful, and it takes a lot of wisdom.

Rearing children involves making many choices. You ought to plan times with your children, and you should not break those engagements indifferently. You don't break your dentist and doctor appointments lightly, do you? You'll sit for two hours and wait for them; but for your kids or even your husband, you break your appointments lightly. Sometimes it means making a choice to say "no" to an unimportant meeting at the church because of a previously scheduled appointment you have made to take your children to the zoo. If you get an unexpected call to come to the church and help with the beginning stages of planning for the Mother-Daughter Banquet one morning, I think the zoo is more important if you have already promised your children you will take them that day. I'd simply say, "I'm sorry. I have a previous appointment." Those calling you don't need to know who it's with or what you are going to do. Your children are important. Do you know what will happen if you break promises to your children to do unexpected things at the church you really don't have to do? They will begin to resent the ministry. That's not fair to them and we shouldn't treat them that way. They are some of our closest neighbors and they ought to have top priority in our lives.

Who's answering your children's questions? Are you there when they bring in that caterpillar and want to show you that wiggly, furry thing? Are you there when that boy comes in and takes a frog or snake out of his pocket?

I was in Dallas visiting my daughter one summer, and I was so thrilled to see pictures all over her refrigerator that Melissa and Michael had painted. Now Linda has a lovely home and those pictures didn't really go with the decor, but their pictures were just covering the refrigerator. When I saw it, I remembered putting up my children's things when they were small. In fact, I still have a little box David made as a junior in Vacation Bible School. I keep my curling picks in it. As I saw Melissa's and Michael's art work I thought, "Kids love that." They love to know their art work and the things they make are so important to you that you would display them for the whole world to see. Melissa had made a sign for the door opening into the kitchen from the garage that said, "Welcome." Of course, it's not a professional-looking sign. It was done by a child. But Linda left it there. I thought it was so sweet.

We need to realize our children want to feel important to us. Who is answering your children's questions? Who is listening to their chatter? I remember coming home from school as a little girl; the first thing I'd do when I came in was call, "Mom?" She'd answer and I'd reply, "Just wanted to know where you were." Now some days I would tell her what happened at school and some days I just wanted to know she was there; but I always hollered her name when I came in the door. I also remember that my mother always smelled fresh and clean when I came home. She always freshened up before we came home, and that made me feel so important. She never looked scruffy and dirty as if she had been cleaning and working all day. I think that's a good way for us to make our children feel important.

Life has many different periods, and the loss of one cannot be made up. You cannot make up for time you lose with those babies, toddlers, adolescents and teenagers. If you lose that time, you'll never regain it. So we need to make the most of every era of our children's lives and make time for them. I realize there are many women who work; I'm not trying to make you feel guilty about leaving your children. I'm simply saying you should make time to be with them and make them feel special when you are with them. Just be sure your children have top priority after God and your husband.

Though my children are no longer at home, I still spend priority time praying for them, calling when I feel the need to call, and so forth. I also give that same type of priority time to my grand-children.

Don't Be Superwoman!

The next priority in my life is myself, because I feel the Bible is so true when it says, "Thou shalt love thy neighbor as thyself." (Matthew 22:39b) If I become a martyr to everyone else and put everybody else's needs and wants ahead of myself, I will get so hateful and resentful I won't be any good to anybody. I feel it's very important for you to put time for yourself in your daily schedule. Be as kind to yourself as you would be to someone else.

Now you would expect that someone my age who is a grandmother and maybe a great-grandmother before too long would get tired and need a nap. But I may not be working as hard as some of you with your little ones underfoot. So consider yourself. Are you getting enough rest? Are you eating properly? Are you getting enough exercise? Are you taking some time just for yourself? You say, "I

don't know where I'd go to get any time alone." Lock yourself in
the bathroom if you have to, but find some time for you. It doesn't
have to be a lot of time, but you are not a super human. There is,
again, no such animal. You must first realize you are important
enough to spend time on yourself. You are very loved by the God
of the universe. He wants you to be healthy both physically and
emotionally.

If you are going through a time when you are under a lot of
emotional stress, you might need to plan some naps for yourself
even if you don't normally need one. Emotional fatigue is harder on
a woman than physical fatigue because we are emotional creatures.
A little extra sleep can replenish you physically and emotionally and
make you able to handle those chaotic times that will come in small
and large ways. Of course, I can usually handle the big things well;
but the run in my stockings will send me into orbit!!

When I know I need to be emotionally strong, I try to be more
careful about my diet. I plan to have some fun and I say things that
make me laugh. I look for the funny side of everything. The Bible
is so practical. "A merry heart doeth good like a medicine."
(Proverbs 17:22a) A merry heart will cause us to have a cheerful
countenance. Now no one wants to see me moping around wanting
sympathy and pity in the midst of trials. But the only way I am
going to keep a cheerful countenance is to have a cheerful heart.
That will come from the Bible, laughter, taking time for myself,
replenishing myself, and doing what I need to do to stay on top.
You must do those things too. You are important.

Some of us need to learn the first word we learned as a baby —
"no!" It is not wrong to say "no." It is not even wrong to say "no"
to good things. You can't do everything. You are only one part of
the body. Your finger can't do what your toe is supposed to do, and
your gallbladder can't do what your liver does. And you are not
supposed to do everything you are asked to do. So often we take on
far too much because we do not have a good sense of self-worth,
and we are trying to prove something. We become a martyr in an
attempt to make people like us or to try to feel good about
ourselves. But that's not the right way to do it. You need to learn

to say "no" and not feel guilty.

For instance, you will have to say "no" to some things at church for the sake of your family and home. Let's say someone calls and wants you to go to lunch on a particular day. Let's also say you have set that day aside to clean your kitchen cabinets. You should simply say, "I'm sorry. I have a previous appointment." Now you probably shouldn't say you have an appointment with your kitchen cabinets. The person doesn't need to know that. But cleaning your kitchen cabinets can be therapy. You say, "Cleaning out cabinets??!" Yes! If it is the only time you have available the next few weeks, it is going to bother you if it doesn't get done. The thing you have been asked to do can wait, it's best for you to clean the cabinets when you have planned to do it. Now, believe me, my husband will not come home and immediately say, "Oh! You have cleaned out the kitchen cupboards!" I have to open the doors and say, "LOOK!" And he says, "What?" And I say, "See that clean shelf paper and all that silverware lined up just right?" **Then** he sees it. But I don't do it for him nearly so much as I do it for me! Learn you can say "no" when there are things you have planned to do that are more important than what you are being asked to do.

You will have to learn to set some rules in your home when you are called upon to keep visiting missionaries or evangelists. You can't allow people to come in and tear your home apart. It is possible to handle situations like this without causing hard feelings. If visitors in your home are allowing their children to run rampant, you should correct them. When my grandchildren come to my home, I don't let them tear up the house. If I will correct my own grandchildren, I will certainly correct someone else's children. In order not to cause hard feelings, you might say something like, "The children are welcome to go to the den and take out all the toys in there, but we try to keep all the toys in one room." That would be better than saying, " Now, look! We don't allow children to run all over the house!" Instead, tell the mother or father which areas you do have for the children to play and eat in. It is also fine to say something like, "I don't mind how many toys you take out in this room. We just ask that you put away anything you take out when you are finished." Once children know they are going to have to put it all away, they usually don't make such a big mess! When children eat in our home, they are asked to eat at the table or take their food outside. Of course, they should wash their hands when they are done. When you deal with people in this way, you might be helping them as well as yourself! Perhaps those parents have never been told that you don't allow your children to eat peanut butter and jelly all over the house. (You know, don't you, one of Murphy's laws is this: "The chances of the peanut butter and jelly sandwich falling jelly side down on the carpet is in direct proportion to the cost and cleanliness of the carpet. And if the carpet has just been cleaned, it will **definitely** fall on the jelly side!") I simply do not see anything wrong with letting your guests know what your house rules are and letting them know you expect their children to abide by those rules.

We must always remember that people are more important than things and schedules. However, you can tell when things are really an emergency and when they're not. Don't try to live up to an image. You are not a perfect anything. You are not a perfect homemaker, wife, mother, Christian or anything else. Now that doesn't mean we have the right to hang out our dirty laundry, but we should take off our masks and not try to make anyone think we are superhuman.

Don't Put Me On a Pedestal, Please!

I don't want to be on a pedestal. The only way you can fall from a pedestal is down. So just don't put me there. I'll tell you right now I am not perfect. If you haven't already found that out, you will if you watch me long enough. So don't even try to live up to the "perfect woman" image. You just can't do it. You might be able to go out in public for a while and keep everything under control, but your perfect facade will give somewhere. Do you know where it will be? When you are at home you will take it out on your husband and your children and you'll just be a witch to live with. I'd rather be a witch outside and be nice at home if I have to choose, but you don't have to be one in either place. The Bible says, "Be ye therefore perfect," (Matthew 5:48a) and we should strive to be the best we can possibly be; but we must realize we won't always reach that goal.

Know your limits. Don't try to please everyone. God and your husband are all you can say grace over. If you please them, you will please most other people. Again let me say you shouldn't try to gain acceptance by taking on more and more. That just won't work. In fact, people will walk all over you like they do a throw rug. People do not accept you just because you are the person who does everything. You won't gain anyone's respect by trying to be perfect, and it won't help you either. So be sure you know your limits and follow them.

Develop new skills that you enjoy. Keep yourself interesting. Keep learning. Jesus increased in wisdom and in stature and in favor with God and man. You need to be doing that regularly. You need to be increasing in wisdom. Learn something. Learn things you can discuss with your husband. If he loves sports, learn enough to talk with him at least a little bit. Always learn. Don't become a stagnant pool. Grow intellectually.

Grow in stature. Grow in stature as a person — in your outward grooming. Learn to be a well-groomed, well-put-together person.

Grow in favor with God — grow spiritually. Don't let your husband get way ahead of you spiritually.

Grow in favor with man. Grow in the social graces. Learn the rules of etiquette; know what's proper to do. Grow constantly.

I, as an older woman, am to teach you to be keepers at home — a good homemaker. I once heard a landlord make this statement about some of his Christian tenants: "They must really be busy, because they surely have dirty houses." That is a shame and a disgrace. Now I'm not saying your home ought always to look like it has just been cleaned. If you have children, you'll be a basket case if you try to do that. But it ought to be clean enough to live in and dirty enough to enjoy. You need to be a homemaker. Your husband needs that haven so he can come home and relax without feeling he needs to shovel a path through the mess to get in the door.

In keeping house, perhaps you need to get rid of some dust catchers while you have young children. Eliminate those things that say to you, "Come clean me." If they are always nagging at you, put them away until you can display them and enjoy them. Whatever you have to do, make your home so that it is not a burden to you but a place you can enjoy and keep nice.

How To Get It All Done

So, according to Matthew 22:35 through 38, we have our priorities in this order — God, husband, children, ourself, our home and our service outside the home. You might not feel that is the right order for you. But, for me, that is the right order. I feel if I have left out any of those first things, I don't have the right to go serve outside the home.

Several times I have been asked to stay from Friday through Monday when I have had speaking engagements in order to save on the airfare. My answer is this: "I don't feel I have a right to come and speak to you on Friday and Saturday if I am not home on Sunday morning to fix my husband's breakfast. I also need to be in my place in my Sunday school class and ready to march into the choir for the morning service. What right do I have to speak to ladies if I am not taking care of my responsibilities at home?" I believe that with all my heart. I know soul winning is everybody's job without exception. The Bible says, "Go ye." But before you "go ye," you ought to make sure you have cared for your priorities at home. It might not be done perfectly or spotlessly, but it should be done.

Let me give you a good tip. A wonderful time saver that helps me is going through the house at night before I go to bed and picking up things. If I do that, I can face the next day without feeling disorganized. It really helps me keep myself together when I get up to an orderly home. If I get up to dishes in the sink and trash that needs to be emptied and magazines and books all over the place, I start my day with a cluttered mind. If everything is neat and in order, it helps me. It just takes a few minutes to walk through the house picking up clutter and throwing away the old newspapers. Now I used to be the kind who picked up the paper on the porch, walked through the house reading it and put it in the trash. I just didn't like **anything** laying around. Now I do give my husband time to read it before I throw it away!

In your service learn that God has given you specific talents and He wants you to use them. If you play an instrument, God will probably use your talent. He gave you abilities for a reason; be sure you use them or you may lose them. So if you do have talents, use them.

Again, remember you are only a part of the body. You are not to do everything. Moses had to learn that. He tried to do too much and he was told to delegate. I think that is something we all have to learn. Sorting out your priorities relieves pressure and guilt. If you live by priorities, those unimportant things that don't get done won't make you feel guilty. You **have** done the most important things. An unchanging fact is no job supersedes your relationship to God and your family.

What Will Your Diary Say?

Remember this: God originated work. He gave it to Adam when man fell in the Garden of Eden. Work is noble and it is good. Often the best thing you can do to get out of the doldrums is to get busy doing a hard task you have been putting off. If a task is worth doing, it is worth doing well.

However, we should also remember on the seventh day God rested. Now He didn't need rest! He wasn't tired! He didn't say, "Boy, I surely am worn out from creating this world and this man and this woman and all these animals!" No, He didn't need rest. He was teaching us we need to plan some time for rest.

Each of our lives is like a diary. Day by day we are writing a page of our lives. When you come to the end of the diary are you going to look back and say, "Oh, that's not at all what I intended to write."? See, one day you will be 70 or 80 or even 90. The only way you can look back at that point and say, "Yes, that's what I intended to write," is by deciding what your priorities are and living by them.

Now perhaps your priorities won't be in the same order mine are. But this order works for me and it seems to be what God has impressed on my heart. Now let me give you some pointers that will help you avoid wasting time.

1. Don't get a late start. I don't care if you aren't a morning person, just get up and get started. If you don't start until 10:30 a.m., then it's too easy to decide you might as well wait until after lunch to get started.

2. Don't be easily distracted. My sister-in-law, Earlyne, will admit this. She says she'll start cleaning out the drawers. Then once she gets everything pulled out, she spends the rest of the day looking at all the mementos and never finishes cleaning out the drawers!

3. Control your telephone. Take if off the hook. I do! If you call me and you get a busy signal for very long, you can be almost certain I have taken the phone off the hook. Learn to say, "Could you call back?" Do you know what? It would do most of us good to just let that old phone ring sometimes. Don't be a slave to the telephone.

4. Be careful about the television. If you watch it at all, do something else while you view it. I sometimes iron while watching television. Perhaps you could do your sewing or mending while you watch. When you watch television, I think a good question to ask yourself is, "Does this edify me?" Now, frankly, there are some old comedies that make me laugh, and sometimes I really need that. Just be sure what you are watching is a help to you.

5. Have a place for everything and put everything in its place. You waste a lot of time looking for things that aren't where they are supposed to be. Now that's a simple principle, but it can really help you. When you're getting ready to go to church on Sunday, do you have to say, "Where are Johnny's socks? Have you seen my keys? Do you see my Bible anywhere?" If things are in their places, you won't have that problem. Remember, time is life; don't waste it!

DON'T BURN YOUR OWN BRIDGE

I am going to address a subject in this chapter you might think is rather strange for a pastor's wife. But it is something you are going to need to know very early in your ministry; in fact, you need to know it right now! You will particularly need it in the ministry.

There really is a disorder called burnout. It can be described as just literally wanting to quit, to give up, or to come to the end of your rope. In my research, I found one of the greatest causes of burnout is bitterness or failure to forgive. I immediately began to study the Scriptures and began thinking about how we can learn to forgive. We are told to forgive, but that is more easily said than done. Have you ever had a difficult time forgiving anyone? Maybe you have even had the problem of not being able to forgive yourself for something that has happened in the past. That is where you need to start. You will never be effective in any kind of work if you do not let go of guilt. Yes, you have made some mistakes. You may have really blown it. However, if it has been confessed, God does not see it any longer. It is removed and He doesn't want you to be constantly remembering it. Now if you remember it to the point that it helps you help someone else avoid doing what you did, that's alright. But don't remember it with guilt and remorse; you have been forgiven no matter what you have done in your past.

As I delved into this subject, I found several causes for bitterness. I want to give you two in particular.

1. A wrong response to adversity. I call that being angry at God. When there are trials and adversities, we must stop and think about Who allows those things into our lives. And He is not the cause. All too often we are the cause. We are reaping what we have sown. Sometimes the cause is other people, but God has still allowed those people to bring adversity into our lives. When we murmur and complain, we are actually complaining against God.

Do you remember when the Israelites murmured and complained? God was very displeased. Remember Miriam? She murmured and she got leprosy!

My study describes murmuring in this way: "It is the opposite of unconditional obedience. It involves opposition to God in expressed, muted, but audible tones." Murmuring is not a pretty thing. This quote caught my eye: "As fever indicates the presence of disease, murmuring indicates bitterness."

So when you hear complaining and murmuring, it is not just coming out of the mouth and head and tongue, it is coming out of the heart where there is bitterness and a failure to forgive. If it is because of adversity, it is God you are murmuring against and He is not pleased. It is one of the greatest sins in the Bible.

I said to someone once, "You know, we have our sins that we preach and teach against because we don't do those things — things like smoking and drinking. But we have our pet sins we hug to our bosoms and we don't call those things sins." Bitterness and a failure to forgive are among those sins. We are going to have to learn how to give and receive forgiveness.

2. **The second cause for burnout is an unforgiving spirit.** When you say "I can't forgive," you ought to say, "I **won't** forgive." One of the first verses I learned as a little beginner in Sunday school was from Ephesians 4:32: "And be ye kind one to another, tenderhearted, forgiving one another, even as God for Christ's sake hath forgiven you." Now I learned that verse years and years ago — but I didn't really **learn** it. You have probably read and memorized that verse too. But let me ask you this. What grieves the Holy Spirit? I'm sure there are many things, but what is one specific thing mentioned in the Bible as something that grieves Him? The verses before Ephesians 4:32 tell us: "And grieve not the holy Spirit of God, whereby ye are sealed unto the day of redemption. Let all bitterness, and wrath, and anger, and clamour, and evil speaking, be put away from you, with all malice:" (Ephesians 4:30, 31)

Now when I think of the word "clamor," I picture two pans banging together. Have you ever heard kids in the kitchen doing just that? That's the way we sound when we are yakking about negative things. Have you ever looked in a mirror when you are upset? If we would do that, we would never get angry again! We just look plain ugly.

Then we come to the verse that commands us to forgive. (Ephesians 4:32) You are going to need forgiveness someday, and if you don't learn to give it, how can you receive it? In fact, the Bible teaches us to pray, "Forgive us our debts as we forgive our debtors." (Matthew 6:12) Does it seem to say to you, as it does to me, unless we forgive we won't receive forgiveness?

Do you remember the story of David and Saul? You know that Saul began to hate David almost from the start because of the women singing David's praises after he killed Goliath. That just didn't suit Saul at all. From that day forward, he tried his best to get rid of David. In fact, he tried repeatedly to kill him! Yet in the first chapter of II Samuel we are told how David lamented upon hearing of Saul's death — the man who had sought him and tried to kill him, the one who had chased him and given him no peace. II Samuel 1:17 says, "And David lamented with this lamentation over Saul and over Jonathan his son."

Perhaps a name comes to **your** mind as you read about forgiveness and you are thinking, "Boy, if that person died, I would have a hallelujah fit. I'd throw a party!" But David didn't. He lamented. In II Samuel 1:24 we read, "Ye daughters of Israel, weep over Saul, who clothed you in scarlet, with other delights, who put on ornaments of gold upon your apparel." We know David loved Jonathan, but he loved Saul too! Would you have forgiven someone who had done you that much wrong? Think about it. Would you forgive someone who had literally tried to kill you, who had pursued you for years, who never gave you any rest or peace? Could you have forgiven that? If you couldn't forgive that, then let me ask you this — what size offense could you forgive? Why even think about size? We are not told to forgive small or large deeds. We are just told to forgive — no matter how big or how small. We need to keep our forgiver in working order.

When you fail to forgive, it is not because you can't, but because you won't. It is important — even urgent — to forgive because, when you work with people, they are going to do things that hurt you. Now I know Psalm 119:165 is still in the Bible. It says, "Great peace have they which love thy law: and nothing shall offend them." But evidently, even though we know that verse is in the Bible, we still get our feelings hurt.

"Be Ye Kind,. . .Tenderhearted"

Let me give you an interesting quote. The late Thomas Hunter, a columnist in Richmond, Virginia, wrote this: "If I ever have to have a trial by jury, I hope it is not made up of good men. Good men have so little sympathy and are so seldom kind." Now that is a sad statement about human nature and Christians in particular. When someone falls and sins, the world doesn't say much because they are guilty of the same thing all the time. But Christians do; they will never let the person live it down until the day he dies.   We Christians must learn it grieves the Holy Spirit and it is a grave sin for us to do that. There is probably no one who will read this who is going to go out and get drunk, but you will refuse to forgive someone and think nothing of it. Let me say you had better learn to forgive. You are going to feel injured — whether the injury is real or imaginary. Your husband is going to hurt you sometime. Maybe a brother or sister in Christ will wrong you. Friends and church members will treat you adversely. You must learn to forgive.

Perhaps there is someone reading this book who grew up as an abused child; maybe the abuse was physical or maybe it was emotional. If you have never dealt with that, I beg you to do so. Learn how to forgive and put it behind you because you will never be effective in any ministry if you are holding on to bitterness over that abuse. I know that must be a terribly hard thing to forgive, but you can do it with God's help. If God had not known we could forgive, He wouldn't have told us to do so. When He tells us to do something, He gives us the means with which to do it. That means is His grace and love and mercy.

Many times I have had to go to the Lord and say, "Now Lord, you know I don't like what was done. But if You will let Your love flow through me, I will just be the vessel and I will love that person and I will forgive." And I have been able to forgive with His help when I never could have done it alone.

I once received a letter from a girl who told me she was glad her mother had died because the mother had sexually molested her when she was a child. Now there is nothing that girl can do about her mother because she is dead and gone. But I wrote her back and told her she must resolve it. She was just stewing in her own juices. She was actually poisoning and killing herself.

True forgiveness is not a casual thing. Matthew 18:21-35 tells the story of Peter asking the Lord how often he should forgive. Peter thought seven times was being very generous. But Jesus answered seventy times seven. And Jesus didn't mean to count it out. He meant that by the time we have forgiven seventy times seven, we are in such a habit of forgiving that we can keep on forgiving. In these verses the Bible goes on to tell about the man who was forgiven the great debt he owed his master. He left being freed of the guilt and weight of owing that tremendous amount he could not pay. But he met a man who owed him a small amount and really let him have it for not paying that debt. Then in verse 32 it says, "Then his lord, after that he had called him, said unto him, O thou wicked servant, I forgave thee all that debt, because thou desiredst me." We have been forgiven so much. How dare we feel we can't forgive anything? No matter what, you can forgive. But it isn't casual — it is very costly.

First of all, we need to recognize we have been hurt. That's not wrong. Just look at it. Recognize that someone has, by their tongue or some other means, truly wronged us. Just to have to think about it is costly in itself. Don't try to dismiss it or repress it if you have truly been wronged. Deal with it because it will fester and surface later if you don't deal with it right away.

Next, you need to give up the right to get even. Give up the right to make the person pay. That's why we don't forgive. It sets someone free and we want them to feel miserable when they see us coming. When we stick our noses up in the air we want them to know that we really mean, "If you think I am going to forgive you, forget it!! You are going to pay the rest of my days or yours — whichever lasts longer." Now we are really hurting them, aren't we? You know what? When they go to bed, they probably sleep soundly. But you lie awake thinking what you can do next to get them back. When they eat their strawberry shortcake, they think the strawberries are unusually sweet this year. But when you eat yours, you think they are tasting flat because you are so bitter that everything is bitter. Give up the right to make someone pay.

Just think a moment. Can you think of Someone in the past two thousand years Who has already paid for the wrong someone did against you? Can you think of anyone? He has already paid. He looked down and knew all those things that were going to be done wrongly against you, and He has already paid for it. Why should someone have to pay for a wrong done against you? I say again I don't care how bad it was. Jesus paid for past, present and future sins. Why should we continue to seek payment? Someone has already paid. So give up that feeling of "I'll make them pay if it is the last thing I do!" It isn't a delicious and wonderful feeling like you think it is. You are only hurting yourself.

Notice this quote: "He who doesn't forgive others breaks the bridge over which he must pass someday." Every person will at some time have a need to be forgiven. Yet when you have a need to go over the chasm on the bridge, the bridge will be washed away if you have failed to forgive those who have wronged you in the past. You'll want forgiveness and you'll want to be cleansed. You won't want to bear that burden of not being forgiven, but **you** will have broken down the bridge; it will be gone.

You are going to wrong someone whether intentionally or unintentionally. I think there are many times when people hurt us inadvertently. But even when the hurt is intentional, forgiving that person can mean freedom from enslavement to the person who has harmed you. When you hate someone, you are attached to that person by chains. When I think of being chained to the person you hate, I think of Corrie Ten Boom. She tells the story of a time after the war when she met a man who had once been her prison guard. During the war she was put in a Jewish concentration camp — the death camp where her sister died. While incarcerated, she and her people were persecuted; they were starved; they slept with lice crawling all over them. They suffered all kinds of indignities; they were stripped naked before guards as they were deloused. Anything you can imagine that would strip a person of all human dignity was done to them. After the war, she came face-to-face with one of the guards who had been the most cruel. As I remember the story, he had gotten saved. Nevertheless, he said to her as he reached out his hand, "Can you forgive me?" I remember reading her words: "I thought for a moment I could not take that man's hand because I saw my sister's death and I saw all that happened to me." Then she thought, "But I must forgive him." So she reached out and took his hand and she said, "In that moment all was washed away of the hate and bitterness I felt." And she was able to forgive just like that. The enslavement to her past that had probably haunted her was broken. That one man had represented all those who had so tortured her. It meant freedom to her. Vengeance or revenge says, "I will forgive after I teach him a thing or two. I'm going to rub some salt in the wound and make him sting a little first. Then after I've seen him suffer a little, I'll forgive." That's not forgiveness. Or maybe you say, "After I've collected a pint or two of tears, after I've seen them cry, then I'll forgive." That's not forgiveness. That's vengeance and revenge.

Vengeance is a game that let's us postpone forgiveness — but it is a slow form of suicide. Who is it killing? The one who won't forgive. Romans 12:19-21 says, "Dearly beloved, avenge not yourselves, but rather give place unto wrath: for it is written, Vengeance is mine; I will repay, saith the Lord. Therefore if thine enemy hunger, feed him; if he thirst, give him drink: for in so doing thou shalt heap coals of fire on his head. Be not overcome of evil, but overcome evil with good."

When we seek vengeance, we are stealing God's job. So you read these verses and say, "Goodie! Get 'em, God! Sic 'em!" Again, that's wrong! We should just let God worry about the vengeance. If He doesn't "sic 'em" as quickly as we think He should, then we begin to think, "Well, He said He would repay and He's not doing it." Then you lose faith in His Word. No, God takes care of things when He gets ready to take care of things.

The Bible says we are not to be overcome with evil. BE NOT OVERCOME! You say, "But Mrs. Hyles, you don't know what that person did to me." No, I don't know. There may be something in your life that is just so big you think you can never forget it. You can because real forgiveness is a gift. It is not earned. You just decide to give it. It is a choice you make and you freely give it. They may not even ask for your forgiveness — they may not even want your forgiveness. But give it anyway because God has said to do so.

The Greatest Example in Forgiving

Luke 23:33 and 34 says, "And when they were come to the place, which is called Calvary, there they crucified him, and the malefactors, one on the right hand, and the other on the left. Then said Jesus, Father, forgive them; for they know not what they do. And they parted his raiment, and cast lots." You know, that forgiveness was free. We did not earn it or deserve it. When Jesus was crucified, we were there in the Roman soldiers and others who scourged him and abused him and spat upon him. We were represented, yet He said, "Forgive them." His forgiveness was freely given and that is exactly the way we ought to forgive.

Now I don't want to, but I am going to tell you about my bad, wicked side. There was a time in my life when someone did something to me I could not forgive. For several years I carried that in my heart. I would go to the Lord and say, "Lord, you know I want to forgive." But I would turn right around in my heart and say, "I just can't! I can't forgive it." So one day I took a piece of paper, dated it and wrote down exactly how I felt I had been wronged. I folded it up, went out in my yard and buried it. Now you may say, "Mrs. Hyles, you're stupid!" I know it, but that represented to me a point of relinquishing something to God I could not handle.

I am not saying I forgot it right away. But every time it came to my mind I would say, "Now Lord, you know I have buried that." I didn't forget it immediately, but the hurt began to leave and I began to be able to desire good for that person. Today I can truly say I love that person.

Let me tell you another stupid thing I did. When I was in the first or second grade, my best girlfriend and I had a fight. For one solid year we didn't speak to each other. Now we went to the same church and school, but when we'd pass each other in the halls we'd go to opposite sides to avoid each other. At the end of the year we decided we would make up with each other, and do you know what? Neither one of us could remember what we had been angry about in the first place. Now that's a bad thing for children to do, but it's even worse when we do it as grown women! It is time we learn to forgive.

Forgiveness should not be used as a form of superiority. We say, "Oh, yes. I'll forgive you." But we have a superior air that shows we don't really mean it and we think we are wonderful for saying we will forgive. Who gets the best end of the deal in forgiveness? The person who forgives does, so we really have no reason to feel superior.

Acts 20:35 says, "I have shewed you all things, how that so labouring ye ought to support the weak, and to remember the words of the Lord Jesus, how he said, It is more blessed to give than to receive." That verse applies to forgiveness too. There's no sense in playing a game of "Let's Pretend." We say, "Oh, just forget it." What we really mean is, "Oh, you dirty buzzard you, you shouldn't have done it and you know it." Don't play games; get the hurt out in the open. Do you know it is always best, whether between two friends or just two people, to admit you were hurt? Say, "Yes, I was hurt. So let's talk about it and get the air cleared." All too often we say, "Oh, it never happened." Well, it did happen! Be honest. Don't play games. Anger cannot be avoided or repressed. It is a little bit like getting a splinter in your finger. If you don't get it out, it will keep festering until it becomes a big sore. So deal with it in the right way. When there is an injury, it must be treated. You must do whatever is necessary to help it heal. When you have been wronged, the only way to heal the hurt is to forgive.

Whenever someone is wronged, there are two injured parties —

the one who has been wronged and the one who is at the mercy of the one who was wronged. Think back to the story about Corrie Ten Boom. That guard knew what he had done. He was carrying the burden of the hundreds of thousands of lives he had seen tortured and killed. Yet just having one woman reach out her hand in forgiveness probably freed him somewhat of the memory of all that he had done or had a part in doing.

Very often the person who has wronged you is suffering greatly. I know. I have talked to them repeatedly. They are hurting, yet they are at the mercy of people who refuse to forgive. What if God had refused to forgive? What did it cost for God to forgive? It cost God Calvary. It is costly to offer forgiveness, with no strings attached.

We must also realize true forgiveness is a necessity if we are to live happily. Luke 6:38 says, "Give, and it shall be given unto you; good measure, pressed down, and shaken together, and running over, shall men give into your bosom. For with the same measure that ye mete withal it shall be measured to you again." But we see in verse 37 right before that, ". . .forgive, and ye shall be forgiven." Again I say if we expect to be forgiven, we must learn to forgive.

Deadly, Destructive, Depressing

An unforgiving heart is deadly. It kills. Think about Joseph's brothers. They hated him; they couldn't forgive him because he was a dreamer and because he was his father's favorite. What did they want to do to him? Their jealousy and failure to forgive made them want to kill him. Of course we don't want to get caught and spend the rest of our lives in prison, so we decide instead to kill people with our tongues. Proverbs 18:21 says, "Death and life are in the power of the tongue: and they that love it shall eat the fruit thereof." But killing a person with the tongue is just as bad as, and sometimes worse than, physical murder. It's destructive and deadly. It destroys you emotionally and physically and it destroys the other person.

An unforgiving heart is depressing. Are you really happy when you refuse to forgive someone? Remember the day you spent just boiling inside because of something your husband said to you? Were you really happy that day? No, you weren't. In fact, you were probably depressed by the end of the day. Someone made this very true statement: "They most live who most enjoy who most love and who most forgive."

When you are hurt, should you seek restitution or revenge? Restitution is not always possible. Of course the ideal situation is one like the prodigal son. He returned and was forgiven and everything was just "peachy-keen." But it isn't always that way. There will be times when the person doesn't give a hill of beans whether you forgive him or not, but you go ahead and forgive anyway! Even if you can never make restitution and become friends again or restore a relationship, go ahead and forgive. Only then will **you** be free. You will have the peace of knowing you have done the right thing.

For whose sake do you forgive? First, we forgive for God's sake. He has said to do so. Ephesians 4:30-32 tells us we grieve the Holy Spirit when we don't forgive. Secondly, we forgive for our own sakes. When you forgive, you will be happier than the person you forgave. It really is more blessed to give than it is to receive. Thirdly, we forgive for the sake of the one who has wronged us. II Corinthians 2:7 says, "So that contrariwise ye ought rather to forgive him, and comfort him, lest perhaps such a one should be swallowed up with overmuch sorrow." Is there someone whom you won't forgive who is actually being swallowed up with sorrow because they can't win your forgiveness? You are going to drive them completely away from God and from good. You are a Christian; if Christians can't forgive, who can?

You are going to need this as Christian leaders' wives. There are going to be people in your churches who are going to do you wrong. There are going to be people who kick you out of conventions. There are going to be people who write you hate notes. There are going to be people who say ugly things to you on your phone. Of course there will be people who love you and do good to you. The bad times are certainly in the minority. However, you need to be prepared for the fact there are people in the world and in churches who like to do harm. Sometimes it seems their chief aim in life is to do all they can to hurt the preacher. We, as Christian leaders' wives and as Christians, must learn to forgive those people.

Another important thing to learn when talking about forgiveness is to forgive yourself. Be as kind to yourself as you would be to someone else. Of course we are going to do wrong. But when we do, we need to learn to ask God for forgiveness and go on. Seek God's forgiveness and then forgive yourself. You know, we are too guilty of going to God again and again about something that happened and was forgiven long ago. He wiped it clean years ago and doesn't even know it happened. So why do you continue to remind Him? Because you haven't forgiven yourself. If my mother had already given me a spanking for getting in the cookie jar, I surely wouldn't keep reminding her of it. Neither should we keep on blaming ourselves for sins that are already forgiven. Perhaps you need to forgive yourself because you had a part in causing the situation where you feel you cannot forgive another person. Forgive the other person, seek God's forgiveness and then forgive yourself.

Forgiveness is basic to character. It is a character flaw when you refuse to forgive and forget. In the case of a great wrong, perhaps you won't be able to forget immediately, but if you forgive, you will eventually forget.

Forgiveness is also basic to your physical health. I believe many people today are sick because they are angry and bitter and they refuse to forgive. This bitterness and hatred is manifesting itself in the form of physical illness.

Forgiveness is also basic to emotional health. You can't be mentally and emotionally healthy if you can't forgive.

Let me say that when I talk about forgiving I do not mean a person should continue to live in any kind of life-threatening situation. I do not mean you should continue to live with someone who is abusing you — even though you must forgive that person. In a case like this, you must seek help as well as forgive. As a Christian leader's wife, you should remember a person should never be counselled to stay in a situation that is dangerous. Whether you are dealing with battered wives or battered children, they should be told to remove themselves from the danger right away. It will probably only get worse.

Something else that will help concerning forgiveness is learning not to be so easily hurt. We won't have to use our forgiver so often if we just won't get hurt so often. If someone doesn't speak to you in the hallway at church, give that person the benefit of the doubt. He probably didn't even hear you speak. If you pass the preacher and he doesn't speak, don't get offended. He might have a heavy burden on his heart from counselling with someone. He might have been praying about it as he passed you in the hall. We are so tacky! We get upset about the pettiest things. You had better get over that before you get out in the ministry.

I will never forget the first church we pastored. The only lady in the church who could play the piano at all played everything to the tune of "The Old Rugged Cross." She also bounced all over the bench; it got a good shine every time she played. But the the church people there said to me, "You mean **you** don't play the piano? The preacher's wife?" Now I could have said, "Huh! I'll never speak to them again!" But that would have been stupid (and wrong) of me. Those people didn't mean to be hurtful. They just thought all preacher's wives played the piano — and I don't! What about when they say, "You mean you won't take the nursery? Our other preacher's wife **always** had the nursery." And you can tell they are thinking, "The lazy good-for-nothing!" You know, you can't just cross them off your list. That's petty. Psalm 119:165 is still in the Bible. "Great peace have they which love thy law: and nothing shall offend them." And of course you will still be offended by wrongdoing, but Philippians 3:3 talks about the fact we should not put confidence in the flesh. Realize people are going to be hurtful. Someone once said, "To live above with those I love — oh, that will be glory! But to live below with those I know — that's another story!"

I hope you see the value of this chapter as you go out into the ministry. People are going to be people, and people will hurt you. However, you can learn to forgive. You can help your husband so much if you will learn this principle. If you don't get offended, he won't either. If you get angry at someone, what's your husband going to do? Remember, he loves you. And because he doesn't want his little sweetie hurt, he's going to get angry at them too. Forget all that petty stuff. Quit getting hurt — and when you do get hurt, just forgive. We must learn to forgive if we are going to be successful Christian leaders' wives and successful Christians.

KEEP AWAY! PRIVATE PROPERTY!

First of all, let me say that marriages must be based on trust. I don't feel we can go through marriages happily if we are always looking around the corner to see who our husbands might be talking to. Yet, God has given us as women a sixth sense where our husbands are concerned. There will be times when we must pay attention to our intuition. Yet in this chapter I am not going to talk as much about the wiles of the wicked women who are out to get your husband as I am about what you can do to keep your husband from being interested in those wicked women.

Something you must realize is a person can be unfaithful without ever having an affair. The reason for that is faithfulness begins in the mind. I Corinthians 10:12 says, "Wherefore let him that thinketh he standeth take heed lest he fall." Every one of you is a potential home breaker. If you were to become lonely enough and begin getting attention from some man, you could easily be drawn to someone and feel it was love, or whatever you want to call it, and run off with that person.

It is possible for us to guard against ever having a man think we have enticed him. If we guard against that, the possibilities are very slim things will progress to interest on both sides.

First, we must decide in our minds not to let such a thing happen. Someone once said there is no such thing as a platonic relationship between a man and a woman. A platonic relationship means a friendly relationship. It is extremely difficult for that kind of friendship to exist between a man and a woman. When a man and a woman work closely together, it is almost impossible to keep the relationship on a basis of strict friendship with nothing else ever entering into it; but there is a way! It starts in the mind — in knowing that you are able to fall into a trap and deciding not to do so.

At this point, I am going to be very, very plain. During my adult life there have been men with whom I have sung on a regular basis. Through all these years, these men have never been anything other than fine Christian gentlemen. But we must keep in mind that fine Christian men are men. So years ago I decided if I was going to continue singing with Christian men, I would be careful to put that invisible shield in my mind that says, "I will never look at these men as anything other than Christian brothers." There are several ways you can maintain a proper distance between yourself and members of the opposite sex. One way I usually maintain that proper distance is to call men by their last names. There is something about calling a Christian man "brother" that automatically gives a reference to that person as a Christian. It puts a spiritual connotation on things that helps you to think of that person in the right way. Now I am sure these men have probably put up a shield of their own, but I believe the burden rests with the woman.

Think of how many times God talked about the strange woman of Proverbs 7 until it can become obvious to us that the woman is the one who is usually responsible when men and women sin together. In fact, the woman is nearly always responsible. A man might make a pass, but a woman can stop it dead in its tracks. She does not have to yield. I believe it is possible to have an attitude that is like an invisible wall. That attitude says, "You come just so close and that is as close as you will ever come." That doesn't mean you are unkind, it doesn't mean you are not a lovely Christian sister to brothers in Christ; it just means a man will know what liberties he **can't** take with you.

Another way to help maintain that distance between members of the opposite sex is to be sure you are never alone with the opposite sex. You can also make it a point to include your families in the conversations you have with other Christian men.

Let me tell you something interesting. In a pastors' wives meeting somewhere in the nation the question was asked, "What do you do if a man makes a pass at you?" I asked for a show of hands from those who had been in this situation — and there were probably thirty or more pastors' wives — and every one of them indicated that a pass had been made at them. Now those women were all sizes and shapes; they were not necessarily gorgeous, voluptuous movie star types. However, every one of them said it had happened to them. So we talked about putting up that invisible wall.

Some might say they only want to carry on an "innocent flirtation." **There is no such thing!** If you decide you will try the "innocent flirtation" just to build up your ego and make you feel like you still "have it," you will be playing with fire. And fires burn down homes. You had better decide you won't be a strange woman and you are going to learn how to handle men in such a way they won't even think you might be interested in them.

You know, it is no feather in your cap when you can get another woman's husband — or any other man who has no right to belong to you — interested in you. Men are just men and it doesn't take much to get their attention. Now when I say that you might think, "Oh, Mrs. Hyles, that scares me." But I don't mean to do that. On one hand we must learn a marriage is built on trust. On the other hand, I want you to be scared enough to realize even strong men are men.

One of my daughters is outspoken and she teasingly told her husband, "Now I love you and I know you love me, but the first time I ever get a hint of you flirting with another woman, you've had it!" And you know, it might not be a bad idea to let our husbands know we plan to be number one with them. Just remember there are ways to keep ourselves number one.   Proverbs 7 talks about the strange woman. Now today I think she would be called the common woman. In Bible days she was strange; today, she is out there right around every corner; and you had better be aware of it. She would just as soon take your husband as look at him.

Who Is the Strange Woman?

We must accept the fact that other women will be involved in our husbands' lives. How we choose to respond is up to us. If we choose to question our husbands, we will probably make them more interested than they would otherwise have been. We must also remember we cannot invade the privacy entitled to the women who counsel with our husbands. Husbands ought not to have to tell us everything about their counselling.

Someone has said that a woman is her husband's antennae. What I mean is God gives you a sense your husband does not have which enables you to see when a woman is doing more than just counselling with her pastor. When you see that, your antennae goes up and signals start coming through it! That is when you need to start saying things like, "Honey, I think I need to go with you when you counsel with her if that's possible. If you don't want me to do that, perhaps someone else could be present or maybe you could leave the office door open to keep the situation from becoming dangerous."

Now you might think those precautions are unnecessary, but I know a pastor who was called to a woman's home one time to counsel with her. When he arrived, the door was open and she called, "Come on in." When he entered, she said, "Come on back here." When he entered the room she was in, her manner was one of obvious seduction and someone was waiting with a camera and snapped a picture. Did you know people are out there trying to set up preachers?

There is a pastor's wife whose husband counselled a teenage girl for some time. She counselled the girl some, but it seemed the pastor/husband had the most ability to help the girl. Then they found the girl was expecting. Someone came to the wife and said, "Your husband is the father." How would you like for that to happen to you? Then it turned out not to be true, and the person who started that rumor came to the pastor and said, "I'm sorry. I was the one who started that rumor." The person asked for forgiveness, and it was given; but the damage was already done. It's kind of like the woman who came to the preacher and said, "Preacher, I know I have started all kinds of rumors about you and I want your forgiveness. I am sorry and I will stop telling lies about you this day."

The pastor answered, "Okay. I'd like for you to take a feather pillow to the top of a tall building. Split it open and shake out all the feathers. Then go and gather up all the feathers." Of course the lady replied that it was impossible and the pastor said, "You can't restore my reputation either. You can never gather everything you said plus what each person who repeated you added to it." People are waiting to damage your husband's reputation. It is up to you to help avoid those situations that can harm him and his reputation.

Proverbs 14:30 says, "A sound heart is the life of the flesh: but envy the rottenness of the bones." You can't go through married life being jealous; there is no place for jealousy in a happy marriage. If you'll work all the time to keep yourself interesting, you won't have to worry about the problem. Jealousy is rotten and it will rot your marriage. I'm not trying to instill in you the thought that all men are dirty old men. No, they are just normal men whom God made to respond to women's wiles; we need to realize that. I believe if we really commit our husbands to God and pray for them, He is able to keep them. Of course there are things we need to do to help, but we need to commit them totally to the Lord. They are His first, and He is able to keep them.

As we look at Proverbs chapter 7 again and talk about the strange woman, I want you to realize she is out there. You also need to realize it is possible for you to be one of them. Before you start condemning those poor, weak nincompoops who are so easily swayed by these women, let's look at Proverbs 7:22-26: "He goeth after her straightway, as an ox goeth to the slaughter, or as a fool to the correction of the stocks; Till a dart strike through his liver; as a bird hasteth to the snare, and knoweth not that it is for his life. Hearken unto me now therefore, O ye children, and attend to the words of my mouth. Let not thine heart decline to her ways, go not astray in her paths. For she hath cast down many wounded: yea, many strong men have been slain by her." Men are easily fooled by this type of woman. What is the woman like who leads these men astray? Proverbs 30:20 says, "Such is the way of an adulterous woman; she eateth, and wipeth her mouth, and saith, I have done no wickedness." She says, "What did I do wrong?" Oh, you have just flirted and dressed alluringly and said flattering words — no, you have done no wrong! But you and I are capable of doing the very same thing and we need to realize that. You need to begin by setting up some invisible walls between you and the men with whom you work closely. Be kind, sisterly and Christian; but realize that men are men.

Look at Proverbs 7:4-7. It says, "Say unto wisdom, Thou art my sister; and call understanding thy kinswoman: That they may keep thee from the strange woman, from the stranger which flattereth with her words. For at the window of my house I looked through my casement, And beheld among the simple ones, I discerned among the youths, a young man void of understanding." Now I don't think that means he was a dumb person. I think it means he was void of understanding in the ways of wicked women — and most men are, by the way! Men do not understand tricky women. They do not understand the danger they are in and that is why it is up to the woman to keep the relationship pure. It is up to us because men are so easily affected by a woman's flattery.

One way you can fight the strange woman is to take lessons from her. We see in Proverbs 7 several particulars we can learn from the strange woman. She flattered him with her words. Now I don't believe in flattery for the sake of flattery, but we can give sweet compliments. I have said many times men are 1% muscle, 1% chivalry, 1% strength and 97% ego. Now that is my personal opinion, but men do love to have their egos fed. When was the last time you told your man how great he is? When was the last time you said, "I am glad I have you. I surely am grateful for the way you provide for our family." If you don't tell him, some other woman will.

When your husband is a pastor, there will be many people who lightly say to him, "I love you, Preacher." We need to be careful about throwing around the word "love." I think we use it carelessly — especially to the opposite sex. Perhaps instead of telling a pastor or any other Christian leader that you love him, you could say that you respect and appreciate him. Those words express so much. We just need to be so careful for we all have the potential of being the strange woman.

Some of you say, "Well, that is just their tough luck if they are dirty old men!" No, they are not dirty old men. They are just men!

They are just like God made them. You see, you don't understand because you don't think the way they do. You are not built like they are — physically or emotionally.

However, we can learn from the strange woman to compliment sincerely. That will offset her flattery.

Proverbs 7 also says the strange woman dressed in a certain way and fixed her room in a very romantic way. Did you know you can be just as alluring and enticing and pretty and sexy as the strange woman when you are in the privacy of your own home? One of the reasons your husband is looking at those strange women is, all too often, he sees you in that dirty housecoat with baby burp on one shoulder and jelly on the other. You smell like B.O. #5 and you haven't combed your hair all day. When I get up in the morning, I put on a clean robe if I don't dress immediately. I keep myself fresh on purpose. I comb my hair and splash my face with water and put on just a little bit of color, especially if I look like death warmed over. I rinse my mouth. I don't want my husband to leave me looking like an unmade bed when he's going out in the world where there are many women who are spiffy-looking and well-groomed. If you don't make an effort to look decent when you are with your husband, you are making a mistake!

Married lady, when's the last time you bought a new nightie? Perhaps you bought a new lipstick or something for the kids instead. Well just let your kids go without and buy yourself a new nightie! Now you may have to go to a thrift store and buy something that's been worn before if money is a consideration for you. But you need to be pretty and you need to fix up at home for your man.

Of course the woman in Proverbs chapter 7 went out in public dressed like a harlot. Certainly I am not saying you should go out in public showing every curve and too much flesh. However, you can be pretty for your husband at home, and you should be. You ought to learn from this strange woman.

Now there is one thing she was that we should learn NOT to be. Verse 11 of Proverbs 7 tells us her feet did not abide in her house. She ran around too much. When your husband is home, you need to try your best to be home too. You need to build your schedule around his schedule. Perhaps you say, "But I am out doing God's work." And I say, "So what?" if you are letting your husband sit at home alone hour after hour with no woman to talk to and no one with whom he can share his dreams, hopes and conversation.

Another verse informs us the strange woman is loud and stubborn. At home, let your husband be the leader. Now it sounds funny to say, "Let him be the leader." But really, some of you are natural-born leaders. Just as a case in point, let me mention Mrs. Elaine Colsten who is a leader of leaders as far as women are concerned. But I have seen her in her home, and guess who is the leader in her home? Bro. Colsten wears the pants in that family.

Letting your husband be the leader may mean you have to switch gears frequently. That happened to be my lot. Because my husband has travelled extensively in the last 25 years, I was often mother, father, repairman and many other things while he was gone. I was constantly switching roles. While he was away from home, I had to tell everyone what to do. So when he came home it took a conscious effort on my part not to order him around too! I had to tell myself, "Oh, you are not the father here anymore. You are the wife and mother. Shut your mouth, Beverly. Don't be so loud now. Just hush. Let him take over." Now that is not always easy, especially if you are a natural-born leader. I am not saying you should not ever be a leader. If God has made you that way, that is exactly what He wants you to be. But at home, temper it.

In verse 13 of Proverbs 7 we see something else we married women can learn from the strange woman. The Bible says she caught him and kissed him. Married lady, when is the last time you just went up and caught him and really laid one on him and said, "You don't really **have** to go to work today, do you?" When he says, "Yeah, I do." say something like, "Well, just wait 'til you get home tonight!" When is the last time you spontaneously went up and gave him a back rub? Perhaps some of you married ladies are thinking as you read this, "Yes, but Mrs. Hyles, I know what comes next!" Well, that's alright. You have a license and a ring on your finger. If your actions bring further amorous attention, you have every right in the world. Remember the Bible says this woman was subtle of heart. That "subtle" is the same word used for the Devil. She was crafty and knew just how to get what she wanted. We are not so much in danger of some glamorous woman stealing our husband as we are from someone who will just give him the attention he is not getting at home. You may be five times more beautiful and you may smell a lot sweeter; but there are women who are crafty and subtle of heart. They know how to get your husband to yield. The strange woman told the young man "void of understanding" that she had been diligently seeking him. She made him feel so important. If you don't let your husband know you desire his company, believe me — there are plenty of women out there who will!

I often say to women that they need a place of refuge in their homes. The strange woman told the young man she had prepared a romantic place for the two of them. She had decked her bed with tapestry coverings and she had perfumed it; then she invited him to come and take his fill of love. If there is any place in your home that ought to be clean and free of any idea of work, it should be the bedroom. That ought not to be the room where the ironing is piled up and all the old stray magazines are stacked to be read. It ought to be a room with soft lights, music, candles, fresh sheets, and a nice romantic color on the walls. If you have to have a quarrel, **don't** have it in the bedroom. If it starts when you are in bed, ask your husband to please get up and go with you somewhere else to fuss. And there will be quarrels — you won't always agree. Mrs. Lee Roberson says in her cute way, "Well, if two people always agree, one of them is unnecessary." And that's true. You are not always going to agree with your husband. Sometimes it is necessary to clear the air on certain points in a very kind way. But don't argue in the bedroom. If you do, it will begin to represent the place where you disagree. Instead, it should be the room that represents calm and peace and harmony. It should represent sweet cleanliness and freshness — it should be a place that naturally lends itself to enjoying one another. It ought to be a haven.

Words Like Apples of Gold

Now I want you to notice in verse 21 what finally caused the young man to yield. "With her much fair speech she caused him to yield, with the flattering of her lips she forced him." (Proverbs 7:21) Now even though all the other things I have mentioned — kissing, touching, romantic settings, being clean and pretty, and so forth — are important, our talk is still important. Can't you just see this woman in a beautiful negligee with luscious perfume on and candles burning in the romantic bedroom saying in a harsh voice, "Well, OK. What'd you do all day? Tell me. I want to know every last detail." Do you think that will entice her man? No. Then there's the woman who says in a sweet voice, "Hon, I bet you're tired. Sit down and tell me about your day." Perhaps she interrupts occasionally to say something like, "You know, you really are wise to give counsel like you do. You really are great to be able to carry on with all you do." I think your husband will like that. I **know** he will! So learn from the strange woman how to counteract the strange woman who will take your husband if she gets half a chance!

Again, please understand you can be that strange woman. You are going to have lonely times. When your husband starts a church, he will have to spend long hours away from home. If you have small children, you can't always go with him. If you don't watch it, you might become interested in some man who has become too friendly when he didn't mean anything by it. However, he just planted a seed that will grow until it is something it was never intended to be.

Perhaps you say, "I am so scared. Why do men have to be this way?" Because God made them that way. God made men to respond to the sight of a woman's curves and flesh and flattering, sweet words. Just **be** sure you are the one who is giving those things to your husband.

Similarly, I would like to address the problem of what you should do when you know some woman is being overly flirtatious or attentive to your husband. Now, first of all, I would say you need to warn your husband. You are his antennae, his radar. Warn him. Most of the time he will probably say, "Oh, you are being foolish!" If that happens, I think you should say something like, "Well, since she's a teenage girl, she surely is not telling you anything I can't hear. Let me come and be in the counselling sessions with you." I also believe there are times when you need to go to the woman and say, "Do you realize what you are doing?" Sometimes they don't. Sometimes things progress too far before the woman realizes what has happened. If you can nip it in the bud before the woman has become too infatuated, that will often divert disaster! By the way, it is very common for women to become infatuated with counselors. When someone is sympathetic and understanding and helpful, we are prone to feel they are so wonderful because it seems they understand us. But you can stop anything from happening by doing the above and, of course, by praying a lot. I think we don't realize how important it is to pray for our husbands.

Keep that husband from the strange woman who is lurking — and she is! Be assured that some woman today is going to tell your husband something nice; she is going to compliment him in some way. Have you? How did you send your husband off to work this morning? Did you say, "We will continue this fight tonight. Just keep it in mind!" That won't keep him from the strange woman!

I do not believe a pastor should refuse to counsel women. But I do believe his wife should do everything in her power to keep it from causing problems.

I believe we women can decide in our minds we will be faithful. The moment a wrong thought comes, quickly drive it away and pray that the Lord will help you never to think that way again. There is an old saying, "You can't keep a bird from flying over your head, but you can keep him from building a nest there!" If some man has been very kind to you, perhaps you can't keep a thought from passing through your mind like, "Oh, I bet he would always be so kind and gentle." But you can immediately say, "Lord, remove that thought. He is just like any other man. He stinks when he doesn't bathe. His breath smells bad in the morning." And if you picture him that way, you will quickly realize he doesn't have a thing on your husband; in fact, he probably doesn't have nearly as much.

There is one short Scripture which probably gives us the best admonition as far as dealing with the opposite sex. I Thessalonians 5:22 says, "Abstain from all appearance of evil."

A FEW DULL MOMENTS, PLEASE!

We are going to deal with ways to handle loneliness. Now I don't have any trouble staying occupied. I never have had. I don't understand women who say, "I have so much time on my hands." Let me give you this little poem entitled, "The Prayer of a Woman."

> I wished for home and husband,
> The wish was given me.
> My heart and hearth are daily sparked with masculinity.
> I wished for children,
> This request was also granted me,
> A nimble five-ring circus performing endlessly.
> I'm ready for my third wish now,
> Though squandered it may be,
> A few dull moments, please, oh please, occasionally.

Let me first suggest some things you might not be doing to prepare yourself for the ministry that is coming in the future. As you are around the house during the day, collect articles from books or magazines you feel might help you or someone else in the future. See, you never know when you might become a speaker or a teacher. Look for things that you think might help your husband too. Perhaps you think, "Mrs. Hyles, I don't think I'll ever need it." You don't know! Someone said to Disraeli one time, "That was a great extemporaneous speech." To which Disraeli replied, "I have been preparing for that extemporaneous speech for twenty years." And many times you will be called on to give a quick answer that for years you have been preparing by reading and studying. So read, cut out articles, save them and make a file of them. Have little 3X5 sectional dividers and divide the articles by topics. Label the box

"Articles for Future Sermons or Lessons."

Perhaps it would help your husband for you to do some typing of correspondence for him. Now I don't type. I took it, but it didn't take me. And I know how long it takes to write things out in longhand. You can save him a lot of valuable time.

If he is already in the pastorate, go visiting with him. You can make hospital calls. Go in your husband's place. Often, if the pastor's wife comes, people will excuse the pastor for not being able to be there.

Maybe you could begin taking piano or voice lessons. You say, "I am too old for that!" No, you're not. Bro. Mike Zachary, a gifted pianist, told me he has a lady who is in her seventies taking lessons from him.

Memorize Scripture. That is a wonderful way to fill your time and avoid being lonely. You know, all the Scripture you memorize as a young woman will stick with you. The Scriptures I remember the best are the ones I memorized as a young girl. Now I still try to memorize regularly, but I better remember those verses I learned as a younger woman. It is amazing how precious it is to you when you need a verse and you don't have time to go look for one and God brings a verse to your mind you know is just what you need.

Spend your day thinking happy, loving thoughts about your husband and children. I mentioned before sometimes we might tell our husband as he leaves for the day, "We have to stop fighting right now, but we'll continue where we left off when you come home!" No, the best way to stop that quarrel is to immediately quit thinking all those negative thoughts and start thinking happy, constructive, positive, loving thoughts. Then by the time he gets home and you greet him with a "holy kiss" (or even one that's not holy), he wonders what on earth happened to the quarrel. After dwelling on the good, you don't want to quarrel. Even if there's something that really does need to be cared for and the air needs to be cleared, you will be able to do it in a positive way and not in an ugly way. So think loving thoughts about your family.

Your phone can be a ministry. I don't like the phone for getting on just to yak, because you can end up staying on the phone too long and things go from constructive business to gossip. But you can use your phone to call someone who's sick, someone who has had an emergency with their family, or to check on somebody who wasn't in church lately. Everyone loves it when they are missed.

You can make a ministry out of writing notes. Everyone loves a note, no matter how brief. If stamps are too expensive, deliver the note in person. It can fill your time and it can be a ministry.

Develop some skills that you enjoy to fill your time. I am a person who from childhood has never minded being alone. That's a gift I think God gave me for which I am very grateful. As a child, I spent half my life up in the top of the chinaberry trees in my backyard dreaming and singing — alone. And I loved it! But I know there are people who just love to be around people. That's the difference in us. However, we all do need to develop the ability to be alone and enjoy it. You can use your time alone constructively.

Let's talk about some skills you can develop while you are home alone that don't require lessons.

What about basket weaving? You say, "Well, what good is that going to be?" I have received so many lovely decorated baskets. As a Christian leader's wife, you could decorate a basket and take it to someone who has been sick. It could also open the door for you to become acquainted with your neighbors; take one as a gift.

Baking — learn to bake. Is there anything that smells better than homemade bread? You could bake small loaves and take them to people as gifts. Mrs. Colsten is great about cooking for people who are bereaved or have problems. Even people in her neighborhood who don't come to our church will often get a gift of food from her in a time of need. That is a great testimony. The skills we develop and use can often even help in bringing someone to Christ.

You can work on your speaking skills by reading books, recording yourself and listening to it with improvement in mind. Most of us have tape recorders. Believe me, when I listen to myself on tape, I declare I'll never open my mouth again. I think I sound like you, and then I hear that I **still** sound like a Texas hick! Now they are **wonderful** hicks, but it does help you to listen to yourself on tape. Practice speaking in front of a mirror. Learn to project and work on your animation. Is there anything worse than listening to a speaker who never changes his facial expression or tone of voice?

You can learn to crochet or knit. That can even come in handy with your own families. Many of you cannot afford to buy very much in the way of gifts at birthday and Christmas. But you can give crocheted or knitted gifts.

Sewing is a useful skill. You can at least learn to sew on buttons, change a hem and do basic mending. If you don't have a machine and can't afford one to make garments, you can at least learn to alter things by learning to sew a straight seam by hand and repair tears and rips and that type of thing. This is a skill that will save you many dollars. The charge at a cleaners for having something like that done is outrageously high.

Needlepoint is something enjoyable for you to learn. Do you know that two of my prized possessions in my home are winter and summer scenes done in needlepoint. Guess who did them? Mrs. John R. Rice. She framed them for me and I will treasure them as long as I live. And there is someone who will cherish a needlepoint gift from you just as I treasure those, especially if you become the wife of a leader in their church.

Perhaps you could learn to quilt. A friend of mine, Mrs. Linda Stubblefield, has learned to quilt and she has given many quilts away. I have two from her — a small lap quilt and one for my bed. She also made one for my mother. I have had other quilts given to me and they are very valuable to me.

Take up cake decorating. Pam Shofroth, a lady in our church, began by taking it as a hobby; now she has a business. She makes almost all the cakes for the weddings at our church. Granted, it is hard work, but it is a business you can do in your home and still be with your children.

Develop skills. Use your time wisely. Don't just sit around watching your television and let your mind go to mush, for that's exactly what will happen. I'm not saying you should never turn the television on if you have one, but don't just sit there hour after hour and waste time. Time is life!

When Paul was in prison, he was sometimes bound to a jailer; but sometimes he was alone. I have been to that jail in Rome. It is way down under the ground. It is cold and damp — there is no way to get rid of water seepage. There is no heat or air conditioning. Yet Paul said in Philippians 4:10-12, "But I rejoiced in the Lord greatly, that now at the last your care of me hath flourished again; wherein ye were also careful, but ye lacked opportunity. Not that I speak in respect of want: for I have learned, in whatsoever state I am, therewith to be content. I know both how to be abased, and I know how to abound: every where and in all things I am instructed both to be full and to be hungry, both to abound and to suffer need." Let's look at several things Paul did while alone in very undesirable circumstances.

First of all, he rejoiced in the Lord instead of grumbling. Now that will change loneliness. Loneliness often brings self-pity and depression. We feel life is not treating us fairly. But if we are rejoicing in the Lord — and there is always something over which we can rejoice — we won't do that.

Second, he rejoiced in the care the people gave him — at least as much as they could — while he was in prison.

Third, he said he had learned to be content. Notice this was something he had to **learn.** You know, I have had to learn to be content with people milling around me. When I go out and speak, I am often put in a beautiful hotel room in which I spend about seven hours sleeping and that's it. Once, in West Virginia, I was given a room that had an absolutely beautiful view of a river. But I didn't get to be in that room a total of one waking hour. I was speaking or signing Bibles or greeting people — and loving it. But, at the same time, a part of me was wishing I could just go enjoy that lovely room and view. Once, when I came in from a speaking engagement, my daughter was at my house letting her Sunday school class go swimming in our pool. Now I had spoken four hours Friday and one hour on Saturday and I was just dead tired. My first thought was, "Oh, **more** people!" Now that's how I felt, but I have had to learn to be content in a crowd even when I would rather be alone. There's a need for both.

Lastly, Paul took time to appreciate. In Philippians 4 there are

several places where Paul took time to think of certain people and
what they had done to help him. In several of his books you will
notice he names people who have helped him. He was grateful to
the people who had contributed to his ministry. Knowing he
thought of them, I think he probably also prayed for them. There
is probably no greater thing we can do when we have time alone
than just to pray. You can pray while you are working with your
hands. When you sit down to work on that basket weaving or
needlepoint, ask the Lord to bring to your mind those for whom
you should pray.

You do need to deal with lonely times, but you don't have to let
yourself feel lonely or bored. As you go through those times when
you don't see your husband much, don't waste time being lonely.
Bloom where you are planted and use your time wisely.

SO YOU'RE NUMBER 10,031
ON HIS LIST, HUH?

Do you resent your husband's service for the Lord? Perhaps he is in full-time service as a preacher or evangelist or bus director. Maybe he is serving the Lord as a layman in the church. Nevertheless, if he is doing it with all his might and spending a lot of time at it, you can find yourself resenting the fact he is gone so much. I am afraid there are far too many of us who have been there. We are resenting when we ought to be praising the Lord. Perhaps when you married him he wasn't saved and you prayed the Lord would save him. Maybe you prayed for quite a while he would get saved and serve God. Then that day came; he got saved. When he did he was like Rover who, when he rolled over, he just rolled over all the way. Perhaps your husband just turned all the way over, too; perhaps he gave everything to the Lord and you think he's spending too much time at it. Or maybe you knew when you married your husband that he was going to serve the Lord. You knew you would be number two on his list, but you had no idea you would be number 10,031! Sometimes, it really does seem that way! However, it is sad for you to resent your husband's service for the Lord when it is the greatest calling a man could possibly have — whether he's in full-time service or a layman in the church.

Let me give you a few thoughts that will help you completely support what your husband is doing without feeling resentful. It is a man's very nature for his work to be his first love. We, as women, can't understand this about a man. But when Adam and Eve fell in the Garden of Eden, God told Adam he would earn his bread by the toil and sweat of his brow. He gave him work to do, and man has been a laborer ever since. Men will love their work if they are doing something they want to do. Consider a doctor who has to spend much, much time at his work. First of all, he spends years preparing; then the nature of his job requires him to spend many hours each day away from his family. The executives in this world spend much time working — that is why they have risen to the top. We find sports figures — professional football players, baseball players and basketball players — who constantly travel without their families. So just stop right here for a minute and realize it is not just Christian men who are gone a lot. In every phase of life, men who are successful spend hours away from their families; that is why they are successful. Don't fall into the trap of thinking that God's servants are the only ones who spend hours away from home. Would you rather have your husband get out of the Lord's work? You might have a little more time with him; but, then again, you might not! That's because every man, if he loves his work, is going to spend many hours at it.

What we need to realize is that being married to one of God's servants certainly has its assets. Let me give you just a few.

If you are married to somebody who is serving God, you get to watch God use him to work miracles in the lives of people. I know, because I have seen this in my own husband's life. I have seen him win people who were in the very depths of sin; now they are upright citizens, soul winners and great servants of the Lord. That is a miracle! I have seen miracles happen year after year and day by day as I have been the wife of a man who has loved his work of serving the Lord.

Another asset is that we are recipients of the blessings of Heaven. Heaven actually opens and the blessings pour out upon us if we are in His service. There is not a time I can remember during our more than forty years in the Lord's work that we have been really hungry. The funds have gotten very low and we have wondered where we would get our next meal. We have wondered where we'd get the gasoline to drive to our church. But do you know what? God always provided. We were serving Him; we were giving Him our tithes. He promises to pour out His blessings upon us, and He has truly done that. He will do the same for you. It is one of the assets of serving the Lord. It is so wonderful to watch Him as He provides for us. He never lets us go without the things we really need. You may not have the things you want, but you will have what you need. And God knows more than we do about what we need!

God's Wonderful People

Another asset of the ministry is the privilege of associating with the greatest people in the world. We have had the blessing of meeting and associating with so many fine people during our years in the Lord's work.

More than twenty years ago, Mrs. Billy Sunday had a meal in our home. Becky and David, though they were quite small, got to eat with her; they will remember it all their lives, and I will, too. It was a privilege to have this great woman in our home. Very early in our ministry we met the John R. Rice family. How grateful I am that God brought these choice people into our lives.   Some years ago, I had a special surprise. I love music. For years I had a special hero whom I loved to hear sing. One evening, a family in our church invited us out to dinner. When we arrived at the restaurant, I was surprised and delighted to see George Beverly Shea and his wife with our hosts.

Yes, we have gotten to meet some of God's choicest servants. And I'm not just referring to those whose names you know. I'm also talking about the ordinary Christian people in the churches where we have pastored. God's people are some of the greatest people in the world! I am not trying to tell you there are no liabilities, but the assets are so much greater!

Our problem comes when we spend too much time concentrating on the liabilities — especially the liability of having a husband who is gone a lot. Now you ought to be involved as much as you possibly can. But, of course, there are years when you need to be at home with your small children. Someone needs to be there to keep the home stable and secure for your children; and that someone is, of necessity, you! Small children need mom whenever possible. But there are still ways for you to be involved in your husband's work. You can be involved even though you are at home. If you will get involved, it will help you avoid the feelings of loneliness and resentment that will come when you are alone.

First of all, what is the goal in your life? I think I can hear most of you saying your goal is for your family to serve the Lord. That is probably the biggest goal in most of our lives. Those of us who love the Lord and have been saved for some time, want to serve Him in whatever capacity He has for us, as long as He will allow. So if that is your long-range goal, what are you doing about attaining it today? Do you think your griping and complaining will help you reach that goal? Have you done anything today that is going to insure the fact you will be serving the Lord twenty or thirty years from now? You must start today. It makes no difference whether you are still in school preparing or in a very small work. I would still say to you, "On your mark, get set, GO!"

Serve Him today wherever you are. Don't wait to be elevated to a higher position or better circumstances. Whatever God has for you is not ten miles down the road; it is facing you right now. Don't wait until you get to that "next place." See, God has a way of looking at people who are doing something for Him in the little places. If you grumble and complain in the small work, I doubt the big work will ever come along. If you are not faithful to serve in a small work, you won't serve in a big work either. Start today where you are. If you are home, tied down by young children, set a goal to accomplish something every day in your personal life that will help you grow as your husband is growing.

Be sure to get into your Bible daily. I know it is hard when you have small children; quiet times and privacy are mighty scarce. You will just have to make time.

Read when you get the opportunity. Read everything you can find that will build your husband and help your mind grow and expand.

Do you have a cup of cold water someone needs today? Give it! It will help you grow. Maybe giving a cup of water is all you can do today, but you will grow as you serve in the small ways. If you don't, you will become stagnant. You will become wrapped up in your tiny little world; bitterly resenting your husband's work and growth. But if you are growing and keeping up with him spiritually, those feelings won't result.

Perhaps you need to train your children better while they are at home. See, you have them; your husband doesn't. Since he is gone, you are the one who has the opportunity to train them and teach them. Maybe you have become lax in this area. You can grow in your personal life as you become the mother you ought to be, and I say to you, "Grow every day!"

Set a goal to do one thing each day that will enrich your life and make you grow personally. As you serve others, as you get into God's Word, as you serve your family in the proper way — grow! Serve wherever you are today.

Secondly, make certain that you align your will with God's will. Bro. Hyles often says, "Don't undo in doubt what you did in faith." Let's say you and your husband knelt somewhere back in the past and dedicated your lives to serving the Lord wherever He wanted you. You gave Him everything — you thought! You had no idea what that really meant. You didn't realize it was going to take your husband away from home a lot in the future. You didn't realize that it was going to leave you home alone with the children and the chores! You just had no idea. **Now** you are thinking, "God's not really very good to me. Here I am, dumped in some little bitsy hole of an apartment while he is out there doing what we both surrendered to do. I am not getting to do anything! I don't know whether I really like this thing of serving the Lord or not."

When you begin to think that way, go back. Realign your will with God's will. Remember that you've surrendered. Don't undo that. Don't take it back. God still has goals for you; He still wants you. When the going gets a little rough, that doesn't mean God has changed His mind — and you shouldn't either. You see, He allows the rough times for our good. If we could only believe that! You know, it seems we trust everybody but God. You have probably trusted many people just today. Maybe you took the kids to McDonald's for lunch. Workers you have never seen and whose names you do not know fixed your food; you trusted them not to put poison in your food. You put your trust in them to give you food that was clean, sanitary and good. Perhaps you also had gasoline put in your car today. You trusted the man who filled your tank to give you gasoline instead of water. If you have been on a plane lately, you entrusted to a pilot — a man you have never seen — your life. Yet, when life begins to hurt a little bit, we immediately begin thinking, "Can God really be trusted? Does He really know what He's doing in this situation?" Yes, He **can be trusted!** God wants the best for you, and you must believe this if you are in His will. Romans 8:28 is still true: "And we know that all things work together for good to them that love God, to them who are the called according to His purpose." If you are lonely, if the burden of rearing your children rests on you, then you must trust and believe it is best for you and the children. God does not allow anything in our lives that is not best for us. So, realign your will with God's will. Don't take back in doubt that commitment you made in faith.

You may feel it would be a terrible risk to align yourself with God's will and surrender to whatever He wants to do in your life. Yes, that would be a risk **if** He were not a God Who cares supremely for us and our welfare. He wants only the very best for us.

Now God is a much greater Father than we are parents to our children, and we want our children to have only the very best. We also know giving them the best sometimes involves taking away things our children think they ought to have. Perhaps your teenager has been careless with his driving and you've had to take away the car. But that's for his best, isn't it? Perhaps you are at a place where God has taken away the companionship of your husband. Just remember God is a loving Father Who wants the utmost for you. So trust Him. Learn to trust and believe He will not bring anything into your life that is not chosen for you.

The Bible goes on to say in Romans 8:29, "For whom he did foreknow, he also did predestinate to be conformed to the image of his Son, that he might be the firstborn among many brethren." The things that are hurting you — the loneliness, the rearing of the children alone — they are conforming you to the image of God. That is why He is allowing these things in your life. Let them accomplish their purpose. If you are filled with resentment, you aren't learning anything. You are not being conformed to His image. You are just kicking against the pricks. Align your will with God's will and don't go back on it.

Thirdly, work on your attitude. See, you think the problem you face today is that you are alone too much. The **real** problem is your attitude. Let me say it this way: the real problem is not the problem but your attitude toward it. As I will discuss in a later chapter, you can actually change your whole world by changing your attitude.

Fourthly, I would like to admonish you to confess and forsake sin in your life. "Oh, Mrs. Hyles," you say, "I am the wife of a preacher or song leader or bus director! I don't drink, smoke, cuss or wear pants!" But I am not talking about that kind of sin; I am talking about sins of the heart — the complaining, bitterness and resentment that come in before you even realize they are there. Sometimes it's just a little festering sore; we don't realize it's there until it ulcerates. You need to look into your heart and see what is really there. Is there something you need to confess to God?

According to the Bible, the sin of complaining greatly displeases God. Miriam complained against her brother, Moses, and she was given leprosy because of it. A man named Korah rebelled against the leadership of Moses and God caused the earth to open, swallow him, all his household, and those who rebelled with him. Discouragement is a sin of the heart. You know, God doesn't bring discouragement to us. It's a tool of the Devil and we fall prey far too often.

I read something the other day that is cute yet so true: "Happy are the people who are too busy to realize that they're not!" Did you get that? If you stay busy, you won't have time to get discouraged! Fill your life to the brim. You say, "I **am** busy, Mrs. Hyles. You just don't understand. I have a sick kid who's vomiting all over the house. The dog has gotten sick, too. Between scrubbing up his mess and the kid's mess, getting the dishes done, serving meals and keeping the house clean, **I'm busy.**" Okay. So while you're busy, make sure your attitude is right and that you are doing your work with the right motives. Happy and fortunate is the person who has work to do.

Discouragement used to be a problem for me far more often than it is now. At this time in my life, I have learned to do some big job I have been putting off or do something for somebody else. Those things keep me from having time to wallow in my self-pity. Sometimes we just have to leave the source of our discouragement with the Lord. You may have a day when you feel that, no matter what you do, you can never throw off that burden. Just get on your knees and say, "Lord, this is one of those times when You are going to have to take this burden. I can't get rid of it." I've done that before. Then I get up and go on with my duties for the day. And do you know what? God answers my prayer. If you will just go on and do what you are supposed to do, God will honor your faithfulness to your duties.

Content in any State

Remember that Paul said, "For I have learned, in whatsoever state I am, therewith to be content." (Philippians 4:11) Paul's contentment was learned; it wasn't a gift. He learned it by being in many different circumstances. Remember he had suffered just about everything—shipwreck, loneliness, persecution, false accusations and imprisonment. And he had **learned** to be content in all those situations. You can learn it, too, but you won't learn it until you get in some of those adverse predicaments. You learn patience by going through a lot of things that try your patience. In addition, you learn contentment by going through a lot of things that test your ability to be content.

You see, the Devil will probably get you down this way more than any other way. Look back and realize the defeats of yesterday are the victories of today. The things in your life, whether years ago or just weeks ago, that seemed so hard are the places where you grew and learned. You look back on them now and think, "Boy, those times were good for me." So realize today that the hard time you are in right now — the time when your husband has to be gone so much — is a time you will look back on and say, "I learned." Consequently, when your husband is away from home so much now, be especially careful about those sins of the heart. You can turn defeat into victory if you will. Learn to guard your heart. Remember the Bible says in Proverbs 4:23, "Keep thy heart with all diligence; for out of it are the issues of life." What you're carrying around in your heart will come out!

You know, if we all had a choice of crosses to bear, we'd all choose our own. Fanny Crosby said, "Oh, what a happy child I am. Though I cannot see, I am resolved that in this world contented I will be. How many blessings I enjoy that many people don't. To weep inside because I'm blind, I cannot and I won't!" And I would like to paraphrase that and say, "How many blessings I enjoy that other people don't. To weep and sigh because I'm lonely I cannot and I won't." It is up to you. Keep your heart clean of those crippling sins. They **will** incapacitate you and keep you from reaching your long-range goal of a lifetime of service for the Lord.

You can plan fun things to do during the time your husband is able to spend with your family. Have a candlelight dinner. You say, "Well, right now, all we're having is cornbread and beans!" Well, **that** even tastes better by candlelight! Plan something exciting to look forward to each and every day.

Every Sunday morning in our house, besides preparing breakfast and cleaning up from that and getting ready for church, I prepare Sunday dinner for eight or more people because my children have a standing invitation to bring their families for the noon meal. This means I have to put my roast in the oven, prepare my vegetables and set the table before I leave for church. Now that's a lot of work, but do you know what? It's such a fun thing. When our family sits down to dinner, though it meant a lot of work for me, it is worth it because we get to have some family time together. Now, you may have to go to some extra trouble to have some family time together, too. Nevertheless, it will be worth the effort. Instead of your brief times alone being filled with fussing and complaining, they will be filled with good times that will make happy memories in the years to come. You can overcome your loneliness if you'll just plan fun times when your husband is at home.

Fifth, keep in mind your value to God. Now I know your husband is the one who is the preacher or bus director or other full-time

Christian worker, but God thinks **you** are valuable, too. Of course, the two of you can't do the same things. You can't get out there and drive a bus or preach a sermon, but you are his helpmeet. You are very important; you must realize the two of you are not equivalent, but you **are** equal. You are somebody. You won't be able to overcome your feelings of loneliness until you realize you are a vital part of your husband's ministry. You really are. Your husband needs you in his ministry. He needs the softening influence you give. He isn't a whole person without you. Remember when Eve was made for Adam? He had to give up a rib. So I say, since then every man is missing a rib and you are that "missing rib" he needs! When you are scrubbing the toilets and cleaning house and taking care of sick kids, keep in mind you are doing one of the most important jobs a woman can do. It is a worthwhile, valuable contribution to your husband's ministry. Don't ever forget that!

Realize you have a high calling. If you like yourself and the work you do, you will like your husband and children more.

If you don't feel you are worth anything, you are going to quit somewhere along the line. You'll get too discouraged to go on. But if you realize your value and the contribution you make to your husband's ministry, you will reach your final goal of a lifetime of service for the Lord. Twenty or thirty years from now you'll still be out there working for God. You'll also have some wonderful memories of the miracles and blessings God has poured out upon you. It's your choice! You can gripe and resent your husband and make him quit either you or his ministry. **Or**, you can grow up and be the woman behind that man who is serving God.

When Lloys Rice told her husband good-bye for three or four weeks at a time, he didn't leave a weeping woman who was saying, "Why are you leaving me? Don't you love me?" NO! She contributed to his ministry for the sake of their long-range goal. And both of them, when they went on to Heaven, were still serving the Lord. They accomplished a marvelous work for God during their lives. Think about this. There are six Rice daughters. When the girls were small, who taught them and reared them while Dr. Rice was away for weeks at a time? Mrs. Rice had to do it! I am not in any way trying to minimize Dr. Rice's influence on his daughters. He was the leader of their home, but Mrs. Rice contributed. She was always glad she did and you will be, too.

Keep your eyes on that long-range goal. Work every day to reach it. If you are still in the Lord's work twenty or thirty years from now, it will be because you do it day by day. You will have to take things one step at a time. Understand that your husband is doing a worthwhile work, and strive to keep yourself from resenting the time he spends away from home. If you will add these thoughts to your life, you will reach your long-range goal — and that's a wonderful, wonderful objective to reach. I challenge you to begin today!

ARE YOU ALL WOUND UP?

Many marriages break up because of many little things rather than one big explosion at any given point. Little foxes spoil the vine, as it says in Song of Solomon 2:15, "Take us the foxes, the little foxes, that spoil the vines: for our vines have tender grapes." "Little foxes" can put enough stress on a marriage to destroy it. Many people are quitting their jobs because of little things adding up and bringing enough stress to cause a complete burnout. We often hear the term, "burnout." I believe it is truly a condition that really happens in people's lives. I want to read a statement by Mr. Minirth of the Minirth-Meier Clinic in Richardson, Texas about burnout and who gets it: "Burnout is when one's attitude becomes 'A job is a job is a job.' In other words, 'Ho hum, who cares anymore?'" And according to psychologist Christina Maslach, burnout is "a syndrome of emotional exhaustion, depersonalization and reduced personal accomplishment that can occur among individuals who do people work." Do you know what this psychologist means by "emotional exhaustion?" When you are emotionally drained, sleep and rest do not replenish you. The exhaustion pervades you more deeply and more deeply, and it takes something other than sleep and rest to replenish you. Another term this author uses is "depersonalization." I can't say I know exactly what she means, but I think she means you forget about yourself and others being people with needs. Instead you simply try to get through each day. By "reduced personal accomplishment" I think she means you just spin your wheels. You feel like you are just going around in circles without getting anything done. I believe stress leads to burnout when we have too much of the wrong kind of stress. I also believe burnout leads to depression or psychological illnesses — even suicide when the case is severe enough. Burnout is most common if you work with people. That is why those little things add up in a marriage and cause divorce. In a marriage, you are often living and dealing with a person who is completely opposite from you.

I feel it is important to give you some information about stress because you will be working with all kinds of people if you are in the ministry. Someone has said, "Stress is the feeling you feel when you feel you're going to feel a feeling you feel you'd rather not feel." And you will feel those feelings because you will be working with people as a wife and mother. We can't get away from people; we live with them. Of course, you might become a hermit; but who wants to live that way?

We live in an age today of fierce competition, busyness, noise, lack of privacy, deadlines to meet, budgets (that we don't meet), and many other things we could name that increase blood pressure and get the adrenalin flowing. Because of the unnecessary adrenalin flow, you can become exhausted when you really haven't done anything to make you tired. In Daniel 12:4 the Bible talks about men living in the last days and running to and fro. If we ever lived in that day, it is today. In fact, doctors say that in the last 25 years we have lived in a state of constant stress. We have noise all around us. When I go in a department store and rock music is blaring at me, I resent it because it puts me under stress. It just unnerves me. That's why my husband sometimes says, "Turn off the radio, turn off the television, turn off all the noise and just listen to the quiet." We need that because we have gotten so used to noise we think we have to have it. Many doctors believe 90 — 95% of the beds in hospitals are filled with people whose illnesses are stress related. Are you all wound up today? Unless you take care of it when you get all wound up, you will eventually wind down.

The Weary Round of Life

In Ecclesiastes 3 the Bible talks about the weary round of life. Do you feel that is what life is like for you? You know, I think it is particularly hard for women because our work is never done. Have you ever heard the saying, "Man works from sun to sun, but a woman's work is never done." And that is true. I made my bed this morning and washed dishes, but I will have it all to do again tomorrow. I wash clothes, but they don't stay washed. All the work we do has to be constantly done over and over again. Trying to keep all the household chores done as well as our other responsibilities can sometimes make life seem like a weary round.

Stress can also be described as your body's response to a threatening situation. Have you ever been out at night and heard footsteps coming behind you? Every time you turned a corner, did the footsteps follow you and you couldn't shake them? Let me describe how your body would respond if this were happening to you. First of all when you are alarmed, your endocrine glands release hormones — that is adrenalin. The heartbeat speeds up, and so does your breathing. Your oxygen-rich blood is directed away from the skin to the brain in order to help you if you need to think quickly to defend yourself. It is also sent to the skeletal muscles — in case you need to deliver a good punch. Your pupils dilate so that your vision is sharpened. Other hormones enter your blood, increasing the speed of coagulation in case you are injured. Your muscles tense — getting ready for injury. Your digestion slows down. All this energy surge, concentration and power enables you to act in crisis situations.

Have you ever heard of a person lifting a car off someone? Is that normal? I read of a case several years ago of a thirteen-year-old boy lifting the front end of a car off a woman who was pinned under it. That is totally abnormal. But under a stressful situation his body gave forth all that was needed to lift that car. Now when the baby messes just before you are about to go out the door somewhere, it does not call for the same type of reaction! Finding a run in your nylons and having no time to change also doesn't call for that type of response! But the fact is we are responding that way to the small stresses. Can't you see what that's doing to us? We are all wound up and we are going to run down. If we let that kind of stress build up over those minor concerns, we are going to be totally depleted. When the stress adds up and all our body's defenses are geared up, we are totally depleted and totally without any physical energy left to fight disease. Our emotional energy is gone; we can't deal with the smallest problems. We just have nothing left with which to cope.

I have often said the person who is ready to jump off a bridge is not thinking, "Life is so wonderful and I am so loved and everything is just going so well." No, they are at the point where stress has so built up and they are so totally burned out over life or people they find there is no longer any reason for which they think they should live. It is so important that we learn to minimize stress because of what it does to our bodies.

One way you can avoid adding to your stress is to give yourself the benefit of the doubt when you aren't reacting like you should to life. Dr. Cal Streeter told me that in a woman's monthly cycle there are no two days when her hormone levels are the same. It's no wonder we feel happy one day and ready to dissolve in tears the next! When you know your state of mind is hormone related, don't heap more stress on yourself by being down on yourself. You are not a bad lady — you are just a lady! Now we should not hide behind our hormones and say, "Well, I am just that way once a month." You don't have to be "that way," and you can learn to deal with it.

We see in the Bible David lived with a lot of stress. Saul just gave David fits for years. David also lived with the stress of his sin with Bathsheba. I think he was never able to forget the consequences of the sin he committed with her. He lost a baby, one other son rebelled against him, and I believe these things were a consequence of his sin. We see in Psalm 55:1-7 how David felt about life at one point: "Give ear to my prayer, O God; and hide not thyself from my supplication. Attend unto me, and hear me: I mourn in my complaint, and make a noise; Because of the voice of the enemy, because of the oppression of the wicked: for they cast iniquity upon me, and in wrath they hate me. My heart is sore pained within me: and the terrors of death are fallen upon me. Fearfulness and trembling are come upon me, and horror hath overwhelmed me. And I said, Oh that I had wings like a dove! for then would I fly away, and be at rest. Lo, then would I wander far off, and remain in the wilderness. Selah."

Now David is saying if he had the wings of a dove, he could have flown off and been rid of his hurting heart and his fear of pursuit by Saul and everything else. But would he have been? No, because he still would have been the same person. You don't need to run away. A lot of women do run away; they think it will solve their problems. However, they only carry the same person with them who has not learned to deal with stress. David was admitting, "I have stress around me constantly and I feel if I could go to the wilderness and remain there, everything would be fine." But it wouldn't be. Even if you go, away from any kind of person or thing that might harm you, solitude is stressful. I have heard one man tell how he dealt with being in a POW camp in World War II. To avoid going insane, he did mental exercises to keep his mind constantly busy. There is stress even in solitude. If you ever feel like escaping your situation, remember that is not the answer. However, David **did** find the great answer. Psalm 120:1 says, "In my distress I cried unto the Lord, and he heard me." David learned that you can take all your stress to the Lord. You say, "Well, God doesn't hear me. My prayers just bounce off the ceiling." Oh, yes, He always hears you. You may not feel like He does, but remember He is always there. Taking our burdens to the Lord is the great answer to stress.

We also need to realize that not all stress is bad. You need a little flow of adrenalin for you to accomplish the work you have to do each day. But you don't need a huge rush of adrenalin over some little minor, silly thing. However, that's what happens.

I can honestly say that in years gone by I would have had a rush of adrenalin like I described earlier if I had found a run in my nylons after I had left the house. But I have learned it is dumb to do that. I have taught my college class at least twice while wearing two different earrings. (And the class I teach deals with wardrobe coordination and grooming!) I have learned not to let little things upset me. They are just no big deal. We **all** do stupid things. Let's learn not to take it so hard. It's not that important. Don't waste ten dollars' worth of energy on a ten-cent problem. Many people do; that is why they are so worn out. That's why people can't cope with life.

Stress is like using spices in cooking. We need a little bit of adrenalin just like certain recipes need a little touch of cinnamon or pepper. Now you don't want the whole box in the pot! A little salt brings out the flavor, but you don't add the entire box. That's the way stress is. It adds spice to life. We need enough of the good stress or adrenalin flowing to make us go. But too much stress makes your brain, spinal cord, lungs, heart, adrenal glands and muscles work very hard. Someone has said we live in a day of three words: "hurry, worry and bury." And that is true. Some people are dying earlier than they otherwise would have simply because they are hurrying and worrying constantly. Do you find yourself hurrying when there is no need to hurry? Do you find sometimes your motor won't quit running? Your body just gets in such a habit of hurrying that it won't quit. Stop and ask yourself if you really need to be hurrying — and slow down if you don't.

Quit Crying Over Spilled Milk

There are three things we need to ask ourselves when deciding whether we can make a difference in our stress levels.

1. Ask yourself, "**Is there really a problem?**" If you are hurrying and you feel worried and anxious, stop and analyze. Let's say your mother-in-law is coming. Is that truly a problem? You know, I am a mother-in-law and I don't go peeking into every corner. I go to have a good time. I am not there to judge. But we are so defensive where our in-laws are concerned. If there is a problem, why not concentrate on dealing with the issue rather than being upset about it?

I remember once when I was being driven to the airport after a large ladies' meeting where I had received a lovely gift. As we drove away from the hotel, there was a group of ladies outside to tell us good-bye. And I had left my gift sitting on top of the car! Everyone was yelling, "Oh, your gift, your gift!" And I was thinking, "Beverly Hyles, you do the silliest things!" But was it a real problem? No. It just gave them all a good laugh, I got a good laugh out of it, and that was the end of it. It was a dumb thing to do, but it was really a funny happening to everyone. However, there used to be a time when that would have been a problem to me and I would have let it get to me.

2. Ask yourself, "**Is this issue important to me?**" Let's say that on an important day you forget to pluck your eyebrows or you find a blemish. Is that an important thing? Perhaps you remember during the middle of the Sunday morning sermon you forgot to put lunch in the oven. Or worse yet, one time I remembered (in the middle of the sermon) I had forgotten to turn the fire off under my green beans before I had left home that morning. At first, panic struck! Then I realized there wasn't a thing I could do about it. The house would be filled with smoke and the pan would be ruined, but I couldn't change it at the moment. So I decided to go ahead and get a blessing from the sermon and worry about the green beans when I got home. I did have to throw out the pan and we didn't have any green beans for lunch that day, but it didn't ruin the world. Don't waste ten dollars' worth of energy on that ten-cent problem. You are only killing yourself.

3. Ask yourself, "**Can I change anything?**" If you cannot change it, then accept it, don't worry about it, and forget it.

A lady I know once lost some precious photographs of her mother when her home flooded; they could never be replaced. She could not change the fact that they were gone. Therefore, she had to change her attitude and accept the situation. You can either accept the things you can't change or kill yourself fretting over them.

Sometimes, when we are running late, we will just sit and fume if we get caught by a train or a traffic light. It doesn't do any good, does it? We might as well find something profitable to do during that time.

When you find that you are unusually stressed, stop and ask yourself the three previous questions. Many times, you will be able to relax when you realize it isn't a problem or an important issue, or there is nothing to be done about it anyway. Much of the solution for stress lies in just simply changing our own attitudes.

We must also consider how we can learn to cope with the normal stresses that do come in our lives as pastor's wives, mothers, homemakers or women working with people. When you are working with people you are subject to stress because people are unpredictable. You never know from one day to the next how they will be.

Practical Ways to Deal with Stress

The first step in coping with normal, everyday stress is to listen to your body. It often tells you much more than your doctor can. Notice if you begin to have headaches that are not normally a part of your physical makeup. Some people have them frequently. I don't happen to be one. So when I get a headache, I stop to figure out why. Headaches can be brought on by an improper response to something that has happened in our lives. Doctors say one of the first places stress affects you is in your digestive system. Perhaps your stomach is upset. Stress slows down digestion and can cause either constipation or diarrhea — and sometimes a mixture of both. When that happens and you know you are not ill, perhaps you have just not responded to stress properly. Perhaps you are having a problem with insomnia. This is particularly true if you are waking up too early. If you can't go to sleep at night, it is usually a sign you are taking your worries to bed with you. But if you go to sleep and then wake up way too early, it is usually an indication you have reached the point of depression.

You need to deal with these things. They are just a few of the signs your body gives you that you need to take a break — you need to slow down. Take a mini-vacation, however short it might be.

How can you take a break? What is a break for you? Perhaps it is having your husband watch the children while you lie down or go out somewhere alone! Perhaps reading a book and drinking a cup of tea is a break for you. Maybe you enjoy taking a walk, sitting in the woods, doing a craft or playing with a pet. Just slow yourself down on purpose!

There are two things that will help you accomplish this. The first has to do with eating. How fast do you gulp down your meals? Slow down! The food is not going to run away; it will stay right there on the plate. Enjoy it and don't eat so fast. Now when we are stressed, our tendency is to eat everything as quickly as we can. Then we think, "Now, where did my food go?" It takes your brain twenty minutes to tell your stomach that you have eaten. So if you are gulping your food down too quickly, then you will eat much more than you need because you will be stuffed by the time twenty minutes has passed. The second thing that will help is to take the necessary time for proper elimination. There are just some things that shouldn't be rushed. I understand that perhaps your children are killing each other outside the bathroom door; but even if you have to let them kill each other, take the time your body needs.

We need to get a balance. This is a Scriptural concept. Mark 6:31 tells us that Jesus said to His disciples, "Come ye yourselves apart into a desert place, and rest a while." And that verse goes on to say, "For there were many coming and going, and they had no leisure so much as to eat." Now if Jesus saw His disciples needed to rest and take a break from the people, don't you think He cares that much about you? Of course He does.

Job 10:1 talks about soul weariness. Job had suffered just about every kind of stress imaginable. He said his soul was weary of life. Now that's real burnout. He had suffered the loss of his possessions, he was sorrowing over the death of his children, he was suffering physically — he had just run the gamut. Then he had those three friends come yakking at him, and I think that was probably the most stressful of all. Yet it seems to me he dealt with it. The Bible says Job didn't blame God.

Jesus tells us this in Matthew 11:28-30: "Come unto me, all ye that labour and are heavy laden, and I will give you rest. Take my yoke upon you, and learn of me; for I am meek and lowly in heart: and ye shall find rest unto your souls. For my yoke is easy, and my burden is light." If we are weary in the work of God, it is probably because we are doing it in our strength instead of in His. We are fretting about it too much, we are worrying about it too much instead of saying, "Lord, I am the vessel. You work through me." Now that doesn't mean we don't need time to prepare — time to get ready for certain things we do. You don't have to worry and fret and stew. You can learn to do your work in His strength because

He says His yoke is easy. Many pastors are quitting the ministry because of burnout. In some cases, I wonder if it's because they are trying to do God's work in their own strength. That is just not possible.

Of course rest is necessary, but we do need to balance our rest with work. You know, work hardly ever killed anybody. In fact, a good day of working at something that gives me a feeling of accomplishment takes stress off me. Work is necessary. But when you are tired, you need to realize you must rest.

So the first step in coping with stress is to learn to listen to your own body. Know yourself well enough to know when some things are wrong with you physically. Often you won't have to go to a doctor if you will just make some changes in your lifestyle to reduce your stress.

Second, reduce stress by learning right priorities. In the second chapter of this book, learning right priorities is discussed in more detail.

Sometimes we just have more on us than we can handle and we must be willing to admit it. Of course, we want to do all we possibly can; but there are times when we must admit that we are not "superwomen."

I know one young mother who finally decided the best thing she could do while her children napped was to take a nap herself. She concluded her nap was more important than trying to get her mending done while the children napped. She realized she was less cranky and irritable when she had rested.

Another little tip that will help you with priorities is to keep a calendar on which you mark the things you have to do each day. Don't rely on your brain. Ann Ortlund, the woman who wrote *Disciplines of the Christian Woman*, said that people often say to her, "You are so organized!" And she tells them **she** is not organized — her **calendar** is!! Really, our minds get too full. Don't depend on your brain to remember where you need to be and when you need to be there. Write down those appointments. I keep a date book in my purse as well as keeping one at home. I keep my appointments in both. In fact, I have three; I keep them all marked. Doing this will reduce your stress.

My husband used to tell me when we were first married that I needed to learn to write down things. I thought, "No I don't! I'm young and I can remember!" But I learned he was right. Even if you think you are young and you can remember, it reduces stress if you will record things. When you run out of an item, write a note to yourself. Just don't stress your mind by trying to remember everything.

Third, organize your home to support you rather than to add more stress to your life. I said in a previous chapter you should make housekeeping simpler. If you are in the busy child-rearing years, put away the precious antique vase that keeps you constantly running behind the children to make sure they don't break it. We tried to teach our children there were some things they couldn't touch. We did that not only to keep them from breaking our things but to keep them from breaking someone else's things when we went out. Sometimes that's not possible. Don't stress yourself by putting out the porcelain vase and then going around in a dither because you expect little Johnny to break it at any moment. Wait and use it later or put it up high enough so little Johnny can't reach it.

Have a place for everything and put everything in its place. Not being able to find your keys can be stressful. Having a pretty little plaque by the door for keys won't do you any good if it is never used.

Have rules for your children's play and eating. Don't let them go all over the house with peanut butter and jelly and crackers and cookies. They ought to have certain places where they can eat and certain places where they can't. That saves you work and it is good for them. They need boundaries and rules. Children are happier (and you are too) when there are rules.

Fourth, plan and take time for leisure. Do this especially when you know you are going through a stressful time. Have somewhere to go where you can regroup. You must have a place where you can be alone to relax and get yourself together. God is a God of order and He wants our minds to be in order. He doesn't want them in a chaotic mess.

Perhaps you can only get away for ten or fifteen minutes. If so, take a short walk. Dig in your flower bed if that's what you enjoy. Or perhaps you could do some special baking for your family. Cooking is relaxing to some folks. I think a wonderful thing we fail to do is just sit in the yard and do nothing for ten or fifteen minutes. We are so programmed to be busy we have almost forgotten how to be still. Psalm 46:10 says, "Be still, and know that I am God." What an important verse! We get so busy it is easy to forget who God is. We don't take time to concentrate on Him. Plan time for leisure. Consider your leisure and your play a service for others, because it makes you better able to cope with others. It isn't necessary to get to the point where you resent your family and all you have to do for them because you never have any time for yourself. Planning time for your own relaxation is essential.

Fifth, get regular exercise and eat properly. When you are under stress, this is very important. Whether the pressure be big or small, if you feel like you are stressed, take special care of your body. I Corinthians 6:19 and 20 tells us our body is the temple of the Holy Spirit. We are responsible for taking care of it because no one else is going to do it for us. We have to learn if we are going to glorify God in this body, which He tells us to do, we are going to have to keep it fit, strong and healthy. For you, exercise might be a good brisk walk. It is said that fifteen to twenty minutes of physical exertion three times a week will lessen your stress, bring down your blood pressure and help tone your body. Don't wait until you feel bad to start exercising — start now while you are feeling good because you won't exercise once you are feeling bad.

It is especially important as we grow older to exercise in order to keep our bodies limber. As we get older, we automatically stiffen. Physical activity will keep that from happening so quickly.

Concerning exercise, remember that it should make you — not break you. Don't take on a regimen that is so difficult it kills you. Exercise is meant to help you. It is not a good idea to exercise strenuously just before going to bed, but exercising during the day will help you sleep. Eating right will also help to reduce your stress. What do you want to eat when you are depressed? Sugar, candy, cookies and pop, of course! Why do you suppose we do that? Do you remember getting a spanking when you were little? After it was all over mom would say, "Now come on to the kitchen and let's have a cookie." Sweets are a reward for many of us. They are a comfort. But that's not what you need. In fact, that's the last thing you need when you are under stress. Too much sugar will make you tend to have quick mood upswings; but, just as quickly, you will have a mood downswing. That's bad when your body is already under stress. We should even avoid those cereals coated with sugar. Eat protein instead.

Are you a breakfast eater? If not, you should at least try to eat something like a half slice of wheat bread with peanut butter and some skim milk. That's protein, and it will bring your blood sugar level up slowly. Now a doughnut will bring it up in a snap and you will think you can whip the world, but an hour later you will think, "Oh, what happened to me?" That's because sugar causes an artificial high. But if you will eat some protein, your blood sugar level will come up slowly and stay there through the morning until lunch time.

Do you ever make cheese toast? My husband is not a breakfast eater. He won't eat an egg. He says he just can't stand one looking at him from the plate. So I will often put a little butter on some wheat bread, grate some cheese on top and put it under the broiler. That's a good source of protein for him. Whatever it takes for you to have protein in the morning, you need to be eating properly.

Be careful not to have too much caffeine. If you are a coffee drinker, don't think drinking cup after cup through the day will give you more energy. It will deplete your energy stores. It will keep giving you a high, but it will make your energy level plummet. That also includes pop and chocolate. Caffeine can be very bad for you.

A good rule of thumb for eating when you are under stress is this: "If God made it, eat it." Now God didn't make Hostess Twinkies! He didn't make Snickers! He made good, crisp apples, oranges, bananas and carrot sticks. You'd be surprised what it will do for you just to change the type of food you eat when you are stressed.

There are certain vitamins that are good for you when life is stressful. The B vitamins are the stress vitamins. As a woman, you ought to be taking a good B complex vitamin as well as a multiple vitamin. Magnesium is a good stress vitamin — especially if you are taking calcium. You have a tendency not to absorb calcium unless you have magnesium. Calcium is nature's tranquilizer. That's why people often recommend drinking warm milk at bedtime — it has calcium. All three of these vitamins — B complex, magnesium and calcium — are good for you when you are under pressure.

I have mentioned previously that eating more slowly will help you greatly. Don't eat for comfort because you will eat the wrong foods and you will eat too quickly. Eat food for the right reasons. Ask yourself if what you are about to eat is going to help your body. If it isn't, don't eat it. I don't mean you shouldn't have an occasional piece of pie or a candy bar. I am just saying you should be more careful in a time of stress, and everyone will have those times.

The sixth thing you can do in dealing with stress is to change your attitude. Anything can be stressful depending upon how we respond to it. One way to look at everything in the right way is to learn to praise God in everything. This is a Scriptural principle. I Thessalonians 5:18 tells us, "In every thing give thanks: for this is the will of God in Christ Jesus concerning you."

There is a reason for everything. When you go to the store for a needed item only to find the store is closed, you can learn from that. It can teach you to call ahead the next time.

Learn to laugh at yourself. One day I got up and, as I always do, I splashed my face, added just a little bit of color, combed my hair, then put on my undergarments and a fresh robe to go down and fix breakfast. That particular morning, my husband was in a very talkative mood. However, I had an early morning college class to teach, so I had to get up from the table to let him know I needed to get a move on. When I got up to do that, I felt something down around my feet. Now we don't have a pet, so I looked down and my slip was encircling my ankles! When I had put on my full slip, I had stepped into it and forgotten to put the straps up on my shoulders. Now I didn't want to laugh, but my husband surely did! Then I thought, "He needed a good laugh so I might as well laugh too!"

Learn to laugh at yourself. I'm sure there have been times when you have thought, "Oh, NO!" But if you will just look at the humorous side of the situation, it is probably hilarious.

Some years back I read about a man named Norman Cousins who had a very serious illness. As I remember there was no diagnosis for it, and he was never free of excruciating pain. He had learned negative emotions caused disease, so he thought to himself if negative emotions caused disease, positive emotions could give him relief from his pain. And he got well! If this man could get well by deciding to laugh, don't you think it would help us to learn to laugh? You can learn to see the humor in almost anything. Our attitude makes all the difference in how we are affected by the things that happen to us.

Relax? What's That?

So often we are tense for no reason at all. We need to learn to relax. Start by taking some slow, deep breaths. Learn to concentrate on relaxing each muscle in your body one at a time. Here's a good formula: Prayer + praise = peace. It really does! Pray about whatever has upset you, then thank God for the situation and peace will come. You can thank God for anything. When you find you have a serious illness, I am not saying you should say, "Thank You, Lord, that I am so sick!" However, you **could** say, "Thank You, Lord, there is medical help available and that I have Your help." No one expects you to giddily thank God for major problems. However, you can thank God for what you can learn while going through the problems and you can thank Him for the good in the problems. There is something in everything for which we can praise God. Learning to praise God in every situation will help you learn to relax.

We are told by those who practice yoga and other Eastern religions that they meditate to learn to relax. Now we have the only real God. Why don't we learn that meditating on His goodness, grace, mercy and love can bring relaxation. Yoga doesn't. Buddhism doesn't. All the strange prayers they pray won't help them at all.

But we have a real and living God to Whom we can talk and upon Whom we can mediate. Find verses in the Bible that give you peace when you think on them. Psalm 119:165 says, "Great peace have they which love thy law: and nothing shall offend them." So learn to relax! You can!

Next, talk out your problems, but **be careful**! It is wonderful to have a trusted friend with whom you can share your problems without her repeating them. But you can **always** go to the Lord and He doesn't ever repeat anything you tell Him. Now sometimes we do need someone in the flesh. As you talk out your problems, try to pinpoint whether some of your stress is caused by unconfessed sin. If it is, confess it. Get it behind you. Perhaps you are holding on to some hidden sin of the heart. Maybe you don't want to get rid of your anger, jealousy or self-pity. If you keep hugging those sins to your bosom instead of confessing them, you will have stress in your life.

You should learn to be the kind of person with whom someone can share their burdens in confidence. It is impossible for you to counsel if you are not the type of person who can keep confidences and not repeat them. You must learn to be that kind of person if you want to help bear the burdens of others.

Stress is here to stay. You are not ever going to be able to get rid of it entirely. In our world as it is today, everyone is in a state of stress. But God still says, "My grace is sufficient." (II Corinthians 12:9) And it is.

Now, what does God expect from us? There are two types of stress problems. First of all are those we **can** change. If it is something you can alter, do it. Perhaps you need to get rid of the stress by adjusting something in your life, or perhaps by just learning to laugh at yourself. Sometimes we put off solving the problem and that causes more stress. So just get on top of the difficulty and solve it. The second type of stress problem is the one we **cannot** change. So what do we do about those? We accept them. We accept them with praise and thanksgiving and endure them with God's strength as Paul did his thorn in the flesh. That thorn in the flesh was evidently a stressful thing to Paul. But God didn't see fit to remove it, so Paul endured; he even went on to say this strength came when he was weak. He even began to see the good that came from the stress God allowed in his life. You can praise God in any situation because He can bring good out of it.

Now let's look at what God expects from us when we are in a difficult situation. The world is looking on and people are watching us as Christians. They know when we are in a stressful situation and they are watching to see how we will handle it.

When we are under stress, we are to glorify God always. Someone has said, "Our lives should be an exhibit to the world." Your life is an exhibit to the world. When you go through those stressful situations that would break most people, you are a greater help and testimony than at any other time in your life. Perhaps you even shed some tears as you go through those situations, but people see the strength and courage you display during the stressful times. So God expects us to keep glorifying Him even during the particularly stressful times in our lives.

Expect God to Keep His Word

What can we expect from God when we are under stress? I want to give you five Scripture promises to help you overcome stress.

1. Romans 15:5 says He's the God of patience. Therefore, we can ask Him to share some of that patience with us in our time of stress. When you are under stress, don't you find that you lack patience? You yell at your children when they really haven't done anything wrong. You are just short-tempered in general. You're a little bit angry at the situation, so you take it out on your family and friends. Romans 15:5 says, "Now the God of patience and consolation grant you to be likeminded one toward another according to Christ Jesus." God will grant you patience if you will ask for it.

2. Romans 15:13 tells us He is a God of hope. Remember this time will pass. The verse says, "Now the God of hope fill you with all joy and peace in believing, that ye may abound in hope, through the power of the Holy Ghost." Believe. God is the God of hope.

When you feel like the world is just caving in, it could be the only thing wrong with you is a low point in your monthly cycle. I have been there. I was just sure the world was ending, but I was simply going through that low point in my monthly cycle. It may be something greater or smaller that makes you feel like all hope is gone, but He told us to believe. He is the God of hope who will bring you joy and peace. Claim it! You can expect it from Him.

3. Romans 15:33 says, "Now the God of peace be with you all." He is the God of peace, the God of order. He doesn't want your life to be filled with chaos. He wants to bring it into order and bring you peace — and He will if you ask Him.

Let me illustrate peace. An artist had a class of just three students and one day he challenged them to paint their idea of peace during their class period. The first artist painted a lake at sunset. The lake was still; there wasn't a ripple on it. The sun was setting. It was just lovely. The second artist painted a sleeping kitten all rolled up in a ball. I don't suppose there's anything more peaceful-looking than that. The third artist painted a raging storm with the trees bending and the water boiling. But in a cleft in a rock, there was a little bird and it was singing. Now the teacher judged that one to be the true picture of peace because we don't live in a world that's like a sunset or a sleeping kitten. We live in a raging storm. But there's always that cleft in the Rock where we can hide and have perfect peace in the midst of the storm. If we can't find peace in the midst of the storm, we are no different from the world. Christianity is more than just getting to Heaven some day. It is something practical that can be a part of our lives every day. We need to claim that peace.

4. I Peter 5:10 says He is the God of all grace. That grace is for you. The verse says, "But the God of all grace, who hath called us unto his eternal glory by Christ Jesus, after that ye have suffered a while, make you perfect, stablish, strengthen, settle you." Now if God's grace was sufficient for Paul, don't you think it is the same today? Sure! He is "the same yesterday, to day and for ever." (Hebrews 13:8) In the time when He does allow stress, He wants to stablish and settle you.

5. In II Corinthians 1:3 and 4 we see He is the God of all comfort:

"Blessed be God, even the Father of our Lord Jesus Christ, the Father of mercies, and the God of all comfort; Who comforteth us in all our tribulation, that we may be able to comfort them which are in any trouble, by the comfort wherewith we ourselves are comforted of God." Why does God allow stressful times to come to us? We can find one reason in these verses. We learn to be comforters by needing comfort! When you think the world is caving in, you get comfort from God. You learn which Scriptures help you and what practical things to do to help yourself. Then when someone comes to you and needs comfort, you can tell them how to find it.

These are promises we can expect God to fulfill during times of stress.

Get a Brand New Start

Perhaps you have already reached the stage today where you'd like to say, "Stop the world; I want off!" Maybe you have even reached a stage of depression where you feel like every day is just a dark, black hole. If you have, there are ways to help yourself. We are threefold beings and we must work on ourselves physically, emotionally and spiritually.

First of all, start working on yourself physically. Exercise. Eat right. If you are dieting, be sure you are getting food from the basic food groups. Diets that involve only drinking liquids or eating only one type of food may make you lose weight, but they aren't good for your body. Get enough sleep. You say, "Well, tell me when and I will do it." I realize getting enough sleep is difficult for many people. But most women do need about eight hours of sleep each night.

I once read a book entitled *Depression* about a pastor who had a terrible mental breakdown. He was out of the pulpit for a number of years. He had to go to a mental hospital and he learned a lot about depression while he was there. Now he eventually discovered his depression was caused in a large part by hypoglycemia. He learned in the hospital when they bring someone in who has attempted suicide, one of the first treatments is to feed them a very high-protein meal. Does that tell you anything about your eating? As I said before, you need to eat protein in the morning. You also need to make sure you are getting enough protein in general. Every cell in your body needs it. It will help you in stressful times.

Secondly, get started back up emotionally by doing the following.

1. Have your laugh each day. When you have a good laugh, you will feel better emotionally. Keep on laughing. Every time you feel down, think of something funny that makes you really chuckle.

2. At the end of the day, ask yourself how much of your talk to yourself was positive that day. You know, we talk to ourselves. Now we don't do it out loud, but we call ourselves "dumb bunnies," etc., where no one else can hear us. Quit talking negatively to yourself. Start talking positively. Say, "My house looks so good. My kids are doing well, and that's partly because I am doing something right. Boy, this supper looks so good tonight. It isn't an expensive meal, but the table looks pretty." Do you tell yourself those kinds of things? Why don't you? You would for a friend if you were visiting. So start talking positively to yourself. We tend to talk to ourselves only when we have bad things to say.

3. At the end of the week ask yourself if you have lived in the present this week. Perhaps you are living in the past, dwelling on past failures. Or maybe you are projecting yourself into the future to something you are dreading. In Matthew 6:34 the Bible tells us that we have enough to say grace over today! "Take therefore no thought for the morrow: for the morrow shall take thought for the things of itself. Sufficient unto the day is the evil thereof."

4. Ask yourself at the end of the week if you have done something at least three times (but preferably every day) for relaxation and recreation. Let me warn you that watching some of the trauma-filled programs on television is not relieving your stress. Of course, soap operas don't relieve stress. They create it. Aside from being wicked and immoral, they are full of problems. They are make-believe life. Instead of sitting down to watch something traumatic, why don't you get up and live life in a positive way? There are many ways to relax that don't cost a cent. You can play tennis, go to the library or take

a walk. A bubble bath is cheap. Once when I was going through a stressful time, a lady in our church sent me a card that said something like, "When I feel like life is treating me unfairly, I take a bubble bath." And then when you opened the card, it said, "I have been in here for three weeks!" Now you probably can't stay in your bubble bath for three weeks, but it is a good idea!

Thirdly, we need to get started back up spiritually.

1. Learn to get into the Bible. Do you enjoy the Bible, or is it just a chore? Get into the Bible long enough for it to become a thrill and really speak to your heart. That will help you recover from depression, burnout, stress or anything else!

2. Do you realize the importance of good music? Play a tape of the hymns of the faith. This can help you so much spiritually. Remember that just as good music can help you spiritually, bad music can pull down. It will make you feel chaotic. Music is so important.

3. Have you applied the Word of God to your life? Do you know what it says without living it? There are practical truths in the Bible. What about, "A merry heart doeth good like a medicine." (Proverbs 17:22) God didn't just put that in there to fill up space, you know. It's for us to apply. Apply I Corinthians 1:3 and 4 — the God of all comfort will comfort **you** in the midst of your trials. Apply the Word!

4. Set a goal of memorizing verses that will help you. Perhaps you can only memorize one verse each week. That is fifty-two verses a year and it will be wonderful to have those verses in your mind and heart when you need them.

5. And then, when you need it, how quickly do you apply I John 1:9? We need to realize we are forgiven if we have confessed our sin. We can forget it and go on. Only then will we have peace and comfort.

These truths will help you in dealing with stress in your life. Don't let stress defeat you. Use it to be a testimony for Christ.

STOP, LOOK, AND LISTEN!

What is counselling? When you ask someone for counsel, what are you asking? You are asking for their advice. Proverbs 11:14 says, "Where no counsel is, the people fall: but in the multitude of counsellors there is safety." And there are many other verses in the Bible that tell us we need counsel. We never get too old nor too smart for guidance.

Sometimes, someone who is considered by the world to be quite unlearned can give us counsel. I will never forget the precious Christian woman in our second pastorate who could raise anything in her garden. So one day I went to her for advice. Now here she was — just a plain old Texas hillbilly, a homemaker who had probably never worked outside her home a day in her life, who probably had never finished school — and she said in her slow drawl, "Well, Miz' Hyles, yuh jis gotta larn ta plant yer crops by tha moon." Well, I never did learn to plant my crops by the moon. However, I believe she could have taught me something about gardening if I'd had time to sit down with her and let her teach me.

We can get advice from everyone really; but we need to be sure when we seek counsel, we are seeking godly counsel. Psalm 1:1 tells us, "Blessed is the man that walketh not in the counsel of the ungodly." And when we give counsel, we need to be sure we are giving godly counsel. Do you know there have been times when I have given advice that is "Beverly Hylesology," counsel that was not based on God's Word? Of course, that's not going to help anybody!

When you are counselling, be very careful about giving advice that goes against some godly counsel the person has received before they have come to you. Let's say a woman came to me and said, "Now the preacher said I should do this, but I don't know if that's right." My response would be, "If you have already talked to the preacher, I would suggest you go back to him again for further advice." I would not **ever** go against any pastor's counsel. There are times when people will come to you just because they didn't get the answer they wanted to hear from the pastor. You must beg for wisdom from God so you will be able to discern situations like this. There are times when you should direct someone to the pastor or to an older Christian for counsel. When we took our first pastorate, I was only nineteen years old. Now I had a lot of common sense. Because I had the Bible taught to me at home as well as at church, I had a good practical knowledge of the Bible. But as a young pastor's wife I directed people to my husband or to an older Christian lady anytime I could. Now I am not saying that I never gave advice, but I wasn't really free with my advice. I was still young and "wet behind the ears" so to speak. Even though I felt like I'd had the privilege of learning a lot I could have given, I still felt I was very young. Now there will be cases where you will actually be much older in Christ than the woman who is asking your advice. In that respect you will have a right to give advice, but you still need to be really careful when you are young.

Proverbs 1:25 and 26 tells us, "But ye have set at nought all my counsel, and would none of my reproof: I also will laugh at your calamity; I will mock when your fear cometh." God says if you don't take His godly counsel or godly counsel that is given to you from His servants, then calamity will come to you and God will laugh. Does God really look down and laugh? Well, He says so. I don't think it pleases God when calamity befalls us. I think He is longsuffering — I know He is because the Bible says He is. But when we go year after year after year and don't take advice we know is godly and right, I believe He finally looks down and says, "I have given up on you. I will just laugh at you because you brought it on yourself." He did that to the people in Genesis when He destroyed the world. The time came when He could no longer put up with their wickedness. Don't think we're any better. When we don't take the advice we know is right to take, God will finally decide that we have had enough time. So, godly counsel must be heeded. You must also be sure you are getting godly advice when you seek counsel. When you are giving godly direction and the person you are counselling will not heed it, you should warn in a loving way that calamity will come. Then that person is accountable to take the advice you have given. If a person doesn't know what the Bible has to say about failing to heed godly counsel, then they are not accountable. But once they are told what the Word of God says, they are then responsible and accountable to take the advice. It is your responsibility to make this clear to those with whom you counsel.

Proverbs 19:21 is another verse dealing with counsel which says, "There are many devices in a man's heart; nevertheless the counsel of the Lord, that shall stand." There are many devices in our own hearts. We have many preconceived ideas and notions. But the counsel of the Lord is what stands. We may have opinions that are not based on God's Word and we need to be very careful about giving our opinions instead of counsel that is based on God's Word.

Hebrews 6:17 and 18 says, "Wherein God, willing more abundantly to shew unto the heirs of promise the immutability of his counsel, confirmed it by an oath: That by two immutable things, in which it was impossible for God to lie, we might have a strong consolation, who have fled for refuge to lay hold upon the hope set before us." That means if God says something, that's the way it is. He doesn't change His mind. So when God gives us His counsel, He never changes His mind. It is always the same. Let's look at the issue of divorce for example. In God's Word He has said that He is against divorce, but because of the hardness of the hearts of the people He made some allowances for divorce. In God's mind divorce is not an option except in the case of adultery. Even then He only allowed it because the hearts of the people were so hardened they would not forgive and try to make their marriages work.

The "Eyes" Have It!

There are three words I believe are very important when you are giving counsel. They are "stop, look and listen." Sometimes when people are asking for counsel, we can hear more with our eyes than we can with our ears. We can often see more from their body language than we can hear from what they are saying to us with their words. Perhaps someone has come to you asking for help in mending her marriage. Let's say you are giving her some verses from the Bible on submission. If she keeps looking away from you and telling you how hard her husband is to deal with, what can you learn from her body language? Perhaps she is guilty of not being submissive and knows she is part of the problem. Perhaps she has already made up her mind she isn't going to do what you are suggesting. Now all these things could be true, but we have to be extremely careful when trying to judge what someone is thinking from her body language. We must constantly pray for wisdom. Even if you feel a person's body language suggests she is turning you off, don't give up on that person. That might not be what she is thinking at all.

When someone is asking for your advice about a problem that could be life-changing, you must constantly keep in mind your responsibility to give the right kind of answer. If you feel totally inadequate to deal with that particular kind of problem, send them to someone else. There is nothing wrong with saying, "You know, I am sorry but I just don't feel I can help you." I have said that many times. If a woman is uncomfortable discussing her problem with your husband once you suggest it, ask for permission to discuss the problem with your husband and get back to her. I don't think it is a good idea for the Christian leader and his wife to share confidences of the people who come to them for counsel. This is especially true if the person has asked you not to share the confidence. But if the person gives her permission, then do it and get back to her with the help she needs. I believe the man of God is given a wisdom from above that far supersedes what we women have unless we are real students of the Word of God.

When someone has told you the problem, I think it is a good idea to sum it up in your own words just to be sure you are getting the correct information. You could say, "Now, what I hear you saying is this." And then go on to tell them what you think they are asking. Some people are people of few words; they get right to the point and you know what they are asking. But others go around the world to get to the question and after they have taken you to "several years ago" and "when I was a little girl," you still don't know what they are asking you. When you tell them what you think they are asking, be careful always to be kind. Don't say, "You sure are wordy. Would you get to the point?" Kindness is very important. Don't ever put someone down who has come to you for advice. If a person is coming to you for advice, she is probably already down on herself and the last thing she needs is for you to put her down too.

Listen with an inner ear to what is meant by their words. Don't just listen to the words they are saying; listen to the tone of the voice and the hurt in the voice. Listen with every fiber of your being. Be sure you are listening in a situation that gives you enough privacy to give your full attention to the person who needs your help.

Listen to the concerns and opinions of the person. Don't be forming your answer **while** they are talking to you. Listen to them until they get done. You already know what you think, so don't get ready to reply before you have listened to the entire problem. They may not get to the real crux of the problem until they get to the last sentence and you will miss it if you are already forming your answers while they are talking. Find out what they think before you decide upon your answer.

Know when to listen without commenting. Be supportive, be quiet, and wait. Be ready to respond but remember sometimes an answer isn't needed. My husband has told me that many times when people come to his office for advice all he does is say "yes" as he listens. When they finish talking they will say, "Bro. Hyles, I can't tell you what your advice has meant to me!" Now we can laugh about that, but what has happened is those people have come up with their own solutions just because someone listened as they talked out their problems. Just because someone listened, the answer became clear to them; they didn't need to be given a solution.

You know, we are getting counsel every Sunday morning, every Sunday night and every Wednesday night if we are just listening for it. But often, when a problem comes, we don't realize we have already heard the advice we need until we talk out the problem. Then a voice tells us, "It seems like I have heard someone give the answer to this problem."

When all you have done is listen and someone thanks you for your help, it is a good idea to say, "Well, rest assured I am going to pray for you." Now if you say you are going to pray for someone, don't be a liar. Write the request down and do pray for that person.

Next, don't judge. Someone once called me for advice and told me before we talked that I would never think the same of her after I had heard her story. I was very quick to assure her I would not think any less of her regardless of what she told me because I was made of the same flesh she was. We must put people at ease. We must make them know we are prone to the same sins in which they have perhaps been entangled. Suppose someone comes to you for counsel who doesn't have your same standards of dress. That is not the time to talk to her about the way she dresses. Take people as they are and don't judge them. They don't need your judgment; they need your help. Let people know you are not surprised by what you hear. We live in a world of sin and degradation and it's only getting worse. No matter what anyone tells me I am not surprised, and I do not feel judgmental. In my heart I am grateful to the Lord that He has spared me from a situation like that, but I am always aware it could still happen to me in the future.

Humor will often go a long way toward making people feel at ease. If there is any way you can laugh with people and make them feel they can be comfortable with you, do so. It helps so much.

Someone has said, "Give every man thine ear, but few thy voice." Concerning counsel, most everyone wants to talk but they really don't want to hear a whole lot. They just want to talk about the problem. Now of course there are times when you know people need advice. But God gave us one mouth and two ears, so I think we should do twice as much listening as we do talking. "Give every man thine ear, but few thy voice."

Any leader can improve his or her effectiveness by learning to listen. Counsellors tell us the greatest form of helping people is learning the art of listening. They say the art of listening is the most effective technique in helping people. So we need to learn what listening really is — we need to put everything else out of our minds except that one person. Zero in on that person.

When you are counselling, be careful not to let people tell you things you don't need to know in order to give them advice. Don't ask for information you don't need to know. If it is a marital problem and they begin to go into intimacies that are not pertinent, change the gist of the conversation. Don't cut them off in a way that will make them feel badly, but don't seek out any information you don't need to know.

You are very prone to make enemies when you are giving counsel. When people tell you their innermost secrets, they are embarrassed by what you know about the situation once the problem has been resolved. If a woman has come to you and told you how her husband or child has wronged her and you take her side and then tell her all the bad things you have seen that husband or child doing, she will be angry at you once the problem is resolved. If you seek out information you don't need to know and let people tell you more than you need to know, you increase your chances of making an enemy. If someone starts naming names, say something like, "Listen, let's don't name names. I don't need to know that." Because if it's not pertinent, you don't!

Let me give you a few things we must do if we are to be effective counsellors.

1. First of all, we must have a clear conscience before God and maintain a daily fellowship with Him. The lines must be clear between us and God. Why is that important? Wisdom cometh from above! We may be ever so smart, but we are not so smart that we don't need God's wisdom. If we are not maintaining a fellowship with God, we have no right to think we are giving godly counsel. We are not ready to counsel unless we are right with God.

2. As counsellors, we must have a healthy sense of self-worth based upon our relationship to God. Not just because we feel good on a particular day or have on a new dress or anything else, but because we are secure in our relationship with God, we can ask God for wisdom and feel that He will give it to us. People who are

insecure within themselves are not good counsellors. In order to be a good counsellor, a good sense of self-worth is essential.

3. We must learn to accept and handle our own emotions. We can't be up and down, fly-by-night people. We must learn to control our own spirits — that is essential. Proverbs 25:28 says, "He that hath no rule over his own spirit is like a city that is broken down, and without walls." Now, why is it important for us to be emotionally balanced? Because we as women tend to take the problems of others home with us. Men don't do that as much. My husband can counsel for hour after hour and come home and put it all out of his mind. But I don't — though I am learning more and more to do so. That's just a woman's nature. We are by nature more emotional creatures and we do tend to take things to heart. We feel with people so much more deeply than a man does. So we must learn to be an emotionally balanced person or we will become so weighted down with problems people bring to us that we become an ineffective Christian, an ineffective wife or a bad mother. And there's no use in being a counsellor if it tears you up to where you are not good in any other area.

4. We must be balanced physically, mentally, emotionally and spiritually. When a person is physically balanced, she takes care of her body. She gets enough sleep and schedules time for play.

I can especially relate to the area of spiritual balance. Some years ago when I first learned about self-esteem in my own life, I tended to see everyone's problem as stemming from low self-worth. Can you see how it might happen that you could get snagged in a certain area? I honestly do believe many, many problems do arise from low self-worth. I haven't changed my mind. But all problems certainly don't stem from low self-worth. Sometimes it's a physical problem that's causing an emotional problem. However, I needed spiritual balance at that time. Self-worth was such a new and exciting thing to me; when I learned you can love yourself, I just wanted everyone to know it. So I seemed to find that as the root of every problem. At the time, I needed more balance in that area.

Emotionally, a woman must have the ability to care without becoming overly involved. Don't take the problems home to bed with you at night. The key to being involved without involving your emotions is to give the situation to the Lord. For instance, there was a time when I had two grandchildren who were both very sick. One day my daughter Linda called to tell me that her daughter, Melissa, was very ill and in a lot of pain. Linda needed to talk, so I said, "Lord, I cannot keep that hurt in my heart. I must give it to You. I know You are going to work it out." Then I was called and my son David told me that his little girl, Bethany, was in the hospital. It was the fourth time in less than a year. That night I went up to stay at the hospital with her while her mom went home to freshen up. While I was there I felt so heavy and I thought, "Now, Lord, I cannot keep this on my heart. I give it all to You." Do you see what I'm saying? We can care and love, but we can't let it weigh us down. It will destroy us. You can't even carry the weight of the problems of your own family members. You have to learn to give those problems to the Lord.

5. Something that is vitally important when counselling is that we must be discreet. The definition of discreet is to be careful of what one says and does.

We must be guarded and able to keep confidences. Now that is a most important point for a counsellor. You say, "But I am just going to tell my ten best friends, and they won't tell anybody." Ha! Ha! A person shouldn't even have to say, "I don't want anyone else to know. Please don't tell." You just assume they have come to you because they trust you. My husband doesn't tell me the things people tell him in personal counselling. I don't tell him either. I just can't emphasize that enough. People won't come to you for help if they find you don't keep their confidences. So you must be discreet about keeping the confidences of people.

"Study to Shew Thyself Approved"

There are some simple and practical things you can do in preparation for counselling.

1. Be well grounded in Scripture. Know the Bible and what it has to say about marriage, child rearing, depression, assurance of

salvation and how to win a soul to Christ. We must know the Bible in order to be able to help people. The Bible is so practical for people's lives. One time when my granddaughter was sick and in a lot of pain, I told my daughter Linda to find something to make Melissa laugh. Now Linda knows that's in the Bible, but she just wasn't thinking about it at the moment. The Bible has so much wisdom for us if we would just learn what it says. Proverbs is particularly full of verses that will help you.

2. Have a broad spectrum of Christian literature. Dr. Ed Wheat is a physician as well as a Christian, and he has written some marvelous material on marriage. Get good books on child rearing. You should have some good books on depression. Be willing to lend out your literature if it is needed. Say, "Let me loan you a book." I don't know how many times I have lent out my copy of the book, *Women in Midlife Crisis*. If you are afraid of losing your materials, you might just tell the person where they can find the book. *CHRISTIAN WOMANHOOD* has a wealth of material on tapes covering every subject imaginable. They have tapes on every subject imaginable. When I am asked for advice, I will often just recommend a certain tape or book to someone. Sometimes I know the material in a certain book or on a certain tape will help more than anything I could say. I will give you one word of caution though. Be careful when choosing your books to find out whether the author is saved. You should also try to determine the school of thought from which that person comes; the humanistic philosophy creeps in before we know it, and of course, the Bible tells us not to walk in the counsel of the ungodly.

3. You need a sufficient background in health and medicine to recognize that some problems are probably physical. Now that doesn't mean you need to go to medical school; you can learn a lot by reading in those areas. If someone is depressed and you can't really pinpoint a specific problem as you listen, you might inquire whether their depression comes around the time of their monthly period. Ask if they have been checked for diabetes or hypoglycemia. It could be high blood pressure or a thyroid condition. Read enough to know there are certain physical problems that can bring on

depression and make little problems seem like mountains.

4. Don't take sides in family disputes. You are probably never going to have a husband and wife come to you for counsel. A husband and wife together will be more apt to see the pastor — and that is ideal. If a woman came to me about a marriage problem, the first thing I would say to her is, "Will your husband go with you to see the pastor? I would rather the two of you counsel together with a man of God." If she tells me ther husband has absolutely refused to get any counsel, and then begins to tell me what a brute her husband is, I NEVER AGREE WITH HER. You see, she is angry now, so he's a brute. But by tomorrow he might be Prince Charming again. Since **you** have agreed with her that he's a brute, she now feels you don't like her husband.

Think about how you are with your own husband. One day you want to kill him, stomp on him or throw him in the river. However, once you get your thinking straight, you want to go home and hug him and kiss him and fix his favorite meal. So be very careful you don't take sides between family members; I think this even applies when counselling friends.

Another thought to keep in mind is that you are only hearing one side of the story. So often when we are seeking counsel, we are making another person look much worse than they really are. We are doing that because we want the counsellor to agree with us. Others will do that to you too, but they won't feel that way for long. So, don't take sides; it isn't fair to the person whose side you are not hearing!

5. Do not over-identify with the person's problem. Be objective. We need to empathize, but not to the point where we lose our objectivity in giving advice.

Let's say that a girl comes to you and tells you her parents just don't give her any time. Naturally your heart just begins to ache for the poor child. Because we hurt for her, we might tell her to look for a mother figure. That's not good advice! The girl needs to be directed to restoring the broken relationship with her parents.

You might counsel some woman about her marriage who has just told you how bad her husband is. If you are over-identifying with her problem, you might say to your husband who walks in the door just after you finish hearing about the rotten husband, "All men are alike! They are just big and bad!"

In counselling, I would make it a point never to say anything that sounds like you are agreeing with a person who is saying negative things. It might even be good for you to say something like, "Well, I haven't heard the other side of the story, and I feel a person needs to hear both sides to be a help. Is there someone to whom you could both go together?" Now be sure you don't say it in such a way the person feels you are calling her a liar. Nevertheless, I think in most situations both sides do need to be heard. That is especially true in marriage. We also tend to want to tell our own experiences, but it is usually not best.

6. As much as possible, allow the person to come to her own conclusion. You'd be surprised at how often that is possible. After the person has finished talking out her problem and you have listened carefully, a good question to ask is, "What do you think should be done about this?" I believe people will very often come up with the right answer unless they honestly don't want to resolve the problem. Usually, if they don't come up with the right solution, they are just seeking someone who will tell them what they want to hear. If they are truly seeking to resolve the problem, they will often come to a conclusion about what they should do as they talk about the problem.

Let me reiterate that you should never act surprised when you are counselling — no matter what a person tells you. Don't ever give a person the idea that you are thinking, "You mean **you** did **that**?" Really, nothing should surprise us because we are all flesh. Avoid exclamations of surprise if you are going to counsel. If you do make those exclamations of shock, that is a put down to the person you are counselling.

7. Avoid making false promises. This is so important. We can say, "If you will go home and do what the Bible says about child-rearing, that teenager is going to turn around." But you don't **know** that. The Bible promises if we "Train up a child in the way he should go: and when he is old, he will not depart from it." (Proverbs 22:6)

However, you cannot promise that a problem is going to be resolved. Now you can say on the authority of God's Word, "If you begin to do what a wife (or friend or parent) ought to do, God is going to bless." Please don't ever make false promises to people that their problems will be resolved immediately. Many times problems take years to resolve. We are so prone to want to see immediate results, and unfortunately, it just doesn't happen that way. I learned this by experience. Many years ago I had a big problem. I went to a wise, godly woman for counsel on several occasions. I remember her saying, "This may never change." But I gave God an ultimatum anyway. You know, we say, "God, I want this to change or be resolved by a certain date." And I did that; but when that date passed and it was not resolved, I remembered her wise words and thought, "What if this never changes?" Now the problem was settled, but it took longer than the ultimatum I had given God. My counsellor's wise words made me deal with the fact God does things in His time. We must not ever presume upon the wisdom of God. We can only advise a person concerning what her own actions should be. We have to leave the rest of the problem to God.

8. Avoid making judgments. Don't say, "Well, you shouldn't have done that in the first place." They probably already know where they made their mistakes; they don't need to be reminded.

Now I do believe there are times when we can point out errors in a kind and loving way. In the Bible we are given an example of a man doing confrontational counselling in a loving way. In II Samuel chapter 12 we see the story of Nathan the prophet coming to David. Nathan told David about a rich man who had many lambs of his own. But when a stranger came and the rich man needed a lamb to prepare a meal for his guest, the rich man took a poor man's only lamb to feed his guest. Nathan asked David what kind of judgment should be put upon the rich man and David replied that he should restore the lamb fourfold because he had killed the poor man's lamb without pity. Then Nathan said, "Thou art the man!" He was talking about David taking another man's only wife when he had a whole harem from which to choose. I think this goes to show us there are times when we can point out to someone their error in a very kind and loving way.

I remember one time when I was counselling with a woman whose son wouldn't do certain things she wanted him to do. Because of that, she wouldn't let him come in the house. This happened during a very hot summer. Now I had to be very careful. I couldn't just come right out and say, "You are handling this situation wrongly!" I had to help her see she could do something that would help the problem. So instead of bluntly denouncing her, I said, "Do you really feel you are helping the problem? Do you see how you are making him hate you by forcing him stay out in the heat?" There are times when it is necessary to point out to someone that what they are doing is wrong. They can't see it. We don't always see what we are doing; we need someone to point it out to us. Also, we have to be extremely careful about judging people.

9. Avoid criticizing and belittling the person. Perhaps someone comes to you and says, "See these little plastic cards? I am over extended on every one of them." So you say, "Are you crazy? You know you shouldn't have done that. Why didn't you cut them up in the first place?" When you say that, you have already lost that person. There is nothing you can do to help. You have criticized and belittled that person. Avoid this at all costs.

10. Avoid burdening the person with your own difficulties. If someone comes to you about their little plastic cards, you could say, "I know. I've got the same problem. I've got some of those plastic cards, too! How in the world do we get into such messes?" But when we do say that, we aren't going to help one bit! Don't burden people with your own problems.

11. Avoid displays of impatience. You know, it is possible to be very impatient when you counsel. You might start drumming your fingers or looking around when it seems a person is never going to finish her story. Some people do go all the way around the world before they zero in on what they are trying to tell you. It can be very laborious, but you've got to listen to get what they are trying to tell you. We must learn patience.

12. Don't become so involved in helping someone that your own

family and obligations suffer. Helping people in need can bring you to that point. Of course it wouldn't hurt any of us to help someone with transportation or some other need once or twice. But don't let it become a thing that robs you of your time with your own family. Don't let helping others disrupt your whole household.

Of course you must realize that, in some people's lives, counselling takes a long period of time before you can help. Just as a case in point, an ex-pastor and his wife joined our church. He had to resign the pastorate because his wife had a mental breakdown. By the time they got to our church she had been to many physicians who had put her on six or seven different tranquilizers. She also had shock treatments and she was just a zombie. So she sought me out for counsel and this situation became a daily phone call. Now there were times when I had to say to her, "I have five minutes to talk and then I have to hang up." And she always told me the same story because she was so doped up she couldn't remember from one day to the next what she had told me the previous day. There was even an occasion when I took her to the doctor when she needed a way. I did take time with her, but I had to be very careful to keep the involvement at a minimum. Now the happy ending to the story is she and her husband are back in the ministry again today. I'm not taking all the credit for that by any means, but I do feel I had a small part in helping her get over her mental breakdown.

When you need to counsel a person more than once, it is perfectly fine to set a time limit. People must understand that you have a life to live. People will respect you more as a counsellor if you don't allow them to just take up all your time and walk all over you and abuse you. They will know you are being professional when you set a limit on the amount of time you have to help them.

13. Avoid arguments. You can't counsel someone if you are going to argue with them. The person didn't come to you to argue. Now you may not agree with their thinking about their problem at all, but don't get into an argument.

14. Avoid blaming the person. It doesn't help anything or anyone.

15. Respect the right of the person to have preferences that are perhaps different from yours. For instance, someone might come in

to see you who is dressed very differently from the way you would dress. Perhaps they enjoy dressing in trendy fashions or following the current fads. If the first thing you do is attack something that is a preference and not a conviction, you are not going to be able to help the person at all.

16. Avoid criticism of any other minister or counsellor. Let's say someone comes in to counsel with you and they tell you they have already counselled with another person and what that person told them to do. If you don't think they got good advice, it would still be a terrible thing for you to say, "I don't agree with that counsellor at all." Now it is fine for you to give an answer based on the Bible. The person you are counselling will be able to see it for themselves if the advice doesn't agree with what they have already been told. Just make sure what you tell the person is God's advice and not your own.

17. Always greet the person you are counselling with warmth. If someone calls you at a very inopportune time, try not to be sharp. If you have cookies in the oven, tell them so. Just say, "You know what? I have cookies in the oven that have to come out in about three minutes. Can we hang up and I will call you back as soon as I care for my cookies. That way, we won't be interrupted." If someone makes an appointment to see you or calls you at a certain time, greet them with warmth even if something has come up that has made that time a bad time. Convey to the person you are glad they sought your help and you want to be a help if possible. So many people need our help, and the Bible does tell us to bear one another's burdens. We can learn to be burden bearers through counselling.

18. Whent someone pauses in what they are saying, don't feel you have to say something in reply right away. The person might just be trying to get up the courage to say something that will get to the crux of the problem. Remember we must stop, look and listen. If there's a pause, you wait. If the person doesn't continue, perhaps you need to ask some question that will get her started again.

Remember that counselling has a two-fold purpose. First of all, it is to give the person some immediate help. If it is a problem that isn't going to go away overnight, give her some immediate comfort from the Bible. Direct her to some tapes or books that can give her help in dealing with the problem even though it might not resolve it completely. Don't give false promises, but do give comfort for the problem. Secondly, give the person help in solving her own problems. Teach her how to use a concordance to find help in the Word of God for dealing with her problems. Then, teach her skills that will help with whatever the problem may be. For example, if the person is having trouble with her husband, teach her how to communicate with her husband to solve the problem.

If a person is unsaved, of course our main goal would be to win her to the Lord. If I am counselling with someone and the person expresses no interest in Scriptural answers, as far as I am concerned I cannot help the person. In most cases, I tell them to find someone else with whom to counsel. Any wisdom I have is from God and I feel my counsel has to be based on the Bible. If the person has no interest in the things of God and what the Word of God says, I don't feel I can be a help at all. If you can't lead her to be saved or help her come back to God if she is backslidden, there is really nothing you can do to help her.

19. Always give the person some kind of prescription. Tell her to go home and get into a certain portion of Scripture, to pray daily about the matter, to listen to a tape, to read a chapter in a book that particularly applies to the problem. Give the person something to do and assure her you will pray for her. Just be sure you do pray for her if you tell her you are going to do so.

You should almost always end a counselling session with prayer. You can even do that on the phone. Sometimes God softens a heart during that closing prayer; then He can reveal things to the person she didn't see during the time of counselling.

I am going to end this chapter on counselling by answering a question that has been asked of me in the past. I think it will help you as well as showing you how to counsel. The question is, "If you are a young pastor's wife (or Christian worker's wife), what is the correct relationship you should have with teenage girls and how do you establish it correctly?" No matter what age you are, you need to be careful how involved you become with a young girl. Many times during our ministries people have called to ask what I think about them taking a young girl into their home. Perhaps this young girl has severe problems at her home; she needs love, counsel and a place to stay. Guess what I say? NO! Now I give this answer for several reasons, but one of the reasons is that I don't think it is a good idea to have a young girl living in the home where there are sons. You are just flaunting great temptation — especially if the boys are teenagers. I also think it is not a wise choice for the husband's sake. Now certainly you need to counsel teenage girls as you would any other girl or lady. But be careful you don't allow a teenage girl to make you her mother figure if she has a mother with whom she can restore a relationship. Dr. Clyde Narramore says there will be a period of two years in every young person's life when he or she rebels against the values and principles of the parents. It may be during the teen years or after marriage, but there will be that period of questioning in every young person's life. It usually happens in the teenage years before marriage; and if a young person is questioning her parents, you don't need to become so important to her she gets farther away from her parents. You need to be directing her toward her parents, even though they might be unsaved. Even unsaved parents many times teach a lot of character. I often say my mother is responsible for my being in church and having been in church all my life and learning spiritual things. But my father taught me more character, and he was an unsaved man until he was age 70. You need to be sure you are getting the true picture of what is going on when teenagers come to you. Teenagers have a tendency to exaggerate. They will misrepresent the truth just a little — or a whole lot — because they want attention from the pastor's family.

Another reason for not having a young girl in your home is your children need a home just as much as you do. They need a retreat that isn't open to outsiders. Teenagers are very crafty and smart, but they do need help. You can give it to them as long as you are careful. In closing, let me give you an admonition from the Word of God. In James 1:19 God says, "Wherefore, my beloved brethren, let every man be swift to hear, slow to speak, slow to wrath."

WHAT MAKES CHAMPIONS?

One of the biggest reasons my husband and I have been able to stand through the battles of our ministry is we committed ourselves to the ministry years ago. When I was a nine-year-old girl, I gave my life to be a missionary during vacation Bible school. I made a commitment. Now of course, as a girl that young, I didn't know exactly what God wanted me to do. Obviously he didn't want me to go to Africa; he gave me four heathen of my own instead! But I committed my life to the Lord, and I meant it. Don't ever take lightly these young people who walk the aisle and surrender their lives. I meant it when I committed my life as a child. Now I have had to recommit myself through the years, but I committed myself long ago. My husband also committed himself to Christ as a young boy.

We, as Christian worker's wives, need to decide whether we are committed to the Lord. We are so afraid of that word commitment. People going into marriage these days are afraid to commit themselves to marriage. They think, "Well, what if he quits loving me? What if he runs around with someone else?" Well, if they have truly made a commitment, they will work at resolving the problem and making the marriage whole again. Anything we do demands commitment if we are going to be successful.

We are afraid of Romans 12:1 that says, "I beseech you therefore, brethren, by the mercies of God, that ye present your bodies a living sacrifice, holy, acceptable unto God, which is your reasonable service." You know, sometimes it is harder to be a living sacrifice than it is to be a martyr. Personally, I would not want to have **my** head chopped off. But sometimes it is more difficult to be a living sacrifice than to die suddenly.

Let's think about being a living sacrifice. What about a pianist like Mike Zachary? What has he had to do? He had to make a commitment as a young boy. He had to determine to work and practice and work and practice. He still has to do that as a grown man. It is a well known fact that the great musician, Paderewski, thought nothing of going over a single bar of music forty times.

Once when he played before Queen Victoria, she exclaimed, "Mr. Paderewski, you are a genius!"

"Ah yes, your Majesty," he replied, "but before I was a genius I was a drudge."

Successful people in any field have to be committed — and I don't mean to an institution! They have to be committed to their work.

Olympic champions are dedicated for years and years and years for one shining moment of glory. I think of Scotty Hamilton back in the Sarajevo, Yugoslavia, Winter Olympics of 1984. He won the gold medal for the men's single competition in skating. As a young boy, he was sickly with a serious disease; but he committed himself and for years he trained toward that Olympic goal. I remember how moved I was when he won that medal and the tears streamed down his face as the American flag was raised. He reached his goal; he reached it because he was committed to it.

Now we need to be at least that committed, and maybe even more so, to Christ. It is no different from being committed to some worldly goal except that our reward will be so much greater. Commitment is not something we should fear. Being completely sold out to the Lord is the only way to find real happiness. Commitment is a positive intangible and you need to think of it as such. Luke 9:24 tells us that only as we lay down or give up our lives — i.e. our ambition to make money, our plans for our lives, our hobbies, our nice houses, or our homeland if we are called to the mission field — will we find our lives. Giving up our own ambitions is the only way to find happiness. Happiness can be likened to chasing a butterfly. It is so difficult to catch one in flight. But if we will just stand still, it will often come and light on our shoulder. If we chase after our own ambitions instead of committing our lives to the Lord, real happiness forever eludes us. But if we just commit ourselves completely to God, we find that happiness just comes and lands on our shoulders.

Unclench That Fist

We need to let go and empty our hands of our own desires. If we don't, the devil will catch us and stop us from becoming what God intended for us to become. Dan Johnson, a missionary to Brazil, has told us how they catch monkeys in Brazil. They hollow out a coconut. Then they put a hole in it just big enough for a monkey's hand to fit inside and they fill the coconut with peanuts. The monkey wants the peanuts so badly that he won't relax his fist and let go of the peanuts in order to get his hand out of the coconut. Of course the coconut is attached to something stationary and he is caught. The Devil catches us in the same way. We have too many things in our hands we don't want to let go. So, we are caught. Relax that fist and commit your life completely to God. The devil will rob you of the real happiness and real joy that true commitment brings.

You know, your husband can't do what God wants him to do if you are not committed. If you are forever tugging at him and pulling him back and saying, "Now, listen. We have had enough of this. Why don't you just settle down and be a normal preacher?" I don't think it's possible, if you are really serving the Lord, to be a "normal" preacher. The Bible says we are a "peculiar people." And peculiar is not normal, is it?

Perhaps you are always saying, "I am sick; I just can't take all this strain." If you do that, your husband will never be what he ought to be. We need to be just as committed to the Lord's work as our husbands are. Remember, commitment is a positive thing!

When we are considering the matter of commitment, we need to consider Matthew 19:29. It says, "And every one that hath forsaken houses, or brethren, or sisters, or father, or mother, or wife, or children, or lands, for my name's sake, shall receive an hundredfold, and shall inherit everlasting life." This tells us God will return to us an hundredfold if we have to give up things. That means we don't sacrifice because God gives back so much more than we ever could relinquish. We say we sacrifice, but we don't according to this verse. We need to remember this verse when we are thinking about the matter of commitment.

Soldiers in a warfare know there is always the possibility they will die. But it is for a cause. When I think of someone dying for Christ, I think of Stephen and the marvelous death he died. The Bible says he died with the look of Heaven on his face as Jesus stood at the right hand of God to welcome him Home. But in most cases today we are not even called upon to die physically for Christ. We have it so easy. Have you ever read *Foxe's Book of Martyrs?* If you haven't, you probably should; just make sure it's not right after a meal! In days gone by, Christians have really had to suffer for the Lord. In the last two thousand years Christians have been boiled in oil, thrown to the lions, decapitated, driven through streets naked, and tortured in countless ways. In some countries, this still happens. However, in America we don't have to suffer persecution for Christ's sake.

Matthew 10:16 through 18 says, "Behold, I send you forth as sheep in the midst of wolves: be ye therefore wise as serpents, and harmless as doves. But beware of men: for they will deliver you up to the councils, and they will scourge you in their synagogues; And ye shall be brought before governors and kings for my sake, for a testimony against them and the Gentiles." He tells us, "Just get ready for it. I am sending you out in the midst of wolves, and you are just little doves. Now you have got to become wise as serpents and harmless as doves because you will be brought before governors, and men will deliver you up." So we may as well expect persecution. If we expect it, we can get ready for it. In Matthew 10:22 the Bible says, "And ye shall be hated of all men for my name's sake: but he that endureth to the end shall be saved." And in verse 24 we see, "The disciple is not above his master, nor the servant above his lord." Now you might say, "Mrs. Hyles, what is **positive** about this type of commitment?" And I say it is a positive thing that God has warned us what the warfare will be like. We just need to prepare our hearts and our minds before we go into the ministry. Be committed as Job was — "Though he slay me, yet will I trust in him." (Job 13:15a) If you are already consigned to doing what God wants you to do, it won't be so hard when the battles and skirmishes come along.

I want to give you an excerpt from the book *The Cost of Commitment*. This is a letter from a Communist to his fianceé. He was writing from Mexico City to break their engagement, and he said, "We Communists suffer many casualties. We are those whom they shoot, hang, lynch, tar and feather and so forth. Some of us are killed and imprisoned. We live in poverty, for what we earn we turn over to the party — every cent. We Communists have neither time nor money to go to the movies nor for concerts nor for beautiful homes and new cars. They call us fanatics. We are fanatics. We Communists have a philosophy of life that money could not buy. We have a cause to fight for, a specific goal in life. We lose our insignificant identities in the great river of humanity. There is one thing about which I am completely in earnest — the Communist cause. It is my life, my business, my religion, my hobby, my sweetheart, my wife, my mistress, my meat and drink. I work at it by day and dream of it by night. Its control over me grows greater with the passage of time. I have already been in jail for my ideas and, if need be, I am ready to face death." Now if a Communist will do that for his cause, can we not do it for the living God Who promises to give us back a hundredfold anything we might sacrifice for him? Certainly! The only cause for which it is worth giving your all is the eternal God. Yet people will commit themselves to such nutty things in this world. We don't need to be afraid to give our all to God.

Again I say that we don't even know what persecution is. Look at Hebrews 11:35b through 38 which says, "And others were tortured, not accepting deliverance; that they might obtain a better resurrection: And others had trial of cruel mockings and scourgings, yea, moreover of bonds and imprisonment: They were stoned, they were sawn asunder, were tempted, were slain with the sword: they wandered about in sheepskins and goatskins; being destitute, afflicted, tormented; (Of whom the world was not worthy:) they wandered in deserts, and in mountains, and in dens and caves of the earth." We are not even worthy to be called by the same name these people were called — Christians. We owe them a debt. After all these people before us have suffered, how dare we be afraid to commit ourselves to the Lord? The day may come in America when we, as Christians, will actually face the gun for our faith. I hope not, but it could happen. Are we ready? How do we get ready? We get ready by suffering the things we are suffering now.

Boot Camp

Sometimes students come to our college who really have to go through the fire before they are finished. I know one particular couple where the man has paid for a semester seven different times without getting to finish because of financial difficulties. When those people graduate after eight or ten years, I am always so thrilled for them. I am sure it is embarrassing for them to admit it has taken them so long to finish school, but that's okay. They had to work harder, lose some credits, suffer a little more than others, and perhaps have some medical debts to pay which prolonged their graduation. However, all those things that happened to them in college are just small skirmishes which are preparing them for the warfare to come. For them, college has been boot camp. When God allows you to go through some little battles, he is preparing you for the day you are going to face bigger battles. As you go through those small battles and recommit yourself to the Lord each time you do, realize that things will only get harder. Now you might say, "What's positive about that?" It is that way with anyone who is successful in any field. It gets harder to stay successful. So if the tests are getting harder, you must be successful!

One way to learn how to suffer persecution is to start by being faithful in small ways. Luke 16:10 says, "He that is faithful in that which is least is faithful also in much: and he that is unjust in the least is unjust also in much." Perhaps you have had to give up a nice home or endure sickness. These things are difficult, but they are probably little compared to what you might have to face later. When you take things like this well, God looks down and says, "She is taking it so well, I know I can entrust bigger things to her and her husband. She is not trying to pull him back or discourage him from going on and totally committing his life." So start being faithful in the little things.

Purpose in your heart that you will stand for Christ in the little things. In Daniel 1:8 Daniel purposed in his heart that he wouldn't defile himself with the king's meat or drink. Now that wasn't too hard. The king sent in a lot of rich food to fatten up the Hebrew children so they would be stronger and better servants. But Daniel knew that food would weaken him, so he sent a request to the king for different food. He took a stand. Then when the big battle came of whether he would pray to God as he always had, he went ahead and prayed. Because he had stood for what he believed was right in the little matter of food, it was easier for him to stand when the hard battle of prayer came. Of course, he was thrown in the lions' den; but he was also delivered from the lions' den. Our God is still the same God. He can deliver us from trouble and He very often chooses to do just that. Don't be surprised when the fiery trials come. I Peter 4:12-14 tells us, "Beloved, think it not strange concerning the fiery trial which is to try you, as though some strange thing happened unto you: But rejoice, inasmuch as ye are partakers of Christ's sufferings; that, when his glory shall be revealed, ye may be glad also with exceeding joy. If ye be reproached for the name of Christ, happy are ye; for the spirit of glory and of God resteth upon you: on their part he is evil spoken of, but on your part he is glorified." The Lord is telling us we should not be surprised when testing comes because that's part of what He is doing to strengthen us as Christians and make us stronger soldiers for Him. These verses also tell us, in a small way, that we are partaking of Christ's suffering when we suffer trials. We can also glorify God by taking the testings in the right way.

I think what throws us when trials come is that we aren't expecting them; but we should be! When I was a young person a common slogan was, "Christ Is The Answer." And He is the Answer, but that does not mean when you become a Christian everything will be smooth sailing from that point on. It won't be. However, He is the Answer when we are going through those trials. We need to learn that being a Christian does not exempt us from trials. In fact, it may mean that we even have a few more.

Does God tell us that when we are reproached for Christ's sake we should go around with a long, gloomy face? No! He tells us we should be happy when we suffer reproach for His sake.

Some of you cause your own suffering and call it suffering for Christ. When you are in financial difficulties because you are not handling your money well, that is not suffering for Christ. If you are suffering because you are not handling your money well, that is another matter entirely.

Now commitment doesn't mean the fun is over! We think if we go to the altar and commit ourselves as living sacrifices, we'll have to wear black and never laugh again for the rest of our lives. That's not the case at all! You will have more fun than a barrel of monkeys! When we serve God, each day is full of amazing things if we are constantly looking for the miracles He is doing in our lives. Serving God will bring you the greatest joy in the world. The Bible doesn't say that Jesus came so that we might have a dull, slow, suffering death. John 10:10 tells us, "I am come that they might have life, and that they might have it more abundantly." You don't have to dry up like an old prune. It's fun to be committed to the Lord.

You must also realize that you cannot serve two masters. One circumstance that sometimes draws us away from commitment is the fear of living on a little bit of money. I told you earlier in this book that our first church paid us the great sum of $15 a month. But you know what? We have never been hungry. We have never gone without having our needs met. We have never gone without the things we truly had to have. Now that doesn't necessarily mean you will drive a Cadillac, but your needs will be met. Contentment is a matter of the heart anyway. If you aren't content with what you earn now, you won't be content even if you are earning fifty times as much. Don't let the Devil keep you out of the Lord's work because you fall into his trap of wanting prettier houses and better cars. I drive very nice cars now, but I haven't always been able to do that. Once we had a car where I had to stick my head out the window to watch at night because we couldn't use the headlights while we drove. If we did, the battery would go dead. I have been in that place. I know it's not fun to drive a car that's not pretty and doesn't work well. But you need to learn to be content; and it is learned. Paul said, "I have **learned**, in whatsoever state I am, therewith to be content." (Philippians 4:11) You can **learn** contentment.

Let me read you a few excerpts of a letter from the wife of a Christian school teacher. I feel the things she says illustrate true contentment. She said, "There is a phrase that is said to me which annoys me. The Holy Spirit impressed upon me that you probably hear it much more often than I do. The phrase? 'It must be nice.' I have a talent for sewing. Someone gave me a nice coat from which I made my daughter a coat, hat and muff for the sum of $5. It would have cost me at least $120 to have bought it." At a later point in the letter she said, "But when I make something like I mentioned earlier, I often hear 'It must be nice.' And yes, it is nice. But it was just as nice not to have it. Whatever God gives is nice. I feel like it's Christmas every day." Now that family doesn't have a lot of money, but she feels like it's Christmas every day. That's contentment, and it goes along with committing yourself to Christ. The problem with us is we don't recognize the gifts as they come to us every day. We just think, "Ho hum. I got another sweet note. That's nice." We need to recognize it as one of God's little gifts He has sent down to encourage us. Someone sends us an apple and we say, "Oh. An apple." But God sent that apple, whereas we just take things and never acknowledge from Whom they have come. You can only serve one master and that master must not be money!

Now God may give you money. Russell Anderson, the co-founder of Hyles-Anderson College, has money, but it is evident he knows how to handle it. The reason I don't have much money is God knows I don't know how to handle it. If I could, I would have some. God knows whom He can trust with what.

See, we are storing up our treasure in Heaven. You do that by using your talents every day all through the week. Use your gifts, your money and your time. Whatever God has given you, use it regularly for Him and you will be storing up treasure in Heaven. You may have more treasure waiting there for you than you could possibly dream. Have you used your talents and gifts this week? Have you encouraged someone today? Have you smiled at someone who perhaps needed it desperately? Have you witnessed for Christ? Have you won a soul? If so, you are storing up treasure.

Is it really a hard thing to commit yourself to the Lord? It shouldn't be. You know, I don't think committing yourself to the Lord is a once and for all commitment. Paul said, "I die daily." I think there comes a time in our lives when we are willing to say, "Lord, I have held back this part. Now I want to make a clean sweep of things and just let you have it all." I am no longer afraid to say, "Lord, you can take even my health." You know, that's rather hard to say. None of us wants to lose our health. But we must get to the point where we totally commit everything to the Lord.

Total Commitment

Let's consider Calvary. Do you think Christ held back anything? No. He was totally committed, wasn't He? He surely didn't have to be. He didn't have to hang on that cross. What held Him there? His commitment to die for us, to make a way for us to get to Heaven kept Him there. Those nails didn't hold Him there. He could have been with His Father whenever He wanted. But He was committed to the plan for His life, which was to die and shed His blood by which we could be saved. That was a commitment for Christ. He always knew the cross was ahead of Him. How could we be afraid to commit ourselves to the One Who loves us so much? Quit fearing it. Make it a positive thing in your life. Yes, you will suffer some trials — just as you do in every other phase of life. However, that's no reason to be afraid to commit yourselves to the Lord.

You know, the way up is down. It was with Christ, and it is for us also. Philippians 2:5-11 tells us, "Let this mind be in you, which was also in Christ Jesus: Who, being in the form of God, thought it not robbery to be equal with God: But made himself of no reputation, and took upon him the form of a servant, and was made in the likeness of men: And being found in fashion as a man, he humbled himself, and became obedient unto death, even the death of the cross. Wherefore God also hath highly exalted him, and given him a name which is above every name: That at the name of Jesus every knee should bow, of things in heaven, and things in earth, and things under the earth; And that every tongue should confess that Jesus Christ is Lord, to the glory of God the Father." Have you stopped to think what that means? He came with a need to be fed and have his soiled clothing changed as an infant. The Everlasting God! In the flesh He suffered the indignities of being a helpless infant and child. He took on the form of man. Now that's a lot just in itself. Yet He did that because He was committed to dying for us. Yes, at first it was down, down, down. He came in the form of man, became a servant and then became obedient unto death. That's going all the way down. But God highly exalted Him, so the way up in the Christian life is down. You go down as you become a servant, as you are willing to be identified with Christ and be called a Christian. You know, at Antioch they called them Christians in a sarcastic way. That name was given to label them in a hateful and spiteful way; and we still carry it. It is truly a sweet and precious name that identifies us with Christ. As we do identify with him and perhaps suffer a little persecution, remember the way up is down!

Have you ever gone soul winning, knocked on a door and had someone slam it in your face when they found out who you were? Well I don't like that! Do you? I consider that just a tiny bit of persecution. But every time you feel like you are going down, remember you are really going up. At the very moment when someone is criticizing you and your church and slamming the door in your face, you feel badly. But later you feel good for going out and doing what God told you to do.

You'll always be happy when you commit yourself to doing what God wants you to do.

TOUGHNESS WRAPPED IN FEMININITY

I am excited to be writing about spiritual warfare. As I have said before, I already know that I am on the winning side. Therefore, warfare is not a frightening thing. However, it is real and we need to face it and understand it.

Let's look at II Timothy 2:1-5: "Thou therefore, my son, be strong in the grace that is in Christ Jesus. And the things that thou hast heard of me among many witnesses, the same commit thou to faithful men, who shall be able to teach others also. Thou therefore endure hardness, as a good soldier of Jesus Christ. No man that warreth entangleth himself with the affairs of this life; that he may please him who hath chosen him to be a soldier. And if a man also strive for masteries, yet is he not crowned, except he strive lawfully." So Timothy tells us that we are committed to a warfare and we are to endure hardness as good soldiers.

First, I want you to notice we are to learn to endure — have endurance. That means you need to develop a little bit of toughness. My two heroines in the faith through my years as a pastor's wife have been Mrs. Lee Roberson and Mrs. John R. Rice. Now to me, they are two very feminine ladies; but there is also a toughness and ability to endure in those ladies. There's a beauty in that. There is loveliness in all women who will endure. All too often we think of the beauties as those women who are soft, namby-pamby and spoiled. But true beauty is in those who learn endurance, and we must learn it.

How do we learn to endure? First of all, we need to realize we only need to fight today's battle. Perhaps today's battle is stretching that one-eighth of a pound of hamburger meat to feed your family of six people. If that's your battle, then just worry about handling that one thing. Your battle may not be dealing with those who are trying to smear your name. It may be just a small battle, but that's the only one you have to deal with today. Don't worry about tomorrow. Face that when it gets here. Sometimes we may find it necessary to make some provisions for tomorrow, but don't fight the battle before it comes.

Don't Spend Your Life
at the Complaint Counter

Live realistically each day. Realize that where you are is God's territory. That's true whether you are in a time of trouble or a time of peace. God is with you even when you don't sense His presence. You might say, "God, where are you? Hey, remember me? I'm the lady who needs some food." Wherever you are, it is His territory and He wants to help you. Have you asked Him to help you spread that food so it will go a little further? Have you asked Him for those clothes you need? He is there whether you feel Him or not and we must learn to live recognizing God's presence.

Realize who you are. Romans 8:37 tells us, "Nay, in all these things we are more than conquerors through him that loved us." Now that verse doesn't say you are a conqueror. It says you are more than a conqueror. We exceed the one who just conquers. No matter how small or large the battle, you are more than a conqueror. So often it's the little battles that the Devil will use to get us down and keep us from living our lives victoriously. Perhaps it's work or school or the heat. These are all little things that can discourage us; but we don't have to let them get us down because we are more than conquerors. So today, as you live realistically, remember who you are.

Live optimistically. Did you get up this morning and put on your blue glasses or your rosy ones? Did you even look for the rosy ones? You are the one who decides whether you look at the world through rose-colored glasses or through blue ones. It's your decision whether you get up and have a bad day and live under the circumstances or have a good day and live above the situations. Happiness is your choice. We can't choose the circumstances, but we can choose to be happy in them. **Don't spend your life at the**

complaint counter! There are more important things to do with your day. There is something good in every day. I Thessalonians 5:18 says, "In everything give thanks: for this is the will of God in Christ Jesus concerning you."

Live cheerfully. Mrs. Marlene Evans often quotes Philippians 4:4 which says, "Rejoice in the Lord alway: and again I say, Rejoice." Do you know that feelings follow actions? Maybe you are really angry at your husband today. You single girls might as well know now we do get exasperated at them sometimes. They are not perfect and neither are we. Do you know how to change those feelings? Do something that you know he will like. Perhaps you could fix his favorite meal or bake him some cookies. Do you know, as you do that, your feelings will fall right into line? How about salvation? Which came first — action or feelings? You went through the action of praying and accepting Christ. Then the feelings came. That's the way life works. If you will just decide to **act** cheerful, you will begin to **feel** cheerful. It really works. As we learn to live this way, we learn to endure the battles we face each day.

So live optimistically, realistically and cheerfully; and just fight today's battles today. Savor each moment of today. Have you told the Lord on this day that you love Him? As you cherish every moment of every day that will help you to endure.

Get Your Second Wind

When we aren't able to endure, it's because we are our own worst enemies. When we think, "I'm just going to give up," it's not the Devil. It's us! We give in too easily. We must develop a toughness instead. Now I don't mean a hard shell; you aren't supposed to be hard. I'm talking about developing a toughness that says, "By cracky, I'm going to endure." Now maybe you say, "I'll swan" instead of "By cracky," but be tough! I believe that both Mrs. John R. Rice and Mrs. Lee Roberson have said that. Realize the Devil has a lot of things he will try to use to stop you. Just refuse to succumb to them.

Now the first thing we need to learn in warfare is to endure. How do we learn it? We learn to endure by obeying orders. Soldiers don't do what they want to do. They have to do what the commanding officers tell them to do. They don't get to set that alarm clock for eight or nine o'clock in the morning. I think reveille is usually more like four or five o'clock in the morning. If a soldier oversleeps, his commanding officer doesn't come with a quiet little voice and say, "It's time to get up now." God is more lenient than the army, but the fact remains that we need to learn to be more disciplined. We need to learn to obey orders. I don't mean we need to do what our bodies would have us do. Our bodies would say, "Sleep in a little later. Eat that extra piece of cake." No, we need to learn to deny ourselves some things we want. That is what develops that toughness I mentioned. When soldiers go to the mess tent, they don't put in an order. They just eat whatever is put on the plate. You know what? What is on the plate is usually something that's good for them even when it isn't really tasty. Soldiers aren't made by sitting in their barracks. They are made by going out on maneuvers and playing war games. And we need to train ourselves for spiritual warfare too.

What is the Battleground?

John 15:18-20 tells us, "If the world hate you, ye know that it hated me before it hated you. If ye were of the world, the world would love his own: but because ye are not of the world, but I have chosen you out of the world, therefore the world hateth you. Remember the word that I said unto you, The servant is not greater than his lord. If they have persecuted me, they will also persecute you; if they have kept my saying, they will keep your's also."

We live in a world that hates righteousness. Why? Because it pricks their conscience. Every time they see a Christian carrying a Bible, it makes them uncomfortable. So they don't like us. God **said** they wouldn't. We need to be wise enough to understand that we live in a world that hates Christ. Therefore, they will hate us because we represent Him. Now they don't hate us personally — we must be able to separate the two. We need to develop a toughness that says, "I want to be identified with Christ. I know He's hated, but it is a privilege to be identified with Him — to be called a Christian."

Don't be surprised at anything the Devil does. And because the Devil won't stop at anything to paralyze Christians, not only do we need to develop toughness, but we need to become "wise as serpents, and harmless as doves." (Matthew 10:16) Many of you probably grew up in Christian homes and good churches. If you did, you probably grew up like I did. I didn't know a lot of things that were going on as far as the wickedness of the world was concerned. But you need to realize the world is wicked and ask God to give you wisdom. I asked my husband for permission to write this story as an example of learning to be wise in our dealings with the world. After all our public services in our church each week my husband counsels our people. He sees just certain groups of people after certain services. On Sunday nights he sees college men. On one particular Sunday night, as he began to see college men in his office, he noticed there was a woman in his line. He also noticed every time a man came and got in line, she went to the end of the line. Now perhaps you might think she was just being kind in letting the men go first since my husband was supposed to be seeing only men that night. But God gave my husband the wisdom to know something strange was going on. Then he became as wise as a serpent. He went out in the hall and got a couple of security guards. He told them to stand near his door to watch and listen. When the woman's turn came, he didn't close his office door as he usually does; he left it ajar. Sure enough, she made a suggestive overture toward him. Of course he immediately yelled for the guards and they came and escorted her out of the church. Can you see what was happening? That was probably a setup to harm him and his ministry. Now if he had shut that door, she could have gone out and claimed that anything in the world happened in that office. But the Lord gave my husband wisdom. You need wisdom like that, too.

Watch Out For Wounded Animals!

I believe the world is so wicked because we are living in the last days. Have you ever seen a wounded animal? Have you ever swatted at a wasp and failed to kill him? Boy, he got mad, didn't he? He really did start trying to sting you then. The Devil is like that wounded animal or swatted wasp today. He knows his time is short and he doesn't have much time left to make Christians fall. Of course, he wants to take every soul to Hell with him that he can; therefore, he is doubling his efforts. He is running to and fro ". . .as a roaring lion, walketh about, seeking whom he may devour." (I Peter 5:8) Therefore, we need to develop a balance between being "wise as serpents, and harmless as doves." Again, Mrs. Rice and Mrs. Roberson are good examples of this. They are like little cooing doves in what I see of their personalities and their love for the Lord. As I have observed them, I have observed the wisdom of a serpent and toughness. You must realize that this isn't just for your husbands. Christian men aren't the only ones in danger. You need to be ready to fight. Now I'm not talking about getting out there and clawing with your fingernails. I'm referring to spiritual weapons. II Timothy 2:15 tells us one way we can become a good soldier. The verse says, "Study to shew thyself approved unto God, a workman that needeth not to be ashamed, rightly dividing the word of truth." Study! Learn the Word of God. It will help you.

Aside from getting wisdom, learning endurance and developing toughness, we are also to "put on the whole armour of God." God has given us specific armor and this is what He has told us to use to fight our battles. It is time we learned to use that armor. Ephesians 6:10-18 tells us, "Finally, my brethren, be strong in the Lord, and in the power of his might. Put on the whole armour of God, that ye may be able to stand against the wiles of the devil. For we wrestle not against flesh and blood, but against principalities, against powers, against the rulers of the darkness of this world, against spiritual wickedness in high places. Wherefore take unto you the whole armour of God, that ye may be able to withstand in the evil day, and having done all, to stand. Stand therefore, having your loins girt about with truth, and having on the breastplate of righteousness; And your feet shod with the preparation of the gospel of peace; Above all, taking the shield of faith, wherewith ye shall be able to quench all the fiery darts of the wicked. And take the helmet of salvation, and the sword of the Spirit, which is the word of God: Praying always with all prayer and supplication in the Spirit, and watching thereunto with all perseverance and supplication for all saints."

Notice the word "whole." That means you need all the armor; you can't leave out one piece. We simply can't fight a spiritual warfare using ordinary means. We can't go out with tanks and guns and start shooting in the air at principalities and powers, can we? No! We'd be thrown in the mental hospital! So let's look at the way God won battles in the Bible. What about Jericho? Joshua was told to march around the city once a day for six days and seven times on the seventh day while shouting and blowing trumpets the last time around the wall. Now if I had been Joshua, I would have said, "No way! We're going to take our bows and arrows and do it that way!" But good soldiers obey orders, so he obeyed God. And what happened? The battle was won because they used God's extraordinary plan to win the battle. They followed God's orders. We must learn we will have to do the same instead of doing what we think is best. When the Israelites were about to be overtaken by the Egyptians at the Red Sea, God told them to stand still and see the salvation of the Lord. I bet they thought, "STAND STILL??? Those Egyptians are gaining on us every second." But then God gave them marching orders and when they did exactly as they were told, the enemy was defeated by unfathomable means. It is the same way today. Spiritual battles are won by God's methods, not ours. God's methods are usually that we don't chase the enemy and we don't answer back. When you do those things, it is so easy to get sidetracked from your real purpose of winning souls and helping people. So just keep on doing what God called you to do with the armor God has told you to put on. Let God take care of the enemy.

Our Weapons

The first thing God tells us to do is have our "loins girt about with truth." That truth is the Word of God. Have you read it today? Are you studying it and memorizing it? You must read it and hide it in your heart in order to have God's whole armor.

When God tells us to use "the breastplate of righteousness," I think He is telling us that righteous living is part of our armor. We are to be separated. No, I don't mean that we will be perfect; none of us is perfect. But part of our armor is righteous living. Why? Because if we are not living righteously, our iniquity will keep God from hearing our prayers. And if we ever need Him to be hearing our prayers, it is when the battles come. Therefore, if we expect God to hear our pleas for help, we must be living righteously.

The next part of our armor is to have our "feet shod with the preparation of the Gospel of peace." How do you feel when you have just won a soul? I always feel as if I have just gotten saved myself. My faith increases when I see God has used my tongue to tell someone His precious plan of salvation. It increases my love for the Lord when I see He is still in the saving business. It is strengthening for me. It covers our feet so we can keep on marching. We need to keep going soul winning in order to keep our feet shod.

Remember, it's the **whole** armor. You might say it doesn't sound like a very good way to win a battle, but it's God's way. It's God's armor. So just as they did at Jericho, we had better follow His plan!

Next in our armor we see, "above all, taking the shield of faith." Now according to the Bible, ". . .faith cometh by hearing and hearing by the Word of God." (Romans 10:17) We need to go to church. We need to be faithful to church; don't look for excuses to stay home. Hear the Word being preached. It helps your faith to grow.

I also think it helps us to go to church just because we see there are other Christians who love us and believe just like we do. We are not alone. It's kind of like the time Elijah told God he was the only one left. God told him that it just wasn't so. There were seven thousand who hadn't bowed their knees to Baal. In that same way, it helps build our faith when we see there are multitudes of people who love God and who are standing for the same faith for which we stand.

Then there's the "helmet of salvation." You don't need to question and reexamine your salvation every day, but you do need to settle it once and for all that you have really been saved. Then when you have it settled, keep thinking about it day by day. Think like this: "I'm saved. They can ruin my name and perhaps even kill my body, but they can't take away my salvation." That in itself is enough to give us endurance.

Again we see the "sword of the Spirit, which is the Word of God" mentioned. We must have the Bible in order to be able to fight our battles and win.

Sometimes when I get in the midst of a battle, I want to fight it my own way. I'd like to give some people a good tongue-lashing. Sometimes I'd even like to poke them with ice picks. However, that's just the woman in me speaking. We get emotional and we want to see blood. But that's not God's plan. So we have to learn to fight using God's armor.

The "sword of the Spirit, which is the word of God," does not complete the Christian's armor. The chapter goes on to say "praying always" which, according to Scofield, is the warrior's resource. To me, concluding with prayer is always the answer to being "strong in the Lord, and in the power of his might."

God is still a miracle-working God. He is still the unseen Captain of our army. We are on the victorious side. Don't let the battles get you down; you are more than a conqueror in whatever you face today.

DAUGHTER OF THE KING, I BOW TO YOU!

I don't think it ever hurts us to refresh our minds about the importance of self-worth. I Corinthians 6:20 tells us, "For ye are bought with a price: therefore glorify God in your body, and in your spirit, which are God's." We are to glorify God. Now the interesting thing is, all too often, what we think glorifies God is the opposite of what really does glorify Him. I have an acrostic for the word "inferiority" I believe you will find interesting.

The "I" of inferiority stands for insecurity. When a person is meek, quiet, and timid, when they always talk about their lack of abilities, we so often think, "Oh, isn't she a humble person?" Well, no! Often those things are just signs of insecurity. An insecure person will hide behind, "I'd rather not."

The "N" stands for a negative attitude. People who don't have good feelings about themselves are usually negative. They constantly find fault and seldom see anything in a positive light. They are kind of like the children of Israel when they sent the spies into the land of Canaan. Only two of those men said, "We can!" Those two realized that one + God = a majority. However the ten, in their own negative insecurity, said, "No! We are like grasshoppers!" Now, were they really grasshoppers? No, they were men. But they saw the people in Canaan as giants. They weren't that small, but their negativism caused them to wander for forty years in the wilderness. Negativism is a terrible thing.

The "F" stands for failure. These people have a failure complex. When you get up in the morning, you are the only one who can decide whether you view the day through rosy glasses or blue ones. It all depends on what you decide to make of the day. If you do something at the beginning of the day that isn't quite up to par, don't let it color your whole day. Put it behind you. Forget about it. If you really did something wrong, confess it and start out again. Make it a good day. You don't have to have a failure complex. I have said before failing does not make you a failure. If it did, we would all be failures because we all fail. Nevertheless, God uses people who fail.

The "E" is for envy. A person who has an inferiority complex is usually someone who is envious of the accomplishments and abilities of others. She can't rejoice in the blessings of God in someone else's life. Have you ever known anyone like that? Everything good always happens to everyone **but** her — according to **her**! But that's not really true. When a person has an attitude like that, she is really resenting God.

That brings us to the "R" of the word inferiority; it stands for resentment. People who resent God might not ever admit it, but they are. God allows the "bad" in our lives for a reason. Yet, if we always feel like we don't ever get anything good, and everyone else has a marvelous, wonderful life, we are resenting God — the One Who allows those things to come into our lives each day.

The next letter is "I" and it stands for internal ear. These people have an internal ear in that they are always thinking in terms of, "What does this mean to me? How is this going to affect me? What am I going to get out of it? How is it going to hurt me?" No matter what happens during the course of a day, they are always thinking of how it will influence them. They even think of the weather in terms of how it will affect them and what they have planned for the day. They think everything should revolve around them.

The person who thinks he is inferior is also overly sensitive. This is the "O." He gets a chip on his shoulder at the slightest provocation. You always feel as if you are walking on eggshells around him. All this is simply an indication the person doesn't feel good about himself; therefore, he is not comfortable around others.

The "R" stands for "reactors." People with an inferiority complex are those who react instead of acting in response to life. Do you react to people, or do you just act? Do you know the difference? Do you act upon what you see? Perhaps someone greets you in a rather grumpy fashion. What do you do? Do you react and think, "Well! That old buzzard. She didn't have to treat me like that!" Or do you act and think, "Wonder if she needs an encouraging word today? I wonder if I can help her in any way?" There's a real difference. If we have a feeling of low self-worth, we will react. But if our feelings of our worth to God are high, we will act and think about the other person's needs instead of our own.

These people are often ill-tempered, another "I." Watch out for the person who is ill-tempered or quick-tempered. Now my husband happens to be a very even-tempered man. He is easygoing and slow to anger. When he does get angry, you will know it! Be that as it may, I would rather have that kind of man than the one who flies off the handle about every little old thing. The ill-tempered person is dangerous because he is not in control.

The "T" stands for the person who is tense. That person is often a perfectionist who always tries to prove his worth by taking on more and more. He never says no because he feels he can only prove his worth by doing everything anyone asks him to do. Now, truthfully, he doesn't prove anything. Actually, the person usually ends up becoming less respected by people because he has taken on more than he can handle.

The last letter is "Y." It stands for those who yield to self-pity. They are very prone to self-pity. And no one ever has a right to be full of self-pity.

You know, I think most of us would be cured of these negative emotions associated with an inferiority complex if we could just see ourselves when we are having those feelings. It's not an attractive sight.

Linda Stubblefield took a picture of me once with my hand up to my mouth. It appeared that I was about to relate a really juicy piece of gossip. I told her, "Well, it certainly doesn't flatter me, but it sure gets the point across!" (I had written a column for CHRISTIAN WOMANHOOD dealing with the tongue.) I really wish we could always see ourselves when we are gossiping or when we are ill-tempered and angry. It's not attractive at all. More important, it doesn't glorify God. Look again at the acrostic for "inferiority."

Does any one of those characteristics glorify God? Then do you think inferiority glorifies God? **No!** Yet we are so brainwashed. If two people gave speeches and one was rather shy and stumbling while the other confidently gave a good speech, we would probably tend to lean toward the one who was shy. If the poised speaker is speaking with a confidence born of a sense of self-worth that is based on the Bible, that is the person we should admire. We have been taught incorrectly. We have been taught that it is wrong to be confident, but what does the Bible say? "I can do **some** things through Christ which strengtheneth me?" Is that right? No! We can do **all** things according to God.

Life Began at Forty

I am a living example of someone who has struggled with low self-worth. For twenty of the more than forty years that we have been in the ministry, I did not have any self-esteem. During the last twenty years I have learned what it means to have it, and the difference is like night and day. I have learned you can accept yourself and that, indeed, you should love yourself. Now for the first twenty years I put on a good front. As a result, it wore me out completely. When I got home, I was tired of putting on a front; I wanted to collapse. During all those years when I felt inhibited and unworthy, I could not truly love God, my family, my friends or those to whom we ministered in our churches. Now I still feel **unworthy**, but I no longer feel **worthless**. There's a difference; we are all unworthy, yet God has chosen to use us. It was a marvelous day for me when I began to learn that God would use a vessel like me. It is imperative for you to learn this — not only for your sake, but for the sake of those with whom you will be working.

What is low self-esteem? How do you describe it? In many cases, it is a feeling of worthlessness. We have already agreed we are unworthy; but when you feel worthless day after day, **that** is low self-esteem. At times, we all experience a bit of anxiety about a certain area of our lives. However, I am talking about a continual feeling that says, "I am no good compared to others. I just don't measure up."

When you feel this way, salvation and regeneration has not reached down into your poor self-image, and oh how it needs to do so. If you are ever going to be a Christian leader's wife who can be used of God to help other people, you must have a healthy self-esteem.

Opposites, But Insecure

A lack of self-esteem will keep us from ever reaching our full potential. There was a wonderful leader in the Bible who I think would never have reached his full potential had not God worked in his life and brought him to the point where he realized his worth. That man was Moses, who was called the meekest man in the Bible. Do you remember when Moses was called by God at the burning bush in Exodus? Notice how he answered once God told him what He wanted of him: "And Moses said unto God, Behold, when I come unto the children of Israel, and shall say unto them, The God of your fathers hath sent me unto you; and they shall say to me, What is his name? what shall I say unto them? And God said unto Moses, I AM THAT I AM: and he said, Thus shalt thou say unto the children of Israel, I AM hath sent me unto you." (Exodus 3:13, 14) I think when God spoke to Moses about leading the children of Israel out of bondage, Moses thought, "Who? Me?!!" In verse 14 when God told Moses what to say, I believe at that moment Moses began to have some self-worth. Now the Bible doesn't say anything about Moses getting or needing self-worth. This is something I am sort of reading between the lines. God told Moses that He was all he would need. And I believe when God says, "I AM," you can fill in the blank. He is whatever we need. He can be our confidence to be a pastor's wife. He can be the love we might lack for people. He can be the compassion we need. He can be our courage to go out and stand. He can be our tongue when our own falters as we lead a soul to Christ. None of this do we have to do in our own strength. I believe when God told Moses to tell the people the "I AM" had sent him that Moses just straightened up and said, "Well, I may be a shepherd, but I am God's shepherd. He is aware of me and that makes one + God = the majority." It does. I think Moses learned his worth at this time.

You know, it really did something for Moses when he discovered: Moses + God = enough. In Hebrews 11:27-29 we see, "By faith he forsook Egypt, not fearing the wrath of the king: for he endured, as seeing him who is invisible. Through faith he kept the passover, and the sprinkling of blood, lest he that destroyed the firstborn should touch them. By faith they passed through the Red sea as by dry land: which the Egyptians assaying to do were drowned." What a difference from that insecure man who thought he was just a shepherd. Hebrews tells us he gained a courage and a faith that led the children of Israel out of slavery and bondage. However, all this was not done in Moses' strength. Something happened to him. He never forgot that God, though He was invisible, was always with him. The same thing can happen to you. The same "I AM" is your God. **You** fill in the blank. What is it you need?

There was another person in the Bible who started out to be kind of braggadocios. He was always spoutin' off when he should have kept his mouth shut. That man was Peter. I don't think Peter had a good sense of his own self-worth to God, because he was always trying to prove something. Look at Matthew 26:33: "Peter answered and said unto him, Though all men shall be offended because of thee, yet will I never be offended." And in verse 35: "Peter said unto him, Though I should die with thee, yet will I not deny thee." Often, conceit or bragging is a big coverup for someone who has no self-worth at all. Peter was really bragging on himself, wasn't he? He really believed what he was saying, I think. You see, he didn't realize how weak and insecure he actually was. This insecurity was proven when the Devil's crowd approached him, and he **immediately** denied he was a disciple. Yet, just hours before, he had said he would never forsake Christ. Be that as it may, here he was now, just jelly — not standing for anything! However, Jesus gave him another chance and one day asked him three times, "Peter, lovest thou me?" Peter had denied him three times so Jesus asked him three times, "Do you love me?" I think Peter searched his heart only to find he loved himself more. Sad to say, it wasn't the self-worth type of love. It wasn't the kind of love able to forget itself. Peter's concept of self-love involved the world revolving around Peter. On the contrary, the Bible kind of self-love makes you love others.

A principle to be learned from both of these examples is the thoughts center on self. That's not inferiority, that's pride. Any time you are insecure, you are thinking about yourself. You can't help it. When we get to the place where we face God and realize He loves us with agape love — unconditionally with a deep, abiding love — we can then begin to give that kind of love back to Him.

Agape Love

You see, God's love never changes. He's just not fond of us on the days we are just as tacky as we can be. He always loves us with agape love and it never changes. We will only begin to love Him and get the security of how much worth we have to Him as we realize how much He loves us.

That's why I tell you over and over you won't make it without the Word of God, His love letter to us. If we are not in the Book, we won't know how much He loves us. Therefore, we can't love Him as we should. If we don't love Him as we should, we can't love others as we should because we do not love ourselves.

In my opinion, Moses and Peter were two very opposite personalities who both lacked self-worth. It was only after these men came to terms with their own self-worth that they went on to do great things for God.

A lack of self-esteem will hinder all our relationships. We won't go toward others. We won't even care if we help other people because we will be too busy thinking about ourselves and the help we need.

I am not talking about self-worth from a humanistic viewpoint. I'm talking about it from the Bible point of view. The world tells us we should think we are so wonderful we can step on anyone in order to put ourselves forward. That is a lot of bunk! That is not at all what the Bible means. Yes, we ought to be our own best friend, but only because we know that God loves us and His love never changes. We build on that foundation and not on the humanistic one at all.

A lack of self-esteem will keep you from setting and reaching goals. William Carey, a noted missionary from the past, made this great statement: "Attempt great things for God and expect great things from God." However, we won't attempt great things for God if we don't feel our God is going to help us reach those goals.

You know, you may find you are married to a man who is doing great things for God though he is really an introvert. He has learned to expect great things from God. My husband is a shy, quiet person — an introvert, if you please. The fact is, he learned one + God = a majority. Also, he learned to set goals with God as his leader. He didn't try to set unrealistic goals; but as God led him, he did attempt great things and expected great things from God. Now who is to say your husband is not to be the next pastor of a great fundamental work? We really need some! So don't you ever doubt what God can do with him and with you! You might say, "Well, I don't think I want to live in that type of fishbowl." Well, I didn't either; but I have found it is fun!

You see, it is not that we can't love people or we can't do a work for God. The problem is we won't let God work through us. I have a "never again" list we all ought to follow.

Never again will I confess "I can't," for "I can do all things through Christ which strengtheneth me." (Philippians 4:13)

Never again will I say "I lack," for ". . .my God shall supply all your need according to his riches in glory by Christ Jesus." (Philippians 4:19)

Never again will I confess fear, for ". . .God hath not given us the spirit of fear; but of power, and of love, and of a sound mind." (II Timothy 1:7)

Never again will I confess doubt and a lack of faith, for "God hath dealt to every man the measure of faith." (Romans 12:3) He will increase faith as we need it and want it.

Never again will I confess weakness, for ". . .the Lord is the strength of my life; of whom shall I be afraid?" (Psalm 27:1)

Never again will I confess defeat, for ". . .thanks be unto God, which always causeth us to triumph in Christ." (II Corinthians 2:14)

Never again will I confess condemnation, for "There is therefore now no condemnation to them which are in Christ Jesus." (Romans 8:1)

You see, the Scriptures are so full of positive truths which are ours to claim. Work on your self-image, your self-worth. You are loved by the God of the universe and you need to realize it moment by moment and day by day — especially as you look toward your future as a pastor's wife or Christian leader's wife. Don't just make it for the future! As you go about your daily tasks today, look for someone you can lift up, someone who may need something that only you can give.

TRUST AND OBEY

As we discuss dying to self in this chapter, let me say this: you cannot truly die to self unless you have a good sense of self-worth. This matter of learning your value to God is not something you can take or leave. We must accept it and believe it. Meditate on it until it becomes a part of you. I wonder what we could do in our lives if we truly gave God the glory? Someone once said, "There remains to be seen what God could do with one man totally dedicated to God." And that is true.

I found a little story once about the man who started the J. C. Penney department stores. Look at your husband in light of what J. C. Penney accomplished. This man was a Christian. The year was 1929. J. C. Penney was a patient in the Kellogg sanitarium in Battle Creek, Michigan. He was broken in health and filled with despair. Getting out of bed one night, he wrote a note telling his wife and son goodbye because he felt he would die very shortly. But the next day brought an experience that changed his life. When he awoke the next morning, he was surprised to find he was alive. As he went downstairs, he heard the chapel service, and voices singing, "God Will Take Care of You." Going into the chapel, he listened with a weary heart that had already despaired of life. Then he listened to the reading of the Scriptures and the lesson and the prayer and he said of that day, "I can't explain it. I call it a miracle. I felt as if I had been instantly lifted out of the darkness of a dungeon into bright sunlight." Now I won't give the rest of what he said, but Penney's chapel lesson dispelled his fears and prepared him for a bright and successful future. He had not at that time established one store. Yet today is there any town of any size in America that doesn't have a J. C. Penney store? This man went from total desperation and having given up on life to finding out God cared for him. He went on to get well and live a very fruitful life. Just

think! What could your husband do if you encouraged him to
believe God will take care of him? What could you do as his wife
if you completely grasped that truth? We don't know our own
potential. The great goal of a Christian should be to die to self.
Perhaps you think that sounds like a paradox in light of what we
said about self-worth. The two don't seem to go together, do they?
But they do.

I Corinthians 15:31 talks about dying daily. Of course we know
dying to self is not something we do once and for all. There has to
be a time when we truly desire to die to self.

Moses and Peter give us two different illustrations of dying to self.
At the burning bush, Moses had to die to self-doubt. His self-doubt
would have kept him from becoming a great leader if he had not
dealt with it. I think many of you feel that way. You think, "Who?
Me? I don't have any talents. I am timid; I'm an introvert." We
must stop doubting ourselves; God will be whatever we need.

Then on the other hand, I think Peter had to die to self-assurance
and doing God's work in his own strength. Some of you are trying
to do God's work in your own strength. However, we must also die
to that. If we don't, we won't succeed as Peter did not succeed. His
strength was his weakness. The fact that Peter was impetuous and
self-assured was his strength. On the other hand, those attributes
were also his weaknesses. See, he knew he was a great Christian, but
he didn't realize even great Christians can fall. Peter had to die and
come to the end of himself by giving up his self-assurance and living
in God's power. I think Peter was perfectly pictured when Paul
wrote in II Corinthians 12:9 and 10, "And he said unto me, My
grace is sufficient for thee: for my strength is made perfect in
weakness. Most gladly therefore will I rather glory in my infirmities,
that the power of Christ may rest upon me. Therefore I take
pleasure in infirmities, in necessities, in persecutions, in distresses
for Christ's sake: for when I am weak, then am I strong."

It was the same for Moses. His meekness is admired. Yet, had
God not intervened and shown him that He was going to be his
power and strength, that very meekness would have kept Moses
from becoming the leader God wanted him to be. He would have

hidden all his life behind, "I can't."

So Moses and Peter both had to die, but in a different way. Whether you have a disposition like Moses who felt inadequate or a disposition like Peter who felt he could do anything in his own power, you need to die to self. Only as you come to the end of your own strength can God's strength be shown and can He really get the glory instead of us.

The Way Up Is Down

In Philippians 2:5-9 we see the same qualities were true in Jesus' life: "Let this mind be in you, which was also in Christ Jesus: Who, being in the form of God, thought it not robbery to be equal with God: But made himself of no reputation, and took upon him the form of a servant, and was made in the likeness of men: And being found in fashion as a man, he humbled himself, and became obedient unto death, even the death of the cross. Wherefore God also hath highly exalted him, and given him a name which is above every name." These are some of my favorite Bible verses. In verse 5, God tells us we need to have the mind of Christ. So in order to die to self, we first need to have the mind of Christ. So look at verse 6: "Who, being in the form of God." Do you know anyone who is made in the form of God? Yes, you are! You are made in God's image in so many ways. For instance, you are a three-fold being made in His likeness with the same emotions and desires He feels. "For we have not an high priest which cannot be touched with the feeling of our infirmities." (Hebrews 4:15) Are we equal with God? Who does the Bible say is a joint-heir with Christ? All Christians, right? Then, in a sense, are we not equal? Isn't Jesus God? I know it's against our nature to say that we are equal with God, but according to that verse and I John 3:1 where it says we are called the sons of God, we are equal with Christ. In a sense, we have already inherited the cattle on a thousand hills. We just can't go out and butcher them quite yet! God says He wants you to have this mind — the mind that says you are made in God's image and you are equal with God's Son in His family. Now have you meditated on that lately? If you had, you wouldn't say or feel things like, "I am nothing and nobody! My husband could never do anything for God because of me!" SHAME ON YOU! I am shaming me too because I have days like that. However, it certainly shouldn't be a way of life for any Christian. This verse even sounds like a commandment to me. We are so funny about the Bible. We think of the commandments of God as just being the ten in Exodus; but there are so many more than just those ten, and this verse is one of them. We need to know our position in Christ. We are to have the mind of Christ. He always knew Who He was. Even as a baby when He had to have His diaper changed, as a toddler when He had to be taught to walk, as a teenager when He worked in the carpenter's shop with Joseph, as a young man when He began His ministry and was often misunderstood, hated and persecuted, He always knew He was God. That knowledge never, never left Him.

In verse 7 of Philippians 2 we see the second step in dying to self. He "made himself of no reputation." The Scofield Bible tells us that means He "emptied Himself." He emptied Himself of the privilege of acting like God. Instead, He walked among men acting as one of them.

Then He took upon Himself the form of a servant. He went around serving. Nothing was too menial for Him. Have you ever had a little child from your bus route throw up on you? Did you feel caring for that child was beneath you? When you are cleaning those toilets at home, do you ever feel like that little man in the boat ought to be doing that job? No, nothing is beneath us because nothing can take away our position as God's child. Even when a child uses the bathroom — in your lap! — you are still a child of God, a joint-heir with Christ. People may blaspheme your name, but you are still a child of God. People may dislike you in the ministry, but it doesn't take away your position as a child of God. Of course, those things still hurt. However, people can't do anything to take away your position in Christ. I think the most humbling thing Christ did was to be made like a man. To think He had to live like we live! He even had to be tempted as we are tempted to show us that we can say no to temptation — as He did. But to think He was willing to suffer hunger and thirst and humiliation just like a mortal man is the worst part. Yet, He was willing to be used. And even though He let people use Him, it did not take away one iota from His Godship. Now I don't mean you ought to let people use you to the point they become freeloaders. But it is not bad to be used.

Jesus was used. Look at the precious verses in John 13:3-5: "Jesus knowing that the Father had given all things into his hands, and that he was come from God, and went to God; He riseth from supper, and laid aside his garments; and took a towel, and girded himself. After that he poureth water into a bason, and began to wash the disciples' feet, and to wipe them with the towel wherewith he was girded." I want you to notice the progression of these verses. First, His mind was focused where it ought to have been — He was God. As God He emptied Himself and took on the garment of a servant and washed the feet of His disciples. Ultimate humiliation, I would say.

Have you ever washed anyone's feet? I remember the first time I ever had to wash my mother's feet. She had come to live with us because of her frail health, and I became aware that her eyesight was no longer adequate for her to be able to clip her own toenails. So before I clipped them, I had to wash her feet and let them soak in order to soften the nails. And do you know what? Though I was caring for my own mother, I couldn't help but identify with Christ. And I thought, "How humiliating!" Yet Jesus was willing to wash the feet of an enemy — a man whom He knew would betray Him to be killed. Would you be willing to wash the feet of an enemy? That would be true dying to self. Perhaps you think you have done things even more humiliating than washing someone's feet. Maybe you have, but it's good for you. When we do things like that, it helps us to identify with the way Christ lived. When we stop to think, it actually elevates us rather than debasing us. It's the life Jesus would live if He were here on earth today.

Lastly, I think dying daily simply means daily obedience. It may not mean physical death as it did for Christ. For Him, that was what death meant; that was what He came to this earth to do. If He had not obeyed the plan made before the foundation of the world for

His death, He would not have died to Himself. For us, dying daily probably means something entirely different from the physical death it meant for Christ. Personally, I think it means becoming obedient. There needs to come a time in our lives when we say, "Lord, I am willing for You to do whatever needs to be done in my life for me to die to self." The fact of the matter is you might as well be willing to die daily. You might as well be willing for God to do whatever it takes in your life for you to die to self. See, whatever is going to happen in your life is going to happen anyway. If you surrender to die daily first, then whatever happens in your life can be used to change your life for the better. If you don't surrender to die daily, those things will just be traumatic incidents in your life instead of things to help you grow. When you die to self, you will see God's hand in the things happening to you. That won't keep those things from hurting, from being painful. But when you are looking for God's hand, you can know you will come out better and with more rough edges chipped off when the trial has passed. Also, you will handle the problem much differently when you see God's hand in the midst of the trial.

Now you might be thinking, "Mrs. Hyles, I don't see how God could ever use me even if I do die to self." You need to take on God's mind of who you are. You say, "I just don't think God could ever use my husband like he has used your husband." May I remind you, I knew Jack Hyles when he was like your husband is now. He was just a timid young man. I well remember his first sermon that lasted only five minutes; I mean, that was it! He just ran out of words. When you think, "God just couldn't use me and my husband," just turn to Romans 3:3 and 4. "For what if some did not believe? shall their unbelief make the faith of God without effect? God forbid: yea, let God be true, but every man a liar; as it is written, That thou mightest be justified in thy sayings, and mightest overcome when thou art judged." Let **God** be true and **you** a liar! Just because you don't believe something doesn't mean it isn't true. Even when you can't see yourself being used of God, just be willing. Be a blessing wherever God puts you. He will use you in the way He wants to use you wherever He puts you. We Christians often talk about the tragedy of unsaved people who don't believe in God or don't believe He can save them. However, many of us are unbelievers, too. We have been saved, but the Christian life is **lived** by faith, too. We must have faith to believe He will do what He has said He will do — daily. You need to come to grips with that. You need to realize we cannot live one day without belief and faith He is going to accomplish in us today what He wants done.

Look For God in Your Dailies

Have you ever had an unusually hectic day? What did you feel in the midst of that day? Were you frustrated and aggravated? Did you know even in those kinds of days we can look for God? Is He trying to teach you to plan a little better or perhaps to teach you some patience? He is in everything if we will just look for Him.

When everything seems to come in on you at once, what could God be trying to teach you? What is one of the best lessons we can learn? He is able! Perhaps we need to learn when everything seems to be happening all at once, it will help to take five minutes just to think about Christ and let Him calm our spirits. I Corinthians 6:20 tells us, ". . .therefore glorify God in your body, and in your spirit." All too often though, our spirits don't glorify Him.

We get so impatient, harried, distraught, worried, fretful and frantic; we even think we have a right to be that way. To be sure, those feelings do not glorify Him. Another command He gives us is to "fret not." Yet we women do all too often.

Someone has said, "Doubt your doubts, believe your beliefs, press forward in faith; you're positively dynamite!" Doubt your doubts. When they start flooding in, restrain them. Then believe your beliefs. When you begin to think you can, believe it. You have Bible ground on which to stand. Press forward in faith because God has said He will be with you. You are dynamite. You are! You can do above and beyond anything you have ever dreamed you can do — with the Lord's help.

So this intangible of dying to self, dying daily, is not negative. What did Paul say? "For when I am weak, then am I strong." (II

Corinthians 12:10b) That's the way it works. If you would master this lesson and get it in your heart, it would revolutionize your life now and in the future. No one knows what God can do with you if you will die to self. Learn as J. C. Penney did, that God cares about you.

REACH OUT AND TOUCH

If we minister to Jesus, how are we going to have to do it? Matthew 25:34 through 40 tells us this: "Then shall the King say unto them on his right hand, Come, ye blessed of my Father, inherit the kingdom prepared for you from the foundation of the world: For I was an hungred, and ye gave me meat: I was thirsty, and ye gave me drink: I was a stranger, and ye took me in: Naked, and ye clothed me: I was sick, and ye visited me: I was in prison, and ye came unto me. Then shall the righteous answer him, saying, Lord, when saw we thee an hungred, and fed thee? or thirsty, and gave thee drink? When saw we thee a stranger, and took thee in? or naked, and clothed thee? Or when saw we thee sick, or in prison, and came unto thee? And the King shall answer and say unto them, Verily I say unto you, Inasmuch as ye have done it unto one of the least of these my brethren, ye have done it unto me." If we are going to serve or minister to Jesus, we are going to have to do so by serving people.

If you are a people person, I think those who have been in the ministry will tell you that one of the greatest sources of problems in church **can** be getting "too chummy" with people — people can be unkind. People are never the same two days in a row. It often seems like the people you invest in the most are the ones who stab you in the back. So what will we do about it? We must somehow learn to love people in spite of their frailties. We are one of them, you know. Since they put up with **our** faults, we must learn to respond to people in the right way even when they disappoint us. We can't let it disillusion us when people don't respond the way we want them to respond.

Think about some time when you have felt down. It probably had to do with a person or people and something that had happened with people. It was probably more than just some circumstance that didn't involve people.

Jesus knew what it was to be disappointed by people. John 7:5 says His own brothers didn't believe in Him. Does that mean that perhaps He had disappointed them? No, I don't believe Jesus ever disappointed anyone. They were just human beings.

Matthew 13:53-58 tells us this: "And it came to pass, that when Jesus had finished these parables, he departed thence. And when He was come into his own country, he taught them in their synagogue, insomuch that they were astonished, and said, Whence hath this man this wisdom, and these mighty works? Is not this the carpenter's son? is not his mother called Mary? and his brethren, James, and Joses, and Simon, and Judas? And his sisters, are they not all with us? Whence then hath this man all these things? And they were offended in him. But Jesus said unto them, A prophet is not without honour, save in his own country, and in his own house. And he did not many mighty works there because of their unbelief." This happened to Jesus, and we can expect the same to happen to us. When you are out in the ministry, people will disappoint you and you won't be able to do what God could use you to do because of their unbelief.

Jesus knew this because of the fact that the people threw stones at Him in John 10:31 and 32. He had done nothing but good, yet they stoned Him. So He knew that people were frail. Now, that hurts! I'm talking here about more than just stones. It hurts your feelings when you have given your life and time and energies, and then they throw stones at you. I'm talking about verbal stones. When things like that happen, it tends to make us say, "Well! If that's the way people are going to be, I won't have any more to do with them." But we can't do that! When we want to feel that way, we must learn to overcome those feelings.

We must remember that Judas betrayed Jesus; and he was one of the twelve. One of his closest followers, Peter, denied Him. Also, those for whom He gave His life cursed Him and spat on Him the very moment He was dying so they might have eternal life! Yet He was willing to do it because He knew the fallen nature of man. Now we must determine in our hearts to realize that man, even when he is saved, still has the old man living in him. People have the old nature, so they are frail. That makes them tend to disappoint us just as we will disappoint others.

One of the keys to staying positive about people is to focus on their good qualities even when they are showing their bad sides. And everyone has good qualities!

A Personal Question

I would like to ask you a very personal question. What is your IQ? No, I am not talking about your intelligence quotient. I am asking about your intimacy quotient. By that I mean how close do you allow yourself to get to people? How close do you allow people to get to you? If you were not reared in a family that was a touching, loving, expressive family, then this is something that you may have to learn on purpose. You may have to learn to express your feelings. Now you might have grown up in a family where everyone hugged and kissed everyone else goodbye every time anyone went out the door. Therefore, you have grown up with a large intimacy quotient. Touching and caring and expressing love is easy for you. But for some, it is not easy. And if it isn't easy for you, it may get stuck in your throat the first time you to try to express your love to someone. The second time, it isn't quite so hard. You **can** change!

One of the greatest soul winners in America had to learn how to love. His wife said in public, "I knew my husband loved me dearly, but he could not express it. I had to teach him how." Perhaps you are the same way, but you can learn just like this man did. He is now a successful associate pastor who expresses himself in a very sincere, warm way. But it is something he had to learn. **You** can learn it, too!

How willing are you to learn and reach out to imperfect people? Yes, they are imperfect and they won't always deserve to be loved. There have been times when I have counselled and helped people whom I know have not totally supported my husband and me during the course of our ministry. With God's help, I believe that I sincerely gave those people the time and help they asked for and needed. You, too, will have times when you have to do something like that.

One way we learn to love is by learning to touch. Now I am not recommending you feel free to touch the opposite sex! However, it has been proven that babies will **die** unless they are touched and cuddled and held every day. Mrs. John R. Rice used to say that we need eight hugs a day to exist. I believe she might have been right! We need physical touch.

We also need to make contact with people emotionally. We need to empathize with those who need to feel our comfort and care. Each of us will have to learn to be that kind of person.

I must share a vivid illustration of what a touch can do. Every Friday when I am in town, I visit in a rest home. Several years ago we were at one of our regular nursing homes preparing for a meeting. We were going to sing, have a lesson, mention birthdays, and have some spiritual time with the residents. When we walked into the room where we were assembling, I saw a frail little old lady sitting in a wheelchair. I honestly thought that perhaps she had died and no one had noticed it yet. I went a little closer and found that she **was** breathing, but her eyes were closed. She didn't seem to be aware of me at all, so I decided not to bother her. We passed out the songbooks and began singing. As we did, another little old lady came in; but she still had a lot of bounce! And do you know what? The first person she approached was that little old corpse. She got right in her face and patted her cheeks — and lo and behold if that little old lady didn't open her eyes! The bouncy little gal smiled right in her face and, when she did, that corpse just came alive. She brightened and started singing with us and participating in the service. My conscience was so stricken! I thought, "Now why did I have to wait for that little old lady to bring her back to life? I could have done that." The truth is I was afraid. I was afraid of disturbing her. We must realize we need to be willing to take the risk of disturbing someone. If we do, we can actually bring life to someone today just by a touch, a smile or an encouraging word. The person might even seem utterly dead, but your emotional touch could resurrect her. The thing is, are we willing to do it? You might be thinking, "But I wasn't brought up that way. That goes against my nature." You can change!

In Luke 18:16 Jesus said, ". . .Suffer little children to come unto me, and forbid them not: for of such is the kingdom of God." The disciples were trying to keep the little children back because they didn't want Jesus to be bothered. But Jesus said he didn't mind the dirty little ragamuffins climbing on His lap. He wanted anyone who would come. I think He wants us to be the same way. No one is too small, too undignified, too dirty, too smelly, too whatever to be able to come to us if they need us. We ought to realize that Jesus welcomed anyone into His circle. Jesus reached out to lepers, blind men, crippled people and people who hated Him; He just reached out to people.

Matthew 14:36 says, ". . .and as many as touched were made perfectly whole." Who could be made whole today by your reaching out to them? One of the telephone companies has had the slogan over the last few years of, "Reach out and touch." We need to learn to do that. Who are we touching when we touch those in need?

We are touching Jesus. We are reaching out to Jesus. Maybe you need to reach out to someone who smells badly; maybe you need to reach out to someone who isn't as clean as others. When something makes it difficult for you to reach out, remember that you are serving Jesus when you serve those people. He is our Pattern; He didn't exclude anyone. We must learn to be a people person. The ability to be close is not fixed at birth, praise the Lord! I used to think that it was; but we can change!

You know, we have certain things we do that help us avoid being close to or reaching out to people. One of the things we do is stay too busy. When someone calls us and says, "Do you have a minute," we say, "No. I'm just too busy right now." Most of us probably are legitimately busy. But remember what I said about priorities. People are always more important than schedules. And somehow, when some unexpected call or need comes that takes some of our much-needed time, God just seems to multiply the time we have left and make it go further. He also makes us a little bit happier because we have helped someone. Realize busyness is just something we use to

REACH OUT AND TOUCH

avoid people.

Another way we avoid helping people is to schedule ourselves so tightly we just don't have any place to put anyone else. Some of you even schedule your time with your husband. If he doesn't fit into your schedule, that's just too bad! But again, people are more important than strict schedules. We avoid intimacy by just filling our schedules to the brim.

Another way we avoid getting close to people is that, when we do get around people, we seek to change what we don't like about them. That drives people away quickly. Most people don't want to stay around those who are always trying to change them instead of accepting them.

We also have to be right even when we know we are wrong. When you refuse to admit you have frailties or you are wrong, people will avoid you. I think we use all these things to avoid getting close to people or to avoid letting people get close to us.

What Good Is a Whatnot?

Someone wrote this as being the typical Sunday morning schedule of the typical "good" pastor's wife:

1. Got up, dressed and drove to church. ✓

2. Walked from the parking lot **in the rain** — and had to straighten my halo because of it. ✓

3. Got a seat and sat quietly. Didn't dare turn around and greet anyone or speak; I was in the house of God. ✓

4. Sang each verse of the songs and smiled appropriately. ✓

5. Gave five dollars in offering and listened to sermon. ✓

6. Closed my Bible and looked pious. ✓

7. Shook hands, quickly left the church and promptly forgot everything I heard. ✓

We are such good Sunday morning Christians. Well, what about the rest of the week when people need us? What about when people want to come to us for help? What are we then? The person who made this list called it "A Touch-Me-Not Whatnot."

Do you know what a whatnot is? Did your mother ever have a

whatnot shelf? When I was a little girl, my mother had a whatnot shelf in the corner of the living room. On it were little doo dads — maybe vases or ceramic animals or little dolls. Those things were to be seen and not to be touched! They were especially not to be touched by clumsy little children with dirty little hands. You were only allowed to look. Is that the kind of Christian you are? Now on Sunday morning and Sunday and Wednesday nights you are a beautiful, highly-polished angelic being — a very pious Christian. But how about the rest of the week when your husband needs you, when your children need you, when your neighbor needs you? What about when someone needs your time and you are busy? I think there are very few women who are not honestly busy. But let's don't be touch-me-not whatnots. We don't have to be and we should not be. That's not what Christianity is all about.

Christianity is not just going to church three times a week. Church is just a filling station. That's where we go to get the fuel to go out into the field and serve. I don't know about you, but I really need the fuel I get at church. It inspires me to go out and help people during the week. So very often I find that the sermons I have heard just the Sunday before help me in the problems I have with people during the week.

Let's think about why we are afraid to get close to people. Why is it people have to **learn** to express love?

One of the primary reasons we don't get close to people is we don't like ourselves. Therefore, we are afraid if people come very close they will see us for what we are and they won't like us. So we set a limit on how close people can get. We won't allow people to get close enough to enable us to help them because we think, "If they get any closer, they will see me, warts and all." Now I don't mean literal warts. I am talking about figurative warts. During the twenty years since I have learned the Bible concept of self-worth, I have also learned to take off the mask and let people see the real me. I am not saying that I was ever a complete hypocrite, but we all are to some extent. However, I have allowed people to see me as I am and I believe people love me more because I have done that. I think people will love you more when you allow them to see you as you really are. All too often we try to put up a front of perfection. I am thinking of a woman now who used to strike me that way, and I didn't like to be around her. I thought she was too perfect for me. She made me feel so small. I used to be that way about my pastor when I was growing up. I didn't like to get too close to him. I thought he could see every sin I had done all week long and it bothered me. People will feel the same way about you when you seem to be just too perfect.

I do think we are afraid for people to get too close to us because we don't think they'll like us. How are we going to correct that? When we accept ourselves with our strengths and weaknesses, other people will also. Now, I am not talking about those blatant weaknesses we ought to change. I am talking about those that are part of us. Perhaps you think your nose is too big or you have a grinding voice. You can be used of God even though you might not like those things about yourself. If you have bad habits that can be corrected, go ahead and correct them. Perhaps you are someone who is always late. Now that bad habit is a thief and a robber. When people have to wait on you, it robs them of precious time. A habit like that can be corrected. Go ahead and do it for your sake and the sake of those to whom you will minister. Perhaps you bite your fingernails. You don't want people to get close enough to you to see that because you know it will reveal your lack of character. Just decide that you will quit. There are many little things you can change that will help you feel better about yourself. It will also help you love people more.

Another reason we avoid getting close to people is that it makes us vulnerable to hurt. Perhaps some of you remember the little boy born in Texas years ago who had no immune system. He was called, "David, the Bubble Boy." He couldn't fight off any kind of disease, so they made a plastic bubble for him to live in. They even made plastic arms in that bubble for his parents to reach in and hug him. They could not touch him with their bare flesh. All the toys that went into the bubble had to be sterilized. For almost twelve years David lived in that plastic bubble; he was able to live that long because the sterilized environment kept out all the bad things. But even though it kept out the bad, it also kept out the good.

You, too, can build a bubble around yourself and say, "I don't want to get close to anyone because I will be hurt." But when you do that, you also keep out the good. You keep yourself from the privilege of being a help to people, of loving those who need your love. It is true that loving people does make you vulnerable. So often the people to whom you reach out and help the most are the ones who end up kicking you in the teeth. Even when that happens, you can know you have still done what is right to do. You will still be rewarded. Just forget people will hurt you and think of the good. There is much more good than bad if you just won't build that bubble around yourself. Yes, you will shut out some hurts; but you will shut out a lot more good when you put up a barrier.

Thirdly, it takes **time** to be a people person — to increase your intimacy quotient. I repeat, it takes time. And most of us just don't have a lot of time to give. Still, we need to take those extra moments when we least have them just to help ourselves care more for people. It will also show us that we **can** fit people in our busy schedules.

When I was sick one time, Mrs. Kris Grafton, the head nurse at our college clinic, came out to my house to bring me some medicine that I needed. When I found out Kris brought the medicine, I couldn't believe she could take the time because of her busy schedule in the clinic. My heart was so warmed to know she took time out of her hectic day to come and drop it in my mailbox. I think it helped her as much as it helped me. She gave some valuable moments from her busy schedule to reach out to someone who needed her.

A friend of mine, Linda Stubblefield, is excellent at this. She is a busy lady who is often in a lot of pain. However, she still takes the time to write a lot of cards and encouraging notes. She is a very thoughtful person who is sensitive and she loves deeply. However, I also think this is something she has developed as she did not grow up in that kind of environment. She has learned to love people and you can too. It is so needed.

". . .Ye Did It Unto Me"

How can we learn to reach out to others? First of all, begin investing in others. Perhaps it is not easy for you to say, "I love you, I care about you, I want to help you." If that is so, you can begin by giving someone a pat on the shoulder. Start investing little bits of your time in people. Now I purposely am not talking about money here. All too often it is easier for us to make a gift of money; we might have more money than time. Your time is one of your greatest treasures. Invest that treasure by making a needed phone call or writing a caring note.

You will find that the rewards are wonderful when you really begin to invest your time in others. Of course we should not do it merely for the rewards. The fact is you will begin to want to invest your time because the rewards are so great. My husband has said publicly that one reason he loves to counsel with people and help people is because he gets so much pleasure out of it. Again, that should not be our goal, but it will come. So start investing.

Secondly, accept yourself as God accepts you — weaknesses and all. Realize that you can forget yourself and go toward other people. When you begin to reach out to people, they are **not** going to think, "Well, you ugly old bat!" They are just going to be appreciative of someone who will take time for them. They will think you are a beautiful person for being willing to help them. You don't have to think about your frailties.

Next, you must realize that each of us is basically alone. Now I know that some of you have husbands, but even your husbands can't understand everything you go through. Some of you have children, but they can't always understand. You have friends, but no one can completely understand another person's problems. I know you have God, but sometimes you just need to talk to someone with skin. When people come to you for help, so often all they need is someone to listen. The Bible teaches us in Galatians 6:2 that we should bear one another's burdens. To me, that sounds like a command. The verse goes on to say we are fulfilling the law of Christ when we do this. Bearing one another's burdens is part of

God's law.

Someone once said we only really live by risking ourselves from one hour to the next. I had a teacher in college who said to me, "Beverly, I think you are inhibited. I think you want to do a lot more and say a lot more kind things and be a more spontaneous person than you are." She challenged me to begin to do that. She encouraged me to go ahead and say something nice when I felt like it without stopping to think first. I challenge you to do that. Risk yourself. Maybe you think, "Well, they won't take it like I mean it," or "They'll think it's dumb." Well, let 'em think that if that's how they are, but I don't think they will.

I was at a car wash one day. I spontaneously said to a lady in a bright yellow sweater that she was like a little bit of sunshine. She looked at me rather strangely and I soon learned that her husband had died just eleven days earlier. She said the compliment really encouraged her. You just never know when your encouragement could be needed. Risk it today! Decide to reach out to people. Consciously nurture an interest in people.

Why should we want to be more aware of people's needs? Because that's the way we serve Jesus. "Inasmuch as ye have done it unto one of the least of these," you have done it unto whom? You have done it unto Jesus. How precious to think we are serving others as unto Him! Again, make people a priority. Someone has said, "Together we stick or divided we are stuck!" We need each other. I need you and you need me. We need people.

Be sensitive to people. You can be around people and sometimes feel their need without hearing a word. That goes back to listening with your inner ear as well as your outer ear. Learn to be a good listener. Anyone can learn to listen to people.

Do you know your neighbors? Many of you do; some don't — probably because they don't want to know you! People are just too busy. All too often the following statement pictures us. "This is the age of the half-read page, the quick hash, the mad dash, the bright night, the nerves that are tight, the plane hop with the brief stop, the big shot in a good spot, the brain strain, the heart pain and the cat naps till the spring snaps and the fun's done!" Life just goes faster and faster and nobody has time for anything. What a shame. Cultivate caring for people.

Paul said in Philippians 1:3, "I thank my God upon every remembrance of you." Now, do you really think he was writing to a perfect church? No! Absolutely not. There is no such thing. Have you been disillusioned by people in church because they are not all perfect? A man came to Charles Spurgeon once and said, "I am looking for the perfect church." Spurgeon's answer was, "Well, if you do find it, don't join it because you'll ruin it!" What a good answer!

Yes, people will disappoint you. You may help them, love them, spend time with them and they might not appreciate it. They may even turn on you. But we still must care about people.

There were 120 people who met in the upper room after the death and resurrection of Jesus. Of course, those people had seen the frailties of one another. They were aware that they all had turned their backs on Christ. Their eyes were wide open to the fact they were a very imperfect people. Yet they still came together in one accord and, after much prayer, they caused an evangelistic explosion that rocked Jerusalem. That explosion is felt today because they decided to come together and accept each other. They resolved to love one another and pray together and work together even though they were aware they all had faults.

Another way to increase your intimacy quotient is by not lending your ear to gossip. Be a peacemaker. If you anticipate someone is about to tell you something negative, stop her! If a person gives you an earful before you can stop her, forget it! Replace it with something good. Hearsay will color your thinking. If you dwell on something bad you hear about someone, that is what you will think about the next time you see that person. Dispel it quickly because gossip is usually just that — gossip!

Don't talk about your friends' faults. Dwell on their good points. Refuse to listen to criticism or to be a critic. You are going to have to learn to stop negative talk in a nice way.

Understand people's weaknesses, but give the gift of confidence anyway. The Bible does say that we are to put no confidence in the flesh, but we can give people the benefit of the doubt while also realizing they are not perfect.

An anonymous writer once wrote, "When we are given our rewards, I would prefer to be found to have erred on the side of grace rather than judgment; to have loved too much rather than too little; to have forgiven the undeserving rather than to have refused forgiveness; to have fed a parasite rather than to have neglected one who was hungry; to have been taken advantage of rather than to have taken undue advantage; to have believed too much in my brothers rather than too little; to have been wrong on the side of too much trust rather than too much cynicism; to have believed the best and been wrong than to have believed the worst and been right." Isn't that good? I think that sums up what I am trying to say. People **will** disappoint us, but we must love them. That's our ministry as Christian leaders' wives. That's the only way we can minister to Christ. So start today to increase your intimacy quotient. Say "I love you" to someone who needs it. It will help you tremendously and just think what it will do for them.

OH, TO BE LIKE JESUS

I looked at my china; it is very, very simple. My husband loves uncluttered things. So, when we went to choose our china, he didn't want all the flowered stuff. He wanted something simple. I am told that you should be able to see your hand through really fine china. I know really fine china has to be fired at a much higher temperature than earthenware. In looking at my silver, I realize silver has to go through the fire and be tested to separate the real silver from the dross. All the useful things in our lives are tested. For example, you see on television where they crash automobiles to find out various things that need to be improved about them. I think, "Boy, they are spending a lot of money doing that." But I am thankful for it, because they test those cars for defects before we buy them. Useful things are tested.

Testings will also come to us in our lives — all through our lives. Why do they come? Why does God allow testings? Now, testings even come in the secular world. Have you ever noticed people who start out to accomplish anything in any area of life have others nipping at their heels? Critics suddenly arise. This happened even in the case of our first lady, Barbara Bush. When she was asked to bring the commencement address at Wellesley College, some critics arose. They said, "What has she ever done? All she does is live in the shadow of her husband's name!" Well, let's think about what she has done. She has been the wife of a man in politics for many years. I certainly don't consider that a simple accomplishment. She is a mother and a grandmother. However, the critics didn't like her list of credentials. Frankly, I think those are mighty good credentials! Nevertheless, because she is in a place of prominence, someone will be picking at her. Isn't that the way it is anymore? It almost makes you want to avoid politics or public life because it does bring criticism.

In our spiritual lives, God often uses critics to test us. In Isaiah 54:16a we are told, "Behold, I have created the smith that bloweth the coals in the fire, and that bringeth forth an instrument for his work." He said, "Now you will have people in your life who will pick at you and try to pull you down. They will work on you and nip at you. But I created the very ones who are putting you through the fire; I created them for that purpose." Now you probably say, "Thanks, Lord! It's getting kind of hot; I don't need this." But He knows it is for a reason. It is for the purpose of bringing forth a useful instrument. God sometimes uses people to make us into useful instruments. You must learn quickly that it is not always bad people who are used to be our blacksmiths, so to speak. Just because God uses someone, like a critic, for the refining of an instrument for His work, it does not necessarily mean the one He has chosen is bad. Also notice verse 17 where He says, "No weapon that is formed against thee shall prosper." God says those who pick at the people He has chosen to do His work will not prosper — whether they are good or bad. He gives us that promise. However, testings do come if we set out to do anything.

Have you heard of a formal, modernistic church having a split lately? Why do those kinds of churches rarely have splits? Because they are not doing anything! They are just playing church and the Devil doesn't care. It doesn't bother him a bit. He won't go to the Lord and say, "Can I go down and test them?" But he will test **you** if you start to serve the Lord. Most of you reading this book do want to do something. I hope you don't want to be ordinary. You want to go out and be involved in your ministry. You want to be involved in something that will win people to the Lord and change people's lives. You want to accomplish a work for the Lord.

Learn to Turn a Deaf Ear

In Nehemiah 2, Nehemiah got a vision from the Lord to rebuild the walls of Jerusalem. In Nehemiah 2:11 and 12 he said, "So I came to Jerusalem, and was there three days. And I arose in the night, I and some few men with me; neither told I any man what my God had put in my heart to do at Jerusalem: neither was there any beast with me, save the beast that I rode upon." He said God had put in his heart a desire to rebuild the wall. Go on to verses 17 and 18a: "Then said I unto them, Ye see the distress that we are in, how Jerusalem lieth waste, and the gates thereof are burned with fire: come, and let us build up the wall of Jerusalem, that we be no more a reproach. Then I told them of the hand of my God which was good upon me." He shared his dream.

First, God gave him a dream to do something. Has God given you a dream? I hope so. Has God given you a goal — whether you are married or not — to go out and do the best for Him that you can possibly do in whatever area. Maybe He wants you to build a good marriage and rear children in the best way possible and then be the best in the ministry in which God has placed you.

Then Nehemiah shared his dream and began to do a work. But notice verse 19: "But when Sanballat the Horonite, and Tobiah the servant, the Ammonite, and Geshem the Arabian, heard it, they laughed us to scorn, and despised us, and said, What is this thing that ye do? will ye rebel against the king?" They were critics nippin' at Nehemiah's heels. Why? Nehemiah had a goal, started out to do it and the critics noticed. That's what happens. You may as well get ready for it if you are going to do something for God. Now, if you just go out and sit in a little church somewhere and don't start a soul winning program, if you say, "It will just be those of us who have been here through the years," you are not going to have any critics or problems. However, you decide to build a wall, the criticism will begin.

Let's look again. Opposition came, and it kept on coming. Look in Nehemiah 4:1: "But it came to pass, that when Sanballat heard that we builded the wall, he was wroth, and took great indignation, and mocked the Jews." Sanballat was angry. He probably said, "You'll never be able to finish that wall!" He mocked them. In verse 2 we see him say, "What do these feeble Jews?" He said, "This little old nation. Who do they think they are?" Look at verse 3: "Even that which they build, if a fox go up, he shall even break down their stone wall." He said, "They are so weak. They will never accomplish it." But verse 6 says, "So built we the wall; and all the wall was joined together unto the half thereof: for the people had a mind to work." They just kept on building. They ignored their critics. They overlooked the opposition and the ridicule. Now let's take a look at verses 8 and 9 where it speaks of what the critics did: "And conspired all of them together to come and to fight against Jerusalem, and to hinder it. Nevertheless we made our prayer unto our God, and set a watch against them day and night, because of them." The enemy began to harass them so badly that half of them had to hold weapons while the other half worked. In spite of the harassment, they kept building the wall. They didn't get much sleep; they had to be constantly on guard. But they kept on building.

In Nehemiah 6:2 and 3 they are still at it: "That Sanballat and Geshem sent unto me, saying, Come, let us meet together in some one of the villages in the plain of Ono. But they thought to do me mischief. And I sent messengers unto them, saying, I am doing a great work, so that I cannot come down: why should the work cease, whilst I leave it, and come down to you?" The last thing the enemy said was, "Okay. You go ahead and build a wall. But come down and have a meeting with us first and let's discuss things." What they were actually trying to do was stop the work and get the Israelites' minds off what they were trying to do. They were hoping they could make them forget their work. But Nehemiah refused to be distracted by the local ministerial association. He told them he didn't have time to leave his work. Notice verse 15 of chapter 6: "So the wall was finished in the twenty and fifth day of the month Elul, in fifty and two days." They didn't let the critics — the testings — God had allowed stop them. This time, God used people and ridicule and talk to try to stop the work He had put in Nehemiah's heart to accomplish. But it didn't work. Nehemiah and his people reached their goal and finished the work. Praise the Lord!

What's Your Test Grade?

What is the purpose of tests in school? They are used to see how much you have learned and to see if you are ready to go on to harder material. Also, their purpose is to see how much you have progressed. Did you ever like tests? I don't think even the best students like them. I was a good student in school; I usually made good grades on my tests, but I still dreaded them. It is the same way in my ministry with my husband.

I will never forget the first test that came to me as a pastor's wife. I told you earlier in this book about my trip down the path looking for the outhouse. But there wasn't any outhouse!! Can you just see prissy Beverly Hyles out there? Now, you might think it's stupid, but that was a little bit of a test to me. It was my first small one, I guess. It was so good for me, because it was a forerunner of more difficult tests to come. What if I had said, "I want indoor plumbing. Forget it, Jack; I'm not going!" However, the tests get harder. Praise the Lord, He is so good to start us off with tests at the kindergarten level and work up to harder things. That way, we can build our spiritual muscles gradually.

In Deuteronomy 8:2 God tells the little country of Israel why they were tested in the wilderness. And they **were** tested! They had to eat the same thing every day; they wandered in the wilderness for forty years. But in Deuteronomy 8:2 He gives three things He allowed testing to do in their lives: "And thou shalt remember all the way which the Lord thy God led thee these forty years in the wilderness, to humble thee, and to prove thee, to know what was in thine heart, whether thou wouldest keep his commandments, or no."

First of all, He needed to humble them. God knows we are proud. If anything ever knocked the pride out of me it was going down the path that day, and I needed it! God needed to see whether I was too proud to work with those sweet, precious country people. I learned to love those people; they surely loved this city girl who was so ignorant of country ways. The need for humbling described the nation of Israel and the same could be true of a church or school or individual. So God sometimes allows testings in order to humble us. We get too big for our britches.

Secondly, He allowed the testing to prove them. I looked up "prove" in the dictionary and it said, "to show it to be true or genuine." That's what happens when china is fired or cars are crashed. It's done to see if they will stand the test of being used. In the same way, God has to prove congregations and individuals — to see if they are genuine and if they can be used.

The third reason He gave was to find what was in their hearts. He wanted to know whether they would keep His commandments. He needs to know what it takes to stop you. Will you just keep on going? God is going to test you to find out what it will take to stop you — just as He did the little nation of Israel.

Job was tested. Do you remember? Historically, as far as we know, Job was the first book in the Bible. I believe Job's story was an example to show us why testing comes. There were two sides to Job's testing. What went on in Heaven? Satan came to God and God asked if he had considered His servant Job. He told Satan Job was a perfect and upright man. Satan said Job was only perfect and upright because of the hedge God had put around him. He asked God to remove the hedge and see what Job would do. And did God allow that? Yes, He did. In your testing today in your life or church or school, realize God could be allowing the same thing to happen to you.

Jack Trieber, pastor of North Valley Baptist Church in Santa Clara, California, has been a guest lecturer at our college recently. I can just imagine Satan saying to God some time back, "Let's just see what he does if You let me take his health away." See, Bro. Trieber has rheumatoid arthritis. Now we will never know for sure what the purpose of his rheumatoid arthritis is until we get to Heaven. It could be to see whether Bro. Trieber can be stopped in his service for God.

Job Made an A+

I don't know the reason for anyone's testing. I do believe Job's testing was an example for us so we could consider its purpose when testing comes to us. There's a warfare going on. Satan wants to take our testimonies; since he can't get our souls. He wants to take away our usefulness. He wants to take away everything he can to see if we will stop. Sometimes God allows that, as in the test case of Job. Three things happened because of the testing in Job's life.

First of all, Satan was proved to be a liar. He said, "You let me touch him and take away his wealth and his family and his health and he won't serve you then. He won't be perfect and upright then." But he was proven to be a liar, wasn't he? What about in your life? Are you going to prove Satan to be a liar when the tests come? If he says you will quit when he tests you, prove him to be a liar. Just say, "By cracky! I'm not going to prove the devil right!"

Second, God was vindicated because Job remained faithful. God's name and God's trust in Job was vindicated because He believed Job would pass the test. I don't think He would have allowed that much testing to come to Job if He hadn't believed Job would pass the tests.

Third, it allowed Job to demonstrate his loyalty to God and to know Him in a better way. He was already a perfect and upright man, but Job 42:5 and 6 tells us he got to know God even better: "I have heard of thee by the hearing of the ear: but now mine eye seeth thee. Wherefore I abhor myself, and repent in dust and ashes." He said, "I see myself now as just nothing. Before, I had heard of You with the hearing of the ear, now I see You through all You have done in my life." Job was brought even closer to God and became an even greater man of God. The Bible tells us that God did more in the latter part of Job's life than He had done in the first part. Job's testing allowed him to demonstrate his loyalty and to know God better.

Sometimes we need to stop and examine our testings. Are they testings God has allowed? Do they have our names on them? Are we being tested because of our rebellion, our sin, our wrongdoing, our stubbornness, or our self-will? A lot of our testings, if we will look closely, will say "Made by Beverly Hyles" instead of "Made in Heaven." They are made by us because we have refused to go the way God wants us to go. The consequence of going our way instead of God's is always that we pay for it. So sometimes, testing is because of wrong choices on our part. If you sow onions, you are going to reap what? You are going to reap onions. Again, God allows it; but we need to realize it is our own doing.

Testings are common to all men — in the secular world as well as in the spiritual. Everybody is tested. I always want to say we, as Christians, are much too full of self-pity when we think no one has it as rough as we do. Everyone goes through testings. The only difference is God's testings always have a purpose with them if we will just submit to them and let Him work His purpose and smooth off the rough edges and separate a little more dross. There's always a purpose. But the world can't see that. They don't understand the purposes of the testings that come. That's why it is important for us to be faithful as the testings come. We may never see, this side of Heaven, why He is allowing the testing; we don't have to see it. He knows and that's what's important!

God comes to test our tempers, our courage, our patience, our love — and He does it in strange ways. You know, you need to be careful how you pray. You say, "Lord, teach me how to love." Do you know what He is just likely to do? He is apt to send the most unlovely people in your path. He's likely to send the people who are the hardest to tolerate. Do you know what He is doing? He is teaching you how to love. That's what you asked for, isn't it? We say, "Lord, teach me how to have patience." And boy, everything goes topsy-turvy, doesn't it? You wish you had never prayed that prayer. What you mean is, "Lord, just help that really sweet feeling of love come over me." But that's not the way you learn. Or, "Just let my days be filled with smooth sailing so I can be patient. Let the kids do everything right and let my husband do everything I want him to do. Don't let anything upset the apple cart." That's not the way you learn patience, but that's really what we mean. We pray for courage. And we think, "Okay, he's just going to come down with a big needle and stick it in my arm and I will suddenly be courageous." That's not the way you get it! You gain courage by facing battles and facing the enemy. The more you face the enemy, the more courage you gain. You need to be careful. Be sure you mean it when you ask for certain things in your life; God's just likely to answer your prayers, but not in the way you expected! He will test you in those areas to see if you truly meant it when you asked for love or patience or courage. I Corinthians 10:13 is still true. It says God is faithful and He will not suffer us to be tempted above that we are able. He will never break us. Testings are not meant to break us but to make us. He will also with the temptation make a way for us to escape. It won't last forever. You will be able to escape it. Satan can and does test — but only to the degree God allows it. It was that way with Job. Satan could not have done one thing to Job unless God had said okay. God is still more powerful than Satan. "Greater is he that is in you, than he that is in the world." (I John 4:4) Satan does have power, but he does not have the power to do anything that God will not allow him to do. Then if God allows Satan to buffet us, it is for our good. I don't think we actually believe that, but it's true.

Chosen in the Furnace of Affliction

Someone once said, "God would have no need for furnaces if there were no gold to separate from the dross." A few years ago Mrs. Evans chose as a *CHRISTIAN WOMANHOOD* Spectacular theme, "I See Gold Glittering!" There is gold hidden in every woman who reads this book. Perhaps it is still hidden because there is a lot of dross. God sees that gold, and He's going to bring it forth if you will allow Him to do so. However, many times we pull away from the fire when it starts getting a little bit warm and the gold never has a chance to come forth.

Tests come for several reasons. First of all, they come because of our own stupidity; they have our names stamped all over them for chastening. They come because we have deliberately chosen to go our way instead of the way we knew God wanted us to go. They come because we are rebellious, hard-hearted and disobedient. When people I love are chastened severely of the Lord because of sin, do you know what my first thought is? "Praise God!" I say that because God says He chastens those He loves. If He doesn't chastise us, we are not His children. Chastening is God's way of proving to us that He loves us. If you are a mom, you don't go next door and spank the neighbor's kid. You spank your own child! So I'll tell you right now I am glad when I get spanked for doing wrong. It confirms to me I am God's child.

Secondly, tests come for purifying. He wants to make us pure and usable. Isaiah 48:10 says, ". . .I have chosen thee in the furnace of affliction." It is in the furnace where the dross is separated from the gold or the silver. Purifying is not necessarily meant to cause suffering but to separate. Refining separates what shouldn't be there so what should be there can come forth and be seen more readily. Luke 22:31 and 32 says, "And the Lord said, Simon, Simon, behold, Satan hath desired to have you, that he may sift you as wheat: But I have prayed for thee, that thy faith fail not: and when thou art converted, strengthen thy brethren." Now when the tests come to purify us, we should remember what God told Peter. He told Peter that Satan would test him to see if he really loved the Lord. Jesus also said he had prayed that Peter's faith would not fail. When he talked about Peter being converted, He didn't mean Peter wasn't already saved. He meant Peter's dross needed to be isolated from the gold; he needed to be purified. Now at first, Peter did deny the Lord. But after the dross was separated; he was purified through that testing and he was used in a great way.

Now let me ask you something. If Jesus prayed for Peter, don't you think He will pray for us too? Certainly He will. He will say, "Father, let her pass the test."

Now, how intense must the heat be? How long must the furnace rage full blast? That's up to us most of the time. It all depends on how long it takes for us to allow the dross to be burned away. It depends upon how stubborn and self-willed we are. You know, many of our testings could be much shorter and less fiery. However, we get in the way. See, the Lord is waiting to see His image reflected in us. And until He does, until all the dross is gone and He can see Himself, the fire will continue to be hot. So we could cooperate and make things a little easier for ourselves. Romans 8:28 and 29 says, "And we know that all things work together for good to them that love God, to them who are the called according to his purpose. For whom he did foreknow, he also did predestinate to be conformed to the image of his Son, that he might be the firstborn among many brethren." So, all the things that come to those who love God do work for good so He can see Himself reflected in us. However, we sometimes slow down that process.

Tests also come for perfecting. I Peter 5:10 says, "But the God of all grace, who hath called us unto his eternal glory by Christ Jesus, after that ye have suffered a while, make you perfect, stablish, strengthen, settle you." Now "perfect" means "complete or mature." Suffering is God's way of perfecting us or making us more mature and complete. Suffering makes us stable; it strengthens us and settles us. It helps us have a calm peace in the midst of turmoil. You see that settled, established peace in the lives of older Christians like Dr. Lee Roberson and his wife. You could see it in the lives of Dr. and Mrs. John R. Rice. We can all have that. Testings are supposed to refine us. Again, perfecting doesn't come in a big needle that we can just take as an injection. It comes by testings.

God wants even-keeled Christians. The keel of a ship keeps it stable and steady in oceans that sometimes are very tumultuous. You know, there is more of a great ship below the water than above the water. And all the ship that is below, including the keel, keeps the ship stable and steady. God wants us to be stable and steady too.

I once read an illustration about Mt. Rushmore in South Dakota where someone chiseled out the profiles of four of the presidents. You know, that job took years. Tons and tons and tons of granite were chiseled and dynamited away to bring out the likenesses of those men. That etching is exactly what God wants to do in our lives. He desires to bring out His image in us. Unfortunately, sometimes we are like that granite in the Black Hills of South Dakota; we are hard. That hardness makes it more difficult for Him to bring out His image in us. It takes a hotter fire and more intense testings for some of us. If we would just be more malleable in His hands, our testings could be finished sooner and less intense as we go through them.

Someone once said, "How can the world know what Christ is like until we show what Christ can make us like?" The world can't see

Him; instead, they see those of us who call ourselves Christians. We bear His name. How can they see what He is like until they see what He can make us like?

Also we shouldn't think of the big trials as the only things that are making us more like Him. The little nitty-gritty happenings of each day are also for the purpose of making us more like Him. You know, God doesn't waste anything. In John 6:12, after the five thousand had been fed, Jesus told the disciples to gather up the fragments. Did He need all those crumbs? Of course not! He had just fed five thousand people. Why didn't he just leave the fragments for the ants and birds? Because He doesn't let anything go to waste! Think about the days you are depressed and the kids are all sick. You might think those are just small occurrences, but there are no "uh ohs" with God. Did it ever occur to you that nothing ever occurs to God? He has planned it all; He has allowed all those seemingly trivial events — don't waste the learning times.

God used Jeremiah's scraps when he was in a fearful, dark dungeon. I believe Satan must have come to Jeremiah and said, "Ha! Ha! Where is your God now? Just show me! Where is He now?" Yet Jeremiah wrote in Lamentations 3:21-23, "This I recall to my mind, therefore have I hope. It is of the Lord's mercies that we are not consumed, because His compassions fail not. They are new every morning: great is thy faithfulness." When we sing the song about new mercies being seen every morning, we think of a lovely sunlit day with birds singing in the trees. However, Jeremiah was in a dark dungeon. But he didn't let that trial go to waste; Jeremiah made an "A" on his test because he didn't let the darkness and dampness of that dungeon take away the realization that His God was still a compassionate, loving God. It would be wonderful if we could learn to do that, wouldn't it?

Wrong Ways to Take Tests

There are some bad attitudes we can have toward testing and we need to avoid them.

1. We become calloused and bitter. This often happens. The

difference between what could happen and what should happen is only one letter — we can get bitter or better. We become calloused or sweeter. How many times have you knocked on a door only to hear someone say, "Don't come to me with that God stuff. You don't know what God did to me! He took my kid!" They are bitter and calloused when they could have allowed what happened to soften them toward God.

2. Secondly, we become complainers and gripers. We say, "God hasn't treated me right. He treats everyone else good, but He surely doesn't treat me right." The children of Israel did that, didn't they? What happened to them? Those above a certain age never got to see the promised land and Miriam was struck with leprosy. God doesn't like complaining, does He? Complaining is a bad attitude toward testing.

3. Thirdly, we criticize the people God uses or we criticize God Himself for our testing. When we criticize the people God is using to test us, we are actually criticizing God Who has allowed them to test us.

4. We grow careless because we forget to look for God in everything. I will tell you something truthfully. Recently I was in a car accident and my car suffered damage to the tune of $4300. Then about two weeks after I got my car back, I pulled up behind one of our church buses at a railroad crossing. Well, the railroad gates started coming down at the crossing and the bus driver couldn't see me in his rearview mirrors. By the time I looked behind me to see if I could back up, my grill had already been smashed. As I sat there I said, "Beverly Hyles, why can't you be more careful?" I was a little careless; I didn't see God in that. I had no idea what God wanted me to learn (I still don't) and for a little while I just bawled! I even decided I wasn't going to teach my Sunday school class that morning! Can you imagine?! I went to the bathroom and cried really good. Now, no one was even hurt! So I had to decide the Lord allowed it, refuse to get indifferent, go home and cry all day because my car grill was smashed. And do you know what? I think I taught a better Sunday school lesson that day than I would have had the accident not happened.

Those are the bad attitudes we can have toward testing. Instead of having those bad attitudes, let's decide to have the right attitudes toward testing.

Ways To Pass With Flying Colors

1. First of all, renew your confidence in God. When the heat is turned up the hottest, say, "Lord, I don't yet see what you are doing, but I have my confidence in You. Whatever You are doing, it is okay. I will just walk by faith with You. Now I don't feel You; all I feel is the heat — and it's hot! In fact, I'm scorching. But I know You know the way I take, and I know that when You are through I will come forth as gold. I am going to renew my confidence in You and let You do Your work." Now can't you see how He can do His work a little bit quicker when you have that attitude?

2. Then pray and believe all the promises He has made about testing. Believe He will do what He says He will do. Psalm 50:15 says, "And call upon me in the day of trouble: I will deliver thee, and thou shalt glorify me." Now God didn't say He would deliver us immediately, but He does promise deliverance. He tells us we can call on Him and He will come immediately to help us bear the testing. So many times in the Bible we read, "And it came to pass." It didn't come to stay; it came to pass! He said if we will call on Him He will deliver us and we will glorify Him.

3. Respond to Him; just keep on obeying and keep on doing. See, that's what I almost **didn't** do when my car was hit. I almost decided, "I'm not gonna' teach that class." And there were about twelve junior high girls who needed to hear the Word of God that morning. They didn't need to hear, "Mrs. Hyles went home because her car got hit." I would have been teaching them by my example it was okay not to come to Sunday school when things go a little bit wrong. And that's what I almost did. We are to keep on responding to Him and doing what we know is right to do in the testing.

4. We are supposed to rejoice. Mrs. Marlene Evans is good at teaching this. Now I can't find any place where the Bible says we are

to rejoice just when things are going smoothly. We are to "rejoice in the Lord alway." We are to give thanks in everything. Sing as you rejoice! Paul and Silas were manacled in prison and they were actually delivered from their prison because they rejoiced and sang.

5. Think of others. II Corinthians 1:3 through 5 are such precious verses. They tell us this: "Blessed be God, even the Father of our Lord Jesus Christ, the Father of mercies, and the God of all comfort; Who comforteth us in all our tribulation, that we may be able to comfort them which are in any trouble, by the comfort wherewith we ourselves are comforted of God. For as the sufferings of Christ abound in us, so our consolation also aboundeth by Christ." Now does this say He is the God of some comfort? No, it says all comfort. Does it say He comforts us in **some** of our tribulations? No, He comforts us in **all** our tribulations. He says, "I am the God of all comfort. I allow the times of testing to come to show you how I comfort you in those times so that you, in turn, can teach someone else how God comforts. And the consolation you give is from Me. I will allow you to console and help those who need it." A purpose of testing is to teach us to think of others.

Because of having been in the ministry for forty years, I have had to have this comfort a lot of times. My husband has always been a rather straightforward preacher. I like it that way! Naming sin and painting sin as it is and calling the Devil what he is — these are the only things that get the job done. I was reared in that kind of church and I like it. But not everybody does. So there have been times when people have not liked us. Isn't that amazing?! So I have had to learn to be comforted. Therefore, I think I am qualified to say God will comfort and help you. It is fun to watch Him as He does it.

The world's way is hard. As I observe the world's way and watch Christians who are sold out, it seems to me the Christian life is definitely the easiest. There will be testings; they will come. Their purpose is to make us useful and usable; they are for our good. Testings burn away the dross so God can see His image in us. Be sure when the testings come, you take the right attitudes. It is your choice! Just submit to God; let Him make of you what He wants to make of you. You say, "Mrs. Hyles, that sounds scary." It really isn't. God doesn't bring tests every day of your life. On the days He doesn't choose to test you, you can kind of relax. But the tests will come, and even the tests are exciting because He is there to help you through them. What will your test grade be?

MAN LOOKETH
ON THE OUTWARD APPEARANCE

I feel it is important for us to consider our grooming and dress. I believe one of the main reasons I surrendered my life to serve the Lord as a young girl of nine or ten and was pleased to surrender my life to His service was because of three ladies in our church who meant a lot to me. Now my mother was the first influence in my life and she was a godly influence. She was always a well-groomed lady, and the three ladies who influenced me aside from my mother were also very well-groomed ladies.

One of those ladies was my pastor's wife. She was a beautiful woman who was prematurely gray, and I just loved to look at her. When I began to go into her home for a trio practice each week, I learned that she was also beautiful on the inside. However, as a young girl I was first attracted to the outside. I believe being a pastor's wife didn't look bad to me because she was such a beautiful role model.

Our church organist was another one to whom I looked as an example. She was simply gorgeous; in addition, she was well-groomed and faithful. She was always at her place. The services were never held up while everyone waited for Luella. She was always there, and that made a great impression on me. But I was first drawn to her looks.

We also had a church secretary who was a great influence in my life. I don't remember her name at all. She was not beautiful as the world counts beauty, but she was a very well-groomed, clean, appropriately-dressed lady. She was the kind you would take a second look at just because she kept herself so nicely. She took the time one day to write me a short note that said, "Beverly, I have watched you and I believe God is going to use you someday." That note made such a great impression on me. I didn't know she knew me from Adam, but I have felt through the years I couldn't let down the church secretary who took the time to write that note to me.

All these ladies first drew me by their outward appearances. Then as I got past that, I was drawn by their character, integrity, faithfulness and loyalty. Even though I eventually saw those character traits, man does look on the outward appearance first. I truly do think we get past that; I do think we can see inward qualities that work out. However, the outward appearance is all we can see at first.

Now sometimes when we get to the inside, the person doesn't look pretty anymore. Psalm 45:13 says, "The king's daughter is all glorious within: her clothing is of wrought gold." The king's daughter is beautiful within and without. We should strive to make our inward and outward beauty agree. I believe the way we dress must be considered when we are working on our outward beauty.

In thinking of how a Christian leader's wife should dress, two words come to my mind first. Those words are "basic" and "classic." I believe a leader's wife should never be a trendy, faddish dresser. Now she doesn't have to be dull or boring, but she shouldn't be the one who first tries all the new fads. A leader's wife should stick with the classics. When I say "classic," I am talking about fashions that don't go out of style. When I say "basic," I am talking about building a wardrobe around the basic colors and adding bright splashes of color with accessories. Now if you are trying to build a wardrobe with the basics and classics, that doesn't mean you can never have a bright red or blue dress. In fact, bright colors are important if you are going to be working with small children. Children are drawn to bright colors. I believe bright colors even help you be a better teacher. They bring you out of yourself. However, you should stick to the basic colors for most of your wardrobe.

Now please don't think I am contradicting myself; I'm not. I just believe a leader's wife ought to begin building her wardrobe around the classic styles in basic colors. Then she should add colors as her budget allows.

In building a wardrobe, we should also consider balance. Did you know you can balance your personality with your clothing? For example, if you know you are a woman who tends to be bossy, wear clothing that makes you feel less so. Softer colors and softer clothing styles will tend to make you a softer person. This can especially help you on a day when you know you will be in a position where you will want to be bossy. On the other hand, if you are a very shy, retiring person and you have been asked to speak for a group of ladies, wearing a bold, bright color will give you the extra confidence you need. Color does affect you! You need to know yourself well enough to be able to balance your personality with color.

You can also balance your figure with your clothing. If you are a tiny, dainty person, you probably ought not to wear big pieces of chunky jewelry or great big hairstyles. On the other hand, if you are a larger person, you need to learn to balance that with larger accessories and hairstyles.

Thus far, we need to think classic, basic and balanced. All these tend to make a pleasant whole. Don't wear things that detract from the whole. The object is to be able to look nice, be well-groomed and then **forget ourselves** after we have done all we can do to look as good as we can. The object is to let those before whom we stand see Jesus and the message we are giving. Now, obviously, they will see us first. But we should make it a point not to be so distracting they can't look beyond us and hear what we are trying to say and see the One we are trying to lift up. That's the whole point of our ministry.

Our clothing ought to be as beautiful as our budgets will allow, and we should be as beautiful inwardly as we will allow the Lord to make us. Our inward and outward beauty ought to agree so when people look at us they can look past us and see Jesus.

Let me give you a few tips about dressing I have learned during my years in the ministry. First of all, whenever you and your husband are candidating for a position in the Lord's work, be sure to wear your best bib and tucker. Dress up! Now that was rather hard for me when we candidated at First Baptist here in Hammond because I was five months pregnant with Cindy. However, I think you can be pretty even when you are pregnant. You need to put your best foot forward. You need to look your best. You need to realize people will be judging your grooming and cleanliness as well as your husband's message and abilities. People examine the wife and children very carefully. Allow those people to see a nice-looking wife who is clean and well-groomed.

Secondly, as a leader's wife, you will more than likely have speaking responsibilities of one kind or another. As we have already discussed in this book, your main duty is to be your husband's wife. Be that as it may, it doesn't give you the right to sit down on that one excuse and say, "I'm not doing anything else!" The Lord has given you talents and He expects you to use them. Now perhaps you will be teaching a Sunday school class — or perhaps you'll be in charge of the church nurseries like Mrs. Lee Roberson was for many years. But as you get up before people to speak, you need to think about certain ways of dressing. These tips, if you will use them, will help people look past you to see Christ.

1. Don't wear things that could distract your listeners. For instance, if I were listening to a speaker who was wearing long, dangling earrings, I would be watching the earrings instead of listening to the speaker. They would distract me. Be careful about wearing patterns that are too busy or outfits that are too fussy. Wear a color that is flattering to you. If you know ahead of time you are speaking, be sure to wear a flattering dress. Now it gets difficult to keep your clothes in order and ready to wear when you are busy. But it is so important to have suitable clothing for speaking that doesn't distract from what you are trying to convey.

2. Make sure your skirt is long enough. You will often be seated on a platform before the audience. Make sure your skirt is long enough to cover what it should while you are sitting as well as standing. When you stand, be sure the skirt moves with you. Realize when you are on an elevated platform, your skirt will need extra length to be modest.

3. I find most books that have anything to say regarding clothing for a Christian leader's wife nearly always suggest a becoming suit

with a feminine blouse as a wise choice for a speaker. Now you might say, "But I don't like feminine blouses," or "I don't like tailored suits." Well, you can have the best of both worlds when you wear a tailored suit with a feminine blouse. Also, if you get too warm, you have the option of removing your jacket. You just never know. You might be asked to speak at a banquet and you just take it for granted there will be an air conditioner. However, you may get there only to find it is 110° in the place where you are speaking. If you are wearing something that enables you to shed a layer, it will help you. Almost without exception, this is what is suggested for a speaker.

4. Always make a last-minute check of your clothing if you are going before a group. It's also a good idea to do this on a regular basis before you leave the house.

You should be careful of your dress whether the group is young or old. I am so thrilled that our primaries get to be under the influence of Mrs. Erma McKinney every Sunday. I believe she is the type of lady little children need to see. I am also glad that for many years the juniors at our church have had the opportunity to be inspired by Mrs. Ann Shoaf who is a lovely Christian lady. Both of these ladies are just the epitome of femininity. They do their jobs so well, and they look as if they have just stepped out of a bandbox. Now that's remarkable because I happen to know they are both extremely busy ladies. Their inward beauty corresponds with their outward beauty. I am thankful these ladies dress nicely for the little ones of our church. It is just as important for the little children to have ladies to emulate and admire as it is for older women. I believe this helps our children want to serve the Lord.

So make a last minute check to be sure your slip isn't showing and you don't have strings hanging from your hem or runs in your hosiery. The last-minute check improves your confidence and helps you forget yourself. Sometimes it will show you something you need to change. But once you have done the best you can do, forget yourself and think about the people to whom you are ministering. That is the whole crux of the matter. It enables you to think of others — and that's so needed.

There are several reasons we, as Christian leaders' wives, ought to look our best.

Does God Want Us to Look Beautiful?

1. People watch you everywhere you go. I remember a time a few years ago when I had showered in preparation for going somewhere in the evening. Before I finished dressing, I remembered I had left my sprinkler running in the yard. I thought, "I know. I'll put on my robe and dash out there when no cars are coming. I can get behind the bush where the faucet handle is, turn off the water and dash back in before anyone sees me. No one will ever know." So I did that. And wouldn't you know somebody just honked and honked their car horn at me while I was out there? I didn't even look up, but the next day a lady said to me, "Ha, ha, ha! I saw you out there in your yard yesterday!" When you are a leader's wife, you can't even turn off the sprinkler or take out the trash unless you are dressed! There is no discharge from being watched. Also, you might not always know who sees you. If you are in a small church, you will know when you are meeting a church member. But in a large church, you might not know everyone! There have been times when people have spoken to me and called me by name in public and I have to say, "I'm sorry. You are going to have to tell me who you are." When they say something like, "Oh, my name is Tom Smith; I have been a member of your church for thirteen years," I want to fall right through the floor! You never know when or how your appearance is going to affect someone. In your position as a leader's wife, you are watched!

2. You are an example. If there ever was a day when we need some examples in Christian feminine dress, it is today. If you go anywhere at all — like a mall or an airport — just watch the women. Sometimes, I am ashamed to be female! Women dress so inappropriately anymore. We, as leaders' wives, need to be pacesetters and examples. That doesn't mean we should wear the trends and the fads; it means we should set the pace for the way Christian women ought to look and dress.

A young lady and her husband left our college several years ago to take a pastorate in a northeastern state. One day she called me to ask for advice. She said since they were in a farming community where the ladies didn't dress up for church. They didn't wear nylons and, in fact, they often came to church wearing the same clothes in which they had done their morning chores! Now, she was a young lady who loved to dress up; she even liked hats! I remembered that, while she was here, she wore hats to church. She was also an excellent seamstress, so she had made beautiful clothing for herself. She asked me if she should stop wearing hosiery and dressy clothes to church. Now, I told her not to do that. I told her she could leave off the fancy hats; those ladies would probably have thought her uppity if she had worn them. They could never have afforded hats like that. They probably couldn't even afford clothes as nice as hers. **But my mother taught me Sundays were different.** I was brought up with Sunday dresses; I was not allowed to wear those dresses to school. On Saturday nights my mother made me polish my shoes and get everything ready for Sunday. That has always made Sunday more special to me. So I told this young pastor's wife she could be an example to those farm ladies. I even told her those ladies would feel better about themselves if they would follow her example of dress on Sundays. Farm women work hard all week; in many cases, they work as hard as the men do. That kind of life tends to detract from your femininity. However, that pastor's wife had the opportunity to show them they had one day a week when they could get all gussied up and go to church in their nice things. They might even want to put on hosiery and high heels and put a little blush on their cheeks. I told her if she could get those women to do some of those things by her example, they would like themselves a whole lot more. I told her she might even want to start a Proverbs 31 class and use it as an opportunity to teach the ladies a little about self-esteem and grooming. You know, she called back a few weeks later to say she had followed my advice and ladies had begun to try and were already looking so much better. She had to compromise a little on her preferences, but it paid off in the end.

3. Your church or school wants to be proud of you. Your people

don't want to have to point to some disheveled-looking woman and say, "That's my pastor's wife." They don't want you to look as if you just rolled out of bed.

4. You reflect your husband. Your dress reflects what you think and feel about your husband. Do you care enough to want to look nice for him? When you don't look nice you are also telling the world, whether it's true or not, that your husband doesn't care enough about you to see you have something nice to wear. Now perhaps you will have to wear the same dress every Sunday, but you can do things with belts, scarves and jewelry to make it look a little different. I Corinthians 11:7 says, ". . .But the woman is the glory of the man." That means a woman is the shining forth or the radiance of her husband. According to the Bible, you **do** reflect him.

5. You are a daughter of the King. A daughter of the King always ought to look attractive. I realize in our day royalty dresses less appropriately than in years gone by. However, we are still royalty and we ought to dress appropriately.

6. You will have more confidence when you know you have done all you can do to make yourself look good.

7. Your appearance reveals your attitude toward people besides your husband.

a. It reveals your attitude toward the Lord. In Psalm 139 the Lord says He has made us fearfully and wonderfully. He says we are marvelous creatures; we ought to look like it! So we reveal our attitude toward the Lord by our dress. If our clothing is indiscreet or immodest, it reveals a rebellious attitude toward the Lord. Now you might say, "Sometimes I wear things that aren't exactly within the rules, but I am not rebellious toward the Lord." Yes, but you need to realize nobody can see your heart; therefore, when your dress isn't within the rules, it looks like rebellion to others.

b. Your appearance reveals your attitude toward yourself. Now I realize there will be times when you have to run to the store at the last minute and you aren't dressed properly. (That's another reason we ought to dress fairly decently at home.) But if you run to the store with great big curlers in your hair, you are saying, "I don't care how I look and I don't particularly care what you think either!!" That's what you are saying whether you mean it or not, and we ought to care more about people than that.

I would hate for people to have to look at me in the morning before I have a chance to do at least a little something to myself. That includes my family. Start with your family. You ought to let them know you care enough to at least run a comb through your hair and splash your face with water before they have to see you. I guess if there is one thing I am glad about it is that my children remember I made an effort to look fresh when I greeted them after school. I changed clothes for them. I tried to look decent to do my day's work, but I did freshen up to greet them.

c. Your appearance reveals your attitude toward other people. When we go out not caring how we look, we are saying we don't care what people think. We can't always base our decisions about how to dress on our own comfort; we have an obligation as leaders' wives. We have to be appropriate as well as comfortable. This is particularly important on those days when you don't give a hoot! When you already feel awful, you had better fix up or you will end up killing someone before the day is over. And you will probably do it with your tongue! We have an obligation to ourselves, the Lord and other people to look our best every day — and that includes around the house!

Preserving the Distinctives

Two people approach, silhouetted against the horizon. Both are in trousers, with hair the same length. We could assume both are men, but that is not necessarily true in our present day. What happened?

In the Garden of Eden, God made two very distinct creatures — male and female. They were very different in body, mind, and emotions all because of **God's design.** We've certainly seen these distinctives broken down in the last two decades.

I own a charm book, copyrighted in 1928, written by Marjery Wilson. She was very prophetic when she stated, "Women must preserve civilization." My own husband has said, as he has travelled in the last twenty years, the greatest difference he sees in our nation is in the women.

Mrs. Wilson also says, "In the coming years we shall need all the charm we can get. It will be the task of women to keep the world from despond, to keep the prettier gestures of good living going." That was over 60 years ago. Did she foresee a time when there would be no more dress codes? I wonder.

I believe doing away with dress codes in schools did as much harm as taking away Bible and prayer.

God gives us some codes. One is in Deuteronomy 22:5 which says, "The woman shall not wear that which pertaineth unto a man, neither shall a man put on a woman's garment: for all that do so are abomination unto the Lord thy God." Women are not to wear that which pertaineth to a man, and vice versa. It's called an **abomination!** I realize we are living under grace instead of the law. I understand that clothing has changed. Yet, God's Word is forever settled in Heaven. Also, the Bible teaches we are to go further in grace than people did under the law.

Another principle is given in I Timothy 2:9, which says, ". . .That women adorn themselves in modest apparel."

The question is what type of apparel is modest apparel? It's at least more than Adam and Eve made for themselves in the Garden of Eden. (Perhaps they made themselves the first bikinis?) God made them **coverings.**

The strange woman of Proverbs 7 wore the attire of a harlot. Her attire was immodest enough to show she was for sale.

The reverse is true of the woman whom the Bible calls "virtuous." She made herself **coverings** of tapestry.

I beseech you, don't be like the dumb little sheep that follows just any path. Don't follow every worldly trend or fad. **Know** what you believe based on the Bible; since the Bible doesn't change, neither should you.

A startling verse to me is Ezekiel 16:44, which says, ". . .As is the mother, so is her daughter." Not only should you and I be concerned for our own precious daughters, we **must** be examples to those who look to us as their leaders. Could we not take the admonition of Romans 12:2, which says, ". . .be not conformed to this world: but be ye transformed by the renewing of your mind."

THE X FACTOR

What are your circumstances where you live today? Would you like to be in totally different circumstances? You can be. You can go to a completely new world — and you can do it by cultivating the right mental attitude.

We need to cultivate the right mental attitude because of the warning we are given in Proverbs 25:28: "He that hath no rule over his own spirit is like a city that is broken down, and without walls." Do you know your spirit is controlled by your mental attitude — the things about which you think? It is so vital for us to learn how to cultivate the right mental attitude. I can't stress enough how important your attitude is. And your attitude about life is your choice.

Again, what is your world like today? If you aren't happy with it, you can change it in a snap! You say you don't have any money? You can change that, too! You say you have illness in your home? You can change that. Perhaps the person won't get well immediately; but your attitude can change, and that will change the whole picture.

A lady in our church wrote me a letter one winter. At that point, their electricity and heat had been turned off. She was cooking and heating water for bathing on top of a kerosene heater. This woman has four children. She said in the note that for the first few days she kind of laughed about it and thought it was fun. But after 18 days, it wasn't fun anymore. Then she went to church and Bro. Hyles preached on being content. Wouldn't you know it? He just loves to meddle! So she went to the altar — and when she went back home she said the situation didn't seem nearly so bad. Now nothing had actually changed as far as her circumstances; she still didn't have electricity or heat. But this woman's mental attitude had changed and that made all the difference.

A healthy mental attitude is the X factor that changes our world. It is the missing facet, and leaders have to cultivate it. We must. We can't be leaders if we don't control our own spirits.

So many times we go to the Lord and ask Him for patience, expecting Him to pour a dose of patience down our throats. Or we ask Him to help us control our tempers and we think He will give us a spoonful of freedom from temper. But it doesn't happen that way. We learn to control our spirits by controlling our mental attitudes.

Learning to control your mental attitudes is a Biblical principle. It does not involve the power of positive thinking that Norman Vincent Peale teaches and preaches; it involves the Bible principle of Philippians 4:8.

Would you agree with me we should heed what God says even if He only says it once? What if He says if two or three or even four times? Wouldn't that make you think God thought whatever He was talking about was very important? Look at Psalm 107:8: "Oh that men would praise the Lord for his goodness, and for his wonderful works to the children of men!" That's once, but some of you are not praising God today for your circumstances. Now let's look at Psalm 107:15: "Oh that men would praise the Lord for his goodness, and for his wonderful works to the children of men!" That's twice. Then there's verse 21: "Oh that men would praise the Lord for his goodness, and for his wonderful works to the children of men!" That's three times. Let's go on to verse 31: "Oh that men would praise the Lord for his goodness, and for his wonderful works to the children of men!" I wonder why God put that verse in the same chapter four different times? I think He did it because He knows how hard it is for us to control our own spirits and because He knows we do not control our mental attitudes. We do not fill our minds with praise for His goodness. Instead, we are looking around at everything else. We look at the negative things instead of keeping our eyes fixed on Him and His goodness.

How do we learn to keep our eyes fixed on the goodness of God?

I believe the answer is found in Psalm 108:1 which says, "O God, my heart is fixed; I will sing and give praise, even with my glory." One commentator says our glory is our countenance or the way we look.

How About Your Heart?

First of all, you need to fix your heart. Just determine to eliminate all those lurking negative mental attitudes. Fix your heart to sing and give praise. How do you see your world today? Is it negative? Is someone sick? Is there too much month at the end of the money? Your world today is whatever you make it.

Back in Civil War days, John Brown captured an enemy arsenal; for that, he was sentenced to hang. The story is told that he sat on his own coffin in a cart on the way to his own hanging. The man who was to do the hanging was in the cart, too; this man was very nervous, agitated and uncomfortable. But John Brown was looking all around saying, "My, what a beautiful country. I have never had time before to look at it."

What an attitude! Could you sit on your own coffin today and say, "What a beautiful day!" Yes, you could — if you fixed your heart to do it. That's too simplistic but it's the truth of the matter.

There is a book entitled, *Happiness Is A Choice.* I haven't read the book, but the title is true. Happiness is a choice. If you are not happy this morning, it is because you choose not to be. If John Brown could be happy sitting on his coffin, you can go back to your world today — whatever it is — and make it a good world. You can look around at all the good things you have never before taken time to see.

Controlling your spirit begins in your head. The poet, Milton, said, "The mind is its own place and it can in itself make Heaven a hell or Hell a heaven." And that's true. Viktor Frankl is a man who spent years in a concentration camp in World War II and survived. He was mentally healthy and reasonably physically healthy even though the prisoners were given very little to eat. Mr. Frankl recounts he constantly exercised positive mental attitudes. He sang, he thought about things he had memorized in the past, and he kept his mental attitude positive. There were men in camp with him who were much stronger physically and had better health, but they lost their mental reasoning, became physically weak and died. However, this man stayed healthy physically and mentally because he got his heart fixed to keep his mind where it ought to be. He decided to make his hell a heaven. If he can do that, you can too.

When you think of Napoleon, do you think of a man who was successful or unsuccessful? Probably you think of a person who was fairly successful. But he made this statement: "I have never known six happy days in my life." On the other hand, Helen Keller, who was blind, deaf and dumb, said, "I have found life so beautiful!" She never saw it or heard it; what was the difference between her and Napoleon? It was a difference in the mental attitudes they took. Obviously, Helen Keller had the right one!

You should be more concerned about getting rid of a bad mental attitude than you are about getting rid of a tumor in your body. A bad mental attitude is more dangerous than a tumor. We are actually being told by physicians today that our mental attitudes affect our illnesses. Now that doesn't mean you shouldn't care for a health problem, but your mental attitude is more important as a whole.

This is very interesting to me; when God made the world in Genesis, He gave man dominion over everything. If God did that, why do we not have dominion over our own spirits and thoughts? Man has tamed all kinds of animals; he has dominion over ground that seemingly would never produce anything, yet he cannot control his own spirit. Now we can, or the Bible would not say we can! Nevertheless, we don't! We don't control our fears, our worries or our spirits.

Changing Your Point Of View

Let me give a list of ten decisions you can make that will help you cultivate a right mental attitude if you will take them to your world and apply them.

1. Decide to be happy. Fix your heart. Choose to be happy.

2. Decide to adjust to the circumstances of your world. So often we laugh at the circumstances we were in once the situation is all over. Isn't it too bad we make ourselves so miserable while we are there?

3. Decide to take care of your temple. Sometimes our mental attitudes are bad because we are eating the wrong things and failing to exercise. We get so sluggish and run down that we can't think positively and we can't look at the world through rosy glasses.

4. Decide to strengthen your mind. Read and learn.

5. Decide to exercise your soul in different ways. Do something for someone anonymously. Perhaps you could even help an enemy or someone you don't particularly like. What will that do for you? You will begin to like that person.

Do two things you don't like to do. Maybe it's something you have been putting off doing. But if it is staring you in the face and nagging at you, that is part of your problem with your mental attitude.

6. Decide to be agreeable. Now, that doesn't mean you should compromise your principles or convictions; just be agreeable!

7. Decide you will live life one day at a time. Don't borrow from tomorrow or worry about yesterday.

8. Decide to live by a schedule that is based on your priorities.

9. Decide to have a quiet time all by yourself. I recommend 30 minutes; if you can't find that much time, find what time you can.

10. Decide not to be afraid. Don't be afraid to be happy! What is an attitude? According to the dictionary, it is our point of view or our manner. Your point of view will affect your manner and the way you live. It will affect the way you greet people and the way you greet the world.

Two men looked out from prison bars. One saw mud, the other saw stars. What was the difference? It was a difference in their attitudes. Some of **you** look out and see nothing but mud. When you are in Christian work, there will be many things that tend to make you see mud. Instead, choose to look at the stars and sunshine! If life has handed you lemons — and it will if it hasn't —

make lemonade!

The story is told of a man who bought a ranch sight unseen. I guess that's a dumb thing to do. When he finally did see it he found it was impossible to transform his land into a prosperous ranch. It was rocky, sandy and full of rattlesnakes. It seemed life had handed him a lemon. Do you know what he did? He started canning rattlesnake meat. He started milking rattlesnakes for the venom — and he made a lot of money doing that because there is a big demand for snake venom in hospitals. This man made money with a lemon! You can too!

Have you got a lemon today? Open a lemonade stand! Is your life a lemon? You can do something about it by changing your attitude.

According to Philippians 2:13 and 14, there are two ways you can change your attitude. The first way is in verse 13: "For it is God which worketh in you both to will and to do of his good pleasure." So since it is God's working in your world, whatever that world is, you accept it. Acceptance is the key. Then in verse 14 we see this: "Do all things without murmurings and disputings." Quit whining and pitying yourself and looking at all the bad things. Instead, praise! Make lemonade! We can change our mental attitudes with acceptance and praise.

Did you know that accepting things takes away their power to hurt us? When we accept what God gives to us as being from His hand, it no longer has the ability to hurt us. It all boils down to your attitude, and your attitude is your choice!

Do you remember the wall of Jericho in the Bible? It is said that the wall was so thick that seven chariots could ride abreast on top of it. Still, how much wall had to be broken down before the enemy could enter? All of it? No! Just one section. Proverbs 25:28 is talking about that very thing. Having a bad attitude or spirit in just one area — like anger, jealousy or self-pity — can let the enemy within your walls. Therefore, a good mental attitude is so vital.

The Praise Principle

There is one mental attitude that could change all the rest and keep our walls fortified if we would just learn it and practice it. That is the attitude of praise and thanksgiving. It is a Bible principle. Philippians 4:4 says, "Rejoice in the Lord alway: and again I say, Rejoice." Have you done it today? Have you praised God for the bad things? If He says rejoice in the Lord alway, He doesn't mean just when you are on top and feeling hunky-dory; He means when you are on the bottom, too. If you can learn this lesson, it will be invaluable to you as a leader's wife. If you will learn to praise and give thanks, it will help you stay on top; it might even help you avoid dragging your husband completely out of God's will someday.

So how do we learn and apply this principle of praise and thanksgiving? First, like Psalm 108:1 says, we get our hearts fixed. We determine we are going to do it. Instead of being a negative person who always looks for the bad, we purpose in our hearts to be a person of praise.

I know a lady who, as long as I have known her, has had an attitude of, "Let's see. What hurts today?" Do you know anyone like that? "What can I complain about today? Do I have a toe ache? Do I have fallen arches? Do I have a sunburn? Do I have a headache? What's wrong today?" Are you that kind? You can change that! You can get up and ask, "What's right today?" You know, you **are** still saved!

Now, if you are the type of person who has never been in control of your spirit because you have never controlled your mental attitudes, you will probably need to saturate your mind with Scripture that will be there for you to call on.

A few years ago, I found myself feeling really grumbly in my heart. Now I hadn't gotten to the place where it was coming out, but what does the Bible teach? "For out of the abundance of the heart the mouth speaketh." (Matthew 12:34) I knew I was very close to beginning to gripe outwardly. As I saw this disgruntled spirit in my heart, I thought, "Okay, what am I going to do?" So I began to memorize Scripture. One of the first verses I memorized was Psalm 13:6: "I will sing unto the Lord, because he hath dealt bountifully with me." Can you say that today? You say, "We have one dollar for gas and food. Is that dealing bountifully?" Yes, He is dealing bountifully with you. But you won't see it until you sing unto Him and praise Him. Then I memorized Psalm 100: "Make a joyful noise unto the Lord, all ye lands. Serve the Lord with gladness: come before his presence with singing. Know ye that the Lord he is God: it is he that hath made us, and not we ourselves; we are his people, and the sheep of his pasture. Enter into his gates with thanksgiving, and into his courts with praise: be thankful unto him, and bless his name. For the Lord is good; his mercy is everlasting; and his truth endureth to all generations." After that, I learned Psalm 69:30, which says, "I will praise the name of God with a song, and will magnify him with thanksgiving."

Does it please God when we gripe and grumble in our spirits? Does it please Him when we are all out of whack and when we don't have control over our spirits? Does it please Him when our walls are broken down and the enemy can enter at will? No! But praise pleases Him. Saturate yourself in Scripture. Learn verses that teach you to praise Him. It will help you so much. Psalm 103:1 and 2 says, "Bless the Lord, O my soul: and all that is within me, bless his holy name. Bless the Lord, O my soul, and forget not all his benefits." And these are only a few of the verses that can teach you to praise if you will only learn them.

When are we to give thanks? We read in Philippians 4:6 and 7, "Be careful for nothing; but in every thing by prayer and supplication with thanksgiving let your requests be made known unto God. And the peace of God, which passeth all understanding, shall keep your hearts and minds through Christ Jesus." You know, it is no wonder people are peaceful if they come to Him with thanksgiving.

Ephesians 5:18 through 20 teaches us to be filled with the Holy Spirit. It is a command. These verses also give us some manifestations of being filled with the Spirit of God. They say we will be speaking in psalms and hymns and spiritual songs. We will be making melody in our hearts to the Lord. We will be giving thanks always. Those things are manifestations of the Holy Spirit. The only way others will know we are living with a consciousness of the Holy Spirit's presence is if we have right mental attitudes and keep our spirits with all diligence.

I Thessalonians 5:18 says, "In every thing give thanks: for this is the will of God in Christ Jesus concerning you." Whatever it is, I challenge you to give thanks to God today for the biggest negative thing in your life. I don't mean you are to have a flippant attitude that says, "Thank you, Lord, that I have leukemia." No; I mean we should say, "Thank you, Lord, for what you are doing. You make no mistakes. Thank you for what I am going to learn. Thank you for the medical progress made in this area so far." There is **always** something for which to thank Him. Learn to do it! It will change you and, in so doing, it will change your world.

To me, a very interesting verse is Psalm 142:7 which says, "Bring my soul out of prison, that I may praise thy name: the righteous shall compass me about; for thou shalt deal bountifully with me." Is your soul in prison today? Is it in a prison of self-pity? Is it in a prison of resentment because of your circumstances? Is it in a prison of discontentment? Is it in a prison of bitterness or hatred? This verse teaches if we will begin to praise God, we can be freed from our prison.

You know, Paul and Silas were **actually** delivered from prison. Do you know what they were doing when it happened? They were singing praises to God. That pleased Him, so He sent an earthquake to free them from prison. Your escape from the prison of a negative mental attitude can be just as real as their escape from prison. This Bible principle can change your world if you will let it.

When he lost **everything** in just a short period of time, Job bowed down and worshipped God. The Bible says in all that he did not blame God. No wonder we talk about the patience of Job! Once again, if we will just accept our circumstances as being allowed by the hand of God we will quit our murmuring and complaining.

Let me ask you this. What if, as a full-time Christian worker, your husband is called to a work and given a place to live? What if it is like my first little parsonage? What if you have a rat, too? If you don't learn this principle, if you gripe and complain and demand repairs, do you think it will be very helpful to your husband's ministry? No! People will be watching your attitudes and your spirit. If your attitudes are negative, people will become disillusioned with you — and your husband — very quickly. Also, your attitude can cause your husband to become so disgruntled and unhappy he may end up leaving the work. That's a tragedy because that ministry, with all its liabilities, was just the place where he was supposed to be.

In Jonah chapter 2, Jonah learned this principle. He was in the belly of a fish. Now I think that would be a hard place to praise. I am just sure you feel your situation is worse, but Jonah was in the belly of a fish. Do you know what the fish did when Jonah praised God? It went to dry land and threw up! The fish said, "I can't stand that crazy preacher in my stomach any more!" Now when Jonah wasn't praising, the Bible doesn't say a word about the fish vomiting him out on dry land. The moment he praised God, he was delivered from the belly of the fish. Not only did the fish get rid of him, it put him out on dry land where it was safe to do so! Good things happen when we praise.

We should also learn when to praise. When should we praise? We should praise all the time. I haven't learned it completely, but I am a whole lot better at it now than I once was. I haven't arrived; I still gripe. If you stay around me long enough, you will probably hear it. But I sure have come a long way, and you can too.

Can the World "See" Your Song?

We must also learn where to be thankful. We should be thankful in this strange land through which we are passing.

> This world is not my home,
> I'm just a passing thru,
> My treasures are laid up somewhere beyond the
> blue;
> The angels beckon me from Heaven's open door,
> And I can't feel at home in this world anymore.

Our citizenship is not here only; it is also in Heaven. We are strangers and pilgrims in this land. We are a peculiar people and the world is watching us. Let's show the world we are thankful.

In Psalm 137 the Bible talks about the Israelites when they were in captivity in Babylon. They sounded so indignant because their captors had required of them a song in Babylon. They asked how in the world they could sing while in captivity. They hung their harps on the willow trees and refused to sing to the heathen people. But that is exactly where they needed to sing! Have you hung your harp on the willow tree? Are you refusing to sing God's song in this land through which you are travelling? Have you forgotten how to praise? Bloom where you are planted! Get your harp out and start playing it again. Sing to the Lord right where you are because the world is watching you.

Psalm 40:3 talks about being lifted up out of the clay and having a new song. It says people will see it and trust in the Lord as a result. I really believe we can win souls by the way we accept our circumstances without whining. People are watching you. Sing a new song! Praise the Lord!

It is a healthy mental attitude that keeps your spirits fortified — that builds the wall around your life so the enemy can't get in. Don't let one part of it break down. Praise can change any negative mental attitude you have if you will just let it.

In James 3, the Bible says the fountain cannot send forth sweet and bitter waters at the same time. The same is true of your heart. You can't send forth sweet praises and bitter attitudes at the same time. It just doesn't work. So dispel the bitter with the sweet. As in the case of the waters at Marah, let the bitter water become sweet by applying the Cross and the blood of Jesus and all He's done for you to your circumstances. When you realize all He's done for you, you just **can't** be negative!

HOW TO KEEP ON KEEPING ON

II Timothy 4:7 and 8 says, "I have fought a good fight, I have finished my course, I have kept the faith: Henceforth there is laid up for me a crown of righteousness, which the Lord, the righteous judge, shall give me at that day: and not to me only, but unto all them also that love his appearing." I want to be able to say I have fought a good fight and finished my course. Of course I'm a little farther down the track than many of you who will read this book, but I could still fail to finish. I could still throw in the towel, but I don't want to do that. I want that prize at the end of the race, don't you? I want it so I can give it back to Jesus to Whom it belongs.

In order to finish a race, what must you do first? The first thing you must do in taking any course of action is start. You begin. Have you begun? That race doesn't begin somewhere out in the future; it begins wherever you are **right now.** Have you perhaps been dragging your feet? Have you begun the race yet?

After you begin, what comes next? You have to run the race. Just keep going; run it. Run it day by day by day. Perhaps you think, "Mrs. Hyles, I can't run very fast. I get sidetracked and discouraged so easily." C. H. Spurgeon said, "The snail finally made it to the ark by sheer perseverance." Have you ever thought about that? How did some of the slower animals get there? By sheer perseverance! That is how you will finish the race you have begun.

Perhaps you say, "But I have so many liabilities. I have so many things to keep me from continuing." Let me give you two very good examples of people who didn't let their liabilities stop them. In the early 1900's, Glenn Cunningham was crippled. He was burned severely over his legs and feet and he was told he would never walk again. However, in 1934, he set the world's record for running the mile. Now no matter what kind of handicaps you have, no matter how slow you think you are, don't hide behind those excuses. You can still finish the race — you might even make a record! Itzhack Perlman was born of parents who were in a Nazi concentration camp. He was paralyzed from the waist down at the age of four. Yet, he has become one of the great violinists of the world. He did not let handicaps or background he could have hidden behind keep him from finishing the course. He didn't let it keep him from mastering the art he wanted to master. Now I'm sure both of these men had setbacks; but they kept going and they finished.

Are you still in the race today? You know, you are going to have setbacks. But you can still finish if you will just keep persevering.

Someone once said the most meaningless statistic in a ball game is the score at half time. Do you feel it is half time in your game with the score 9 — 0 and you're losing? That score means nothing! In many ball games the team being tromped on at half time ended up winning the game! You can tromp on the Devil, too! I know you can! Are you in the midst of a setback today? Are you sidetracked? Did your shoelace come undone and you had to leave the track a little while to tie it up again? Maybe you got a cramp in your leg and had to stop the race for a bit. What do you need to do now? Get back in the race!

Maybe you are wanting to get out of the race today — permanently. I read a little book once by Oswald Chambers called, *My Utmost For His Highest*. It contained a little devotional that goes along with getting out of the race. First of all, he says you must have a vision before something becomes real. Then Satan comes in with his temptations, and we are apt to say it is no use to go on. We want out. We want to throw in the towel. But we need to realize God gives us the vision then takes us down into the valley to batter us into shape. Yet it is in the valley where so many of us faint and quit. I don't like the idea of being battered, do you? But we need it. We need to realize every vision will be made real if we will just have patience. God has to take us into the valley and put us through the fires and floods to get us into shape. If you have ever had the vision of God, you will never be satisfied with anything less — no matter how hard you try! God won't let you be satisfied with less.

Have you ever known anyone who quit the race when the going got rough? Are they happy? I have never seen more miserable faces than the faces of those people. I know one preacher well who quit the ministry early in his life; he's one of the most miserable-looking men I have ever seen. He's not the only one; his wife and family are miserable too. God is not going to let you be happy if you give up before the race is over.

Remember, everything that is going well today wasn't always going so well. You think, "Mrs. Hyles, we are so far from being like First Baptist of Hammond!" But, years ago, First Baptist Church wasn't like it is now. That church has been through many setbacks. It has persevered through hard times, loss of some members and criticism — all the usual things. But what did they do? They just kept on going down the racetrack. Now their success didn't come overnight. You don't just arrive at your destination in a snap. It takes perseverance. We must keep on keeping on. If you could learn this one thing and determine to do it, you would be certain to finish the course someday and hear the Master say, "Well done." And that will be worth it all.

We see the pattern so often in the Bible; it is especially obvious in the little nation of Israel. So many times they would begin their course only to backslide or come to a setback. Then God would restore them and they would start over again.

I think of Noah. He began to walk with God. God told him it would rain and he was to build an ark. He did, and the people began to laugh at him and ask him what he was building. When he told them what it was, they laughed even harder. Now he could have said, "I don't have to take this." But if he had, he would have died too. Instead, he finished his course.

What about Joseph? He dreamed his dreams. Now he had setbacks — many of them, in fact. What if he had decided it was enough when he was in jail for doing right? What if, when they called him to come interpret Pharaoh's dream, he had said, "Not on your life! I have been treated badly and I am not doing one good thing for this cotton-pickin' kingdom!" If he had said that, he would have forfeited being in the exact place God had been preparing for him for a number of years! He would have missed the opportunity toward which God had been leading him. He not only wouldn't have saved the kingdom, he wouldn't have been able to save his own family.

You may not understand why God is doing what He is doing to you in the race today. But don't quit before you get to where He is trying to take you — to the finish line. It is so sad when someone quits just before they reach that goal line. We need staying power; we need perseverance like Joseph and Noah. Just learn to hang in there in spite of the things that happen. You **can** learn that.

Climb a high mountain mentally right now. From that high peak, look down on your life up to this point. Also, project yourself into the future. As you reach toward that goal you and your husband have set, as you see the whole in your imagination, I think it ought to excite you. As you look back and see how far you have come, you can say with the songwriter,

> We've come this far by faith,
> Leaning on the Lord;
> Trusting in His Holy Word:
> He's never failed us yet.

Maybe you **have** had some tough times, but He hasn't failed you yet, has He? As you go toward the goal, He will **not** fail you. So, mentally, look at how far you have already come and realize He always came through and He always will. He has promised He will never leave us nor forsake us and He always keeps His promises. To keep going, always look beyond today!

The Bible says we are not to borrow from tomorrow's troubles but we are to reach toward a goal for tomorrow. Paul said in Philippians 3:13 and 14, ". . .forgetting those things which are behind, and reaching forth unto those things which are before, I press toward the mark for the prize of the high calling of God in Christ Jesus." That is what I am saying. Look toward the goal. If you are in the muck and mire of financial problems, realize you

probably will get out of it somewhere along the way. Eyes to the
front! Don't look back; that's what Paul said. Do you know what
that does for you? It gives you hope — and hope is like medicine.
Doctors tell us hope actually produces two hormones — cortisol and
prolactin. And those hormones produce health. Hope — you need it.
Look forward and find it.

Envision the finish line with the words "well done" being said to
you. I want to hear that; don't you? First of all, you have to get
started. You must begin. Ephesians 2:10a says, "For we are his
workmanship, created in Christ Jesus unto good works." You ought
to have already begun being His workmanship in His hands. Let
Him do His bidding through you even now.

It also helps to realize Jesus knows our feelings. Look at Hebrews
4:15: "For we have not an high priest which cannot be touched with
the feeling of our infirmities; but was in all points tempted like as
we are, yet without sin." You may ask how He could know what it
feels like to be a wife and mother with no food to put on the table
for supper. I don't know, but He does. He says He knows our
feelings. I believe He looks down with sympathy. He is not up there
laughing at us and making fun of us. Oh, no! He is glad for what
hardships do in your life; but, at the same time, He sympathizes
with those things that temporarily take you out of the race or make
you stumble. We have a loving God; He is not a bully. He wants to
help. Hebrews 2:18 says, "For in that he himself hath suffered being
tempted, he is able to succour them that are tempted." He wants to
lift you back up and put you back on the racetrack and get you
going again. He won't let you do it by yourself. He will aid you and
He will bring you through. II Corinthians 2:14 says, "Now thanks be
unto God, which always causeth us to triumph in Christ." And He
will cause you to do that!

You're a Diamond in the Rough

Hang in there! Someone once said, "A diamond is just a piece of
coal that stayed on the job." Did you know diamonds come from
coal? There is a diamond in you little pieces of coal if you will just

hang in there and stay on the job. Mrs. Marlene Evans has a tape that talks about seeing gold glittering in people. I believe there is gold glittering in those of you who are reading this book. You may not believe that about yourself, but I do. Remember you are a diamond already; maybe you are a diamond in the rough, but you **are** a diamond. Hang in there.

I consider my husband a diamond — a sparkling diamond of many carats. But did you know there was a day when he wanted to quit? He wrote out his resignation and read it to me. We both felt sorry for ourselves and cried together. We had been kicked out of the Southern Baptist Convention, we had lost friends, our church had not yet gotten back on its feet, and then a tornado came through on a Saturday night and took the roof off our building. So he said, "That's it. Poor us! I just can't take anymore. Surely Job never had it this bad!" We both felt that way, so he wrote out his resignation. He was planning to read it in church the next day. We went to church and his sermon was from the book of Job. Well, the Lord had him accidentally turn to a verse he wasn't planning to use. He looked down and silently read Job 38:1 which says, "Then the Lord answered Job out of the whirlwind." As he read that, I was looking at his face and I knew something had happened. After that, he wound up and preached a lambasting sermon. He said, "Put your seat belts on. We are off for a new beginning." And I thought to myself, "What happened??!" What had happened was he had just gotten completely off the track in the race. But God said, "Hey! I've got a verse in there to tell you what happened. I sent that whirlwind, but I wanted to tell you things are not over. Just get in there and fight!" And God began to work and the church grew. They did a greater work than ever before. What would have happened if we had quit that day? We would never have made it to First Baptist Church of Hammond. There would be no Hyles-Anderson College. We wouldn't have seen the thousands and thousands saved who have been saved since then. Doesn't that show you the importance of perseverance?

Something else you can learn from this illustration is how important it is that you never allow yourself to get down at the same time as your husband. That was one of the few times in our lives when my husband and I were both down at the same time. It is so vital that you refuse to get down when your husband is down. Pull him back up. When you are down, he can do the same for you. My husband is a diamond who stayed in there when the going got tough. You learn to do that also.

There are three ways the Devil tries to discourage us and get us off track. The first thing he does is have you look at yourself and say, "I will never make it. I am just not made of the right stuff. I don't have enough character and stickability." Well, get it! With God's help, you can! That's the Devil who is saying you can never make it. Secondly, Satan will tell you to look at everyone else who is failing. He will tell you if **they** quit, **you** can surely never hold on. Yes, you can! Just don't look at those who quit. Don't pay any attention to the quitters. Just keep on going anyway. Thirdly, he tells you, "You are really having it rough." He just loves to use that line. That's the one he was using on my husband and me when we had both decided to quit. Now we **were** having it tough; it was hard. But God said, "I am not through. Yes, perhaps it is rough, but I am not through with you. Just get back in the race." We need to learn how to take hurt. In Acts 20:24 we see this: "But none of these things move me, neither count I my life dear unto myself, so that I might finish my course with joy, and the ministry, which I have received of the Lord Jesus, to testify the gospel of the grace of God." Now do you think Paul had some setbacks? A lot of 'em. Do you think he had some hardships? A lot of 'em. Do you think he had some pain? A lot of it. Do you think he had physical afflictions? Sure he did. But he decided none of those things would stop him from finishing his course. He decided it would be worth it to hurt a little while if he could finish the course. So just learn how to take hurt. Realize setbacks are of little consequence compared to finishing the course.

You know, these forty years haven't always been easy, but they have always been exciting. I wish I could impart to you the excitement and wonder of the ministry. There is joy in watching God work miracles and learning not to major on the minor. The little hurts and setbacks are so unimportant. Also, they make us what we are.

We have a model for ignoring pain. In Hebrews 12:2 we see Jesus despised the shame. He didn't love what He had to go through. However, for the joy that was set before Him — dying on the cross — He endured it. His goal was dying on the cross, so it was a joy to Him. To finish His course made the pain and blasphemy He had to endure as nothing. He's the model, so we can learn to have the same feelings.

Are you finding it rough to go on today? Perhaps it is tough; but realize the pain is so short-lived compared to the reward. Think about this: God is so powerful He could take away your difficulty right now if He so chose. He's still a miracle-working God. He could heal you in a moment. He could remove disagreeable circumstances and people in a snap. But if He did, has the difficulty lasted long enough to help you — to change you? Let's be careful not to want our difficulties to end before they have done their work. What He can do in your life through the difficulty is a greater miracle than having the difficulty taken away. Sure, He could remove all the difficulties; the race could be smooth going from here on out. But if that happened, you would not become all you can become with the things He allows in your life. Don't quit because of hurt; just learn how to take it!

Observations About Quitting

1. Everyone gets to the point of wanting to quit at one time or another. You need the commitment of the old school when people who married were just determined to keep on and not quit at marriage. I have talked to women who have been married fifty years or more and they have said they wanted to quit the whole thing many times. But they didn't! With anything, there will be times when it seems like it would be easier to quit. But it's not. Charlie Brown says he has often wanted to know where to go to give up, but he can never find the place. I hope you don't find it either.

2. There's a room called the "Throw-In-The-Towel Room." Now, it's really big, because a lot of people go there. Are you going to join them? Do you know what? That room is full of people who look miserable and they are all making excuses for why they are there. Don't join them; they are a miserable lot. There's plenty of room for you there; the room is made big for quitters. Just make it a point not to end up there.

3. You don't have to quit. Maybe you have quit; or maybe you have just thought about it. But Proverbs 24:16a says, "For a just man falleth seven times, and riseth up again." Just get up and begin again! Perhaps you have gone completely back to the very beginning. That's okay. Just start running again right from the beginning. You don't have to quit. When you are tempted to quit, think of Brahms. It is said it took him seven years to write his lullaby because he kept putting himself to sleep!!

You know, the ultimate reason people quit is they just wander away a little bit at a time. Most people who are away from the Lord got away in such small degrees they didn't even realize it was happening. That's why it's so important for us to refocus our eyes on the goal daily. Then we won't wake up to find we have gradually slipped completely away from the Lord.

Develop staying power. You can. Learn to complete small things and just don't give up. As you learn how to complete small things, you will learn how to complete larger tasks.

You might say you are getting winded in the race; you might say that the race is hard. But let me tell you it is a lot harder not to run the race. If you quit, you will never, never be happy. If God has given you a vision and the grace to run, you will never be happy if you quit.

A father once gave his son a lecture on quitting. After he did, he asked, "Do you remember George Washington?" Of course the child replied he did. "Do you remember Abraham Lincoln?" Again, the boy remembered. "Do you remember Thomas Jefferson?" Of course, he did. So the dad said, "Well, they all had one thing in common. They didn't quit!" Then the father asked, "Son, do you remember Ozodora MacEngle?" The puzzled child answered he had never heard of him. "Do you know why? Because he quit!" Don't quit!

BEHAVIOR THAT BECOMETH HOLINESS

In this chapter I want to talk to you about your behavior in your private world. I believe this is the place where the Devil will attack you the most. This is the area in which most Christian leaders' wives fall; it is the thing that most often takes people out of the ministry. It is wonderful to learn what to do in your private world. In this chapter I would like to share with you what God says about your private world.

Titus 2:3 through 5 says, "The aged women likewise, that they be in behaviour as becometh holiness, not false accusers, not given to much wine, teachers of good things; That they may teach the young women to be sober, to love their husbands, to love their children, To be discreet, chaste, keepers at home, good, obedient to their own husbands, that the word of God be not blasphemed."

The first thing these verses say I am to teach you is to be sober. Now I don't think that means you are to go around with a long face and black stockings and tie your hair in a bun just because your husband is in Christian work. I think it means you are to be sober about the position of being in the ministry. There is no higher calling. If you aren't married yet and you desire to marry a man who is going to serve God, good for you!! I believe that's a higher calling than to be the wife of the president of the United States. A pastor has the opportunity to mold and change lives with God's help, and that will do more for our country than the president ever can do. The Lord's work is a high calling and we need to realize it is something about which to be sober. We need to guard that calling carefully if we have it.

Now there are some liabilities that go with the high calling of the ministry. I told you about the fact that Edith and Joe Boyd joined our church in Texas when he was travelling as an evangelist. One morning, when Joe came home after being gone several weeks, his little boy came in the room where he was shaving and said, "I know who you are. You are Joe Boyd!" If your husband is called to be away from home a lot, that is a liability. But the Lord's work is still the highest calling in the world; we ought to be sober about it.

The second thing I am to teach you is to love your husband. Men who love their work often get so caught up in it that they get preoccupied. I am so glad my husband loves his work and is totally at home with it, but he can get preoccupied. Your husband will, too, if he loves his work.

Does this sound familiar to you?

PREOCCUPIED

My husband is frequently preoccupied. Understandably. He has a lot to be preoccupied about.

We were expecting company for dinner, and I asked him what he would like to have on the menu.

"Uh-huh," he grunted. I knew he was with me in body only, and decided to have some fun.

"I thought we'd start off with tadpole soup," I began.

"Uh-huh."

"And there is some lovely poison ivy growing in the next cove which would make a delightful salad."

"Uh-huh."

"For the main dish, I could try roasting some of those wharf rats we've been seeing around the smokehouse lately, and serve them with boiled crabgrass and baked birdseed."

"Uh-huh."

"And for dessert we could have a mud souffle and..."
My voice trailed off as his eyes began to focus.

"What was that you said about wharf rats?" he
asked.

— Ruth Graham

I think those words are so cute — I guess because I have been
there! My husband has come home with news I told him a month
before! Our men will often be preoccupied, but we need to be
understanding about it. They have a lot about which to be
preoccupied. Maybe they don't say "I love you" as often as they
should, but you just have to be understanding and love them
anyway.

Once a lady came to me for counsel and said her husband didn't
express his love verbally as much as she would like. Maybe you
think you have that problem. Let me remind you of some ways your
man is telling you he loves you without saying a word. Does he take
out the trash without being asked? Does he play with the baby
while you rest? Does he bring you a card on your anniversary? Does
he kiss you good-bye or goodnight, or both? Does he put gas in
your car? Does he pat you as he walks by? If he does any of these
things, he is communicating his love in his own way even if he
doesn't do it verbally. When he seems to be preoccupied, look for
things that say "I love you." Does he provide for you? He loves you.
I feel the greatest way my husband says he loves me, our children
and grandchildren is that he keeps on going — trying to help
preachers all over America keep fundamentalism alive and keep the
freedoms alive we have enjoyed during our lives. I consider that an
act of love to me as well as to other people.

I found the following in a book by Dr. Ed Wheat, and I think it
is a good formula for you to follow every day with your husband.

B — Bless your husband. Now I don't mean bless him out! Praise
him every day. Tell him how much you need him. Bless him. Let

him know that he is the most important person in your life. Let him know how great he is to you.

E — Edify him. What do you do when you edify? You build him. No matter what mood he is in, build him. Don't ever compare him unfavorably with another preacher or Christian worker. My husband knows, as far as I am concerned, he is the greatest preacher in the world. Your husband ought to be the greatest to you. Now when he starts out, he probably won't be. He may stumble and fumble and you might wonder if he has really been called. But build him and say things like, "You can do it. Everybody has to start." Always edify. If your man is already an accomplished preacher, find some way every day to build him up and let him know that he is great in your eyes. He wants to be the leader of your parade and it is up to you to make him that!

Do you ever remember as a young girl having a boyfriend who did all kinds of crazy antics in front of you to show you how wonderful he was? Perhaps he rode his bike without hands or turned somersaults. He did that because he wanted to seem important in your eyes. Well your husband is the same way, and he never outgrows it.

S — Share with one another. Share your feelings. Perhaps you say there is an area in your life he just doesn't satisfy. Have you ever told him in a kind and loving way? Share those feelings with him. You say, "Well, he should know I need help with the kids on Sunday mornings!" Why should he know? He is a man. We don't think like men do and they don't think like we do. Therefore, we need to communicate. Keep the line of communication open.

Did you know it is better to argue in a nice way than not to talk at all? You should learn how to argue. There is a way to argue. Never throw around blame-filled statements or accusations. You take the blame. Say, "I feel like I was slighted in this certain area." Don't say, "You hurt my feelings!" Learn how to argue. Keep the lines of communication open.

Some of you might feel it is better to be quiet rather than to argue, but my husband has often made this statement: "Sometimes there has to be a war before there can be peace." Now I am not talking about open battling. It is never proper for a husband and wife to air their differences in front of their children. You are **not** always going to agree, but those disagreements must be handled the right way. That's the only way to keep the lines of communication open between the two of you.

You should also allow your husband to share his feelings with you. I was once asked by a young lady if she should allow her husband to talk to her about his first wife who had died. I believe, in a situation like that, you should allow your husband to talk to you as much as he needs to in order to work through his grief. It will bring the two of you closer together if he can work through his grief by sharing it with you. Someone with whom you can share your grief is going to become more dear to you. Some women feel threatened when their husbands talk about first wives who have died, but I don't see it as a threat at all. I think it is a compliment to you if he feels free to talk to you about the subject. It doesn't mean he loves you any less. The fact that he can share his grief with you indicates he feels very secure about your relationship. Give him the freedom to share his feelings.

T — Touch your husband. Now I am not referring here to intimate touching. I'm talking about just patting each other. Hold hands with him. Rub his neck. It has been proven that everyone needs to be touched, and your husband needs **your** touch. Do it every day.

If you will follow these guidelines, they will help you have God's best in your marriage and it will be a wonderful haven for both of you.

As I said earlier, faithfulness to your husband begins in your mind. Always be faithful to him. A young lady whom I know shared a story with me that I believe will be a help to you in this area. She and her husband were pastoring the fastest-growing church and the most successful church in the state where they lived. But this pastor's wife became unfaithful to her husband because of her service for God. Now you might wonder, "How in the world could anyone do that?" She got so busy she didn't have meals cooked, she wasn't spending enough time with her children and her marriage was suffering. Now, she was out doing many wonderful works for

God; she was spending time working on her bus route and going soul winning. But her suffering marriage was evidence that her service for the Lord was out of balance. Things got so bad she even left her husband for awhile. Praise the Lord, they are together again. They have both taken full blame for what happened and they have rebuilt their marriage. Please learn from this example. Don't get so busy with the Lord's work that you become unfaithful to your husband and children. Remember, too, that a man will and should spend more time doing the Lord's work than you can or should. Keep in mind that it is possible for you to make him jealous of God, and that's wrong.

Always give your husband your full attention in church. Look as if you are the most interested person in the congregation. If you begin to do that, you will be. You will enjoy his preaching so much you won't want to miss any part of it.

One night in church I noticed my watch had stopped, so I took it off to set it. Then I thought to myself, "I don't ever do this kind of thing sitting up here in the choir in front of the whole church!!" And even though I didn't miss a word of what my husband said, I shouldn't have done that. Someone probably saw it and thought, "She's not paying attention to the sermon." Our husbands should always have our full attention. How can we expect the congregation to pay attention if we don't?

Thirdly, I am to teach you to love your children. Have you ever taken a dog to behavior school? Well, here are the basic rules for dogs in obedience school. They will work very well with your children!

1. Keep commands simple and at a minimum. Use one word at a time like, "Sit, stay, heel, and down." Simple one-word commands should do the trick. When you say "no," your children should be taught it means no.

2. Be consistent. As mothers, we certainly need to do this. One day we spank them because they get into the cookies and the next day we just let it go. Be consistent!

3. Be persistent. Follow through. Never give an instruction and allow your children to ignore you.

4. When the dog (or child) responds correctly, praise him. Don't reward with food, but with praise. Children love to be praised!

It's true in all too many cases that our dogs are trained better than our children.

I have four guidelines I would like to give you to help your children as they grow up in the homes of full-time Christian workers.

1. Love them.
2. Love them.
3. Love them.
4. Love them.

Love them unconditionally and let them know you are on their side. You should do this because they will have a lot of people who aren't on their side. Pastors' kids are very visible. You have probably heard the old saying, "The reason pastors' kids are so mean is they run with deacons' kids!" However, they are just children. Allow them to be children.

Teach them. If you love them, you will teach them and train them and discipline them. You will follow through and be consistent.

Your children have a right to a happy, normal home. Just because you are in the ministry, your home should not be Grand Central Station. You should have a hospitable home, but your children deserve a normal home.

Have family altar, but don't have a revival meeting every night. When our children were at home, people often asked me how we got our children to sit still through family altar. I said, "We just make it short and sweet. We don't prop them up and put toothpicks in their eyes to make them stay awake." Now there were nights when we began to memorize whole chapters of the Bible together. We have learned many chapters together as a family, and those times are precious to me. But when the kids were small, we limited our family altar time to perhaps ten minutes. For small children, that's probably as much as they can take in. However, they will always remember those times; it will make impressions upon their hearts they won't forget. People were often shocked when I told them of the brevity of our family altars, but we just prayed, read the

Bible, sang and had some fun. My husband sometimes took that opportunity to teach the kids. He might teach them how to answer the phone or the door. He might teach them to make introductions or how to shake hands. The times were fun and not very long.

If you were to ask my children if they have memories of their dad being gone all the time, they would tell you "no." They remember going out in the yard to play ball. They remember going on picnics and having fun with dad. And I am so glad. When they talk to me about their memories, it always thrills my heart to know they enjoyed living in a pastor's home. It isn't always easy. You have to work to make it so.

Realize you must relinquish your children to God. They are His first. They have been loaned to you to train. After a while, you have done all you can do. You must realize pastors' children sometimes take the wrong course. Remember the Devil wants to destroy the very best. The more you train your children, the more the Devil will go after them.

Another thing is that you will never quit being a mother. If anything, your prayers probably need to become more fervent the longer your children live. The problems your children have don't end when they leave home. I have often tried to find a place to turn in my motherhood badge, but I can't seem to locate it! Of course, I'm teasing, but the problems seem to grow bigger to a mother. You never stop loving them or being concerned about them, and you never should because children measure God's love by their parents' love. If you give up on them when they have problems, they will think God has given up on them too.

The next thing I am to teach you is to be discreet. That means you are to be careful about what you say and do. Did you know you can make your husband give up on the ministry just by what you say? He might be on fire for the Lord, he might be building a fine church. But you get disgruntled in some small area and you take all your little gripes to him until he says, "What's the use?" You just keep nitpicking at every little thing that goes wrong in the church and you keep on dumping every gripe you have on him until he quits. When he does, who is the cause of it? You are! You might have even done it innocently; you had no intention of his ever quitting the ministry. But you have piled too much junk on him because you have not been discreet in your conversation. I have seen this happen and I know what I am talking about.

I am to teach you to be chaste. That means you are to be decent. Be modest, be simple in style and be honorable.

I am to teach you to be keepers at home. Make your home a home. I remember the day we arrived at our new parsonage in Hammond, Indiana. It was 100° and I was six months pregnant. As we arrived, people were everywhere! It was a brand new home the people of the church had built for our predecessor who left before it was completed. They were washing windows and cleaning cupboards and putting food in them. People were scrubbing everywhere. And I thought, "Oh, no! Is this the way it's going to be? People everywhere?" But, when they left, my home was spotless, my cupboards were stocked and for the next few days no one came by or bothered me. The former pastor and his wife had already paved the way. In a kind and loving way, they had taught their people that their home was **their home**; it was not just an extension of the church. Your people need to be taught that. Fortunately, my husband didn't have to teach that to our people. Someone came before us who had already done it. We have never had the problem of people just popping in unannounced, and that's very important. Your family deserves privacy. Your home ought to be as normal as possible.

Keep your home clean. I don't mean it has to be spotless every minute of every day. You can't live in your home and keep it spotless, but you can keep it clean. I have often said I would love to have one house to live in and one for show. Unfortunately, we have one for both! You can learn to keep the portions of your home visitors see presentable. I think it is a great travesty when we have such cluttered, dirty homes that people just take it for granted Christian workers serve God too much to keep their homes clean. That is a disgrace! You need to keep a clean home for your husband's sake. Can you study and concentrate with clutter and disarray? I can't, and your husband probably can't either. Now perhaps your husband won't have his study at home; if he has his office at the church, that's wonderful. That way, he will probably do most of his counselling and studying at the church and your home will be more private. My husband does most of his work in his office at the church, and I love it that way. Nevertheless, keep a clean home for your husband's sake.

Now I am not telling you people are never counselled in our home. Always let people know they are welcome to come if there is an emergency. I would never say to someone in need, "Now, look! This is our home. You make an appointment at the office if you need to see my husband!" No! There must be a balance between hospitality and Grand Central Station. You must learn to be hospitable, but not to the point where you are bombarded with guests all the time. Your home needs to be, as much as possible, a place where your family can relax. You all need to feel like you can just kick off your shoes and be yourselves!

I read a book written by a pastor's wife in 1984; in it, she talked about what a wonderful time she was having as a pastor's wife and what a wonderful marriage she had. I really enjoyed the book. Then in 1988 I noticed a book written by her husband; naturally, his name caught my eye. The book was written in 1987, and the title is, *Rebuilding Your Broken World*. As I opened the book and read the flyleaf, I noticed their world had fallen apart since 1984; but it was their private world. It wasn't a problem caused by anything in the church. Now the happy ending is they did rebuild their marriage. The Devil wants to come into your private world to destroy it, and the world is just watching and waiting for it to happen; they love juicy gossip. So this is a day in which we have to be doubly careful about our private worlds. One way to keep your marriage from falling apart is to work as hard as you can to keep it together. No other woman is going to look as good as you if you do everything you can to have a good marriage. Your private world is vitally important. You can't very well go to church and put on a happy face if you don't live it at home. If your happiness isn't genuine, it will come through eventually. Whether you are ever in full-time work for the Lord, it is so important to guard your private world.

LIFE,
AS VIEWED FROM THE GOLDFISH BOWL

As a child, I often had a goldfish that I would keep in a small glass bowl. I would clean the bowl and feed my fish daily; after a while, it would die and be "flushed."

I loved to watch the fish as it would swim and eat. However, I never thought about it from the fish's perspective. And the more I think about it now, the funnier it becomes. We are being told today that watching fish in an aquarium is a stress reducer. But what about the poor fish?

I must admit, I love to go into my sister-in-law's office and watch the beautiful fish in her small aquarium. I feel almost "hypnotized" by their lazy, flowing movements. Sometimes a fish will turn toward me, and it seems to be looking right at me. I began to wonder what it might be trying to say to me. Could it be, "Knock it off! I've been watched enough today?" Or perhaps it is trying to say, "Be kind in your criticism. I can only be what I was meant to be and do what I am equipped to do."

I know that some species of fish are more timid than others. They try to hide among the plants and rocks in the bowl. However, how much can you hide in a glass bowl?

As a pastor's wife, I've been a "fish" in the fish bowl of a church with only 19 members. I was a different "species" since I was a city girl in a very rural area. Fortunately, those people allowed me to be what I was. Their kindness allowed me freedom to grow and learn about country people. I learned about their character, diligence, generosity and plain old "salt-of-the-earth" goodness.

Time took me to a larger glass bowl where I was watched by many more eyes. Sometimes, those eyes were less kind. I have never learned to be completely comfortable with being scrutinized; I am basically a very private person. But since that goes with living in a fish bowl, I accepted it. However, when I had to go be a cheerful, exuberant person after being up all night with a colicky baby or some other happening, I would want to say, "Knock it off! I'm like you. When I don't get enough sleep, I'm cranky!" (Do fish get cranky?)

As time went on, there were four "little fishes" whom I wanted to protect from prying eyes. But I found they had to accept the glass bowl, too.

As I looked back from inside the bowl, I often saw hilarious scenes with which I could find fault. Perhaps this helped to teach me that we are all made the same, with the same common frailties. It taught me to bestow charity and to realize I was to put no confidence in the flesh; only my God has earned that.

When the big, enormous aquarium became my lot, I was older and wiser — but able to cope? No. I'm still a private person. Now I am in a place where my mid-life crisis can be watched, my newly-formed bulges are observed, and (horrors!) each new wrinkle is seen through the magnification of glass! But I thank God that I have a husband who, when he realized I still needed my privacy when hundreds of people watched, didn't draw undue attention to me by talking about me too much. (I requested that because red faces don't belong in glass bowls!)

Do I know how a timid goldfish feels? I believe I do. However, I wouldn't trade my place in the goldfish bowl for anything. Please realize that those who live in "glass bowls" may not always look, dress or act just like the last "species." Learn to be charitable to them.

I must conclude that there have been times when I thought I would die and be found floating on top — stinking. But it hasn't happened. I haven't been flushed yet and I don't intend to be!